NUCLEAR VERDICTS®

THE APEX

BREAK THE PATTERN

NUCLEAR VERDICTS®

THE APEX

BREAK THE PATTERN

ROBERT F. TYSON, JR.
CAYCE E. LYNCH
with ASHLEY PAIGE FETYKO

LAW DOG
PUBLISHING LLC

First Edition: October 2025

Cover Design by Mario Yepez
Graphic Design by Mario Yepez & Kira Giannoni

Apex Defense Consulting
www.apexdefenseconsulting.com

Tyson & Mendes, LLP
www.tysonmendes.com

ISBN: 979-8-9938778-0-8 (KDP Paperback)

ISBN: 979-8-9938778-1-5 (Ebook)

ISBN: 979-8-9938778-2-2 (Hardcover)

Published by Law Dog Publishing, LLC

LAW DOG
PUBLISHING LLC

Law Dog Logo Design by Kira Giannoni

This book is dedicated to our families.

THE APEX

Defuse Anger
Tell Your Story
Care
Responsibility
Reasonableness
Common Sense
Personalize the Defendant
Accept Responsibility
Give a Number
Argue Pain and Suffering
CORE FOUR
Be a Good Human

TABLE OF CONTENTS

INTRODUCTION

THE PROBLEM OF NUCLEAR VERDICTS

"Collecting data is only the first step toward wisdom but sharing data is the first step toward community."
—Henry Louis Gates, Jr.

THE ERA OF NUCLEAR VERDICTS: HOW DID WE GET HERE?

WE TRAVEL A LOT FOR work. As national law firm leaders and frequent speakers on Nuclear Verdicts®,[1] we often travel coast-to-coast to visit with clients and our branch offices. Sometimes we play a little game to break up the monotony of travel by counting how many attorney billboards we see between the airport and our final destination in our arrival city.

Mile by mile, we count billboards like this:

"Big Verdicts = Bigger Insurance Bills. Guess Who Pays?"

"Inflation Hits the Courtroom Too. Nuclear Verdicts = Higher Prices for Everyone."

1 Tyson & Mendes, LLP holds the trademark to the term Nuclear Verdict® and iterations thereof.

"You're One Lawsuit Away from Higher Rent, Insurance, and Healthcare."

"Nuclear Verdicts Burn Us All."

"Justice ≠ Jackpot"

...

Just kidding. These billboards do not exist. The billboards we see on our travels are the same plaintiffs' attorney advertisements millions of Americans see every day:

"Hurt in a Wreck? Get a Check!"
"One Call, That's All!"
"Accident? Call Us Before the Insurance Company!"
"Insurance Companies Have Lawyers. So Should You."
"Visit SueTheTruck.com"

Nuclear Verdicts are out of control in the United States and are a growing problem across the world. All research suggests things are getting worse for defendants each year. Americans seem more likely to get a Nuclear Verdict or "Nuclear Settlement" if they file a lawsuit than they are to win the lottery.

At the risk of getting the Talking Heads stuck on a loop in your head, we must ask, "How did we get here?" And, more importantly, what can we do to stop it?

THE MODERN MCDONALD'S HOT COFFEE CASE: $47 MILLION MORE EXPENSIVE

Let us go back to 1994: a year that brought us NAFTA, the public release of the World Wide Web, *Pulp Fiction* (Bob's Favorite), *Lion King* (Cayce's favorite), President Nelson Mandela, the O.J. Simpson car chase, and possibly the world's first (and most famous) runaway jury award: the McDonald's hot coffee case.

What was the jury's verdict in that case? $5 million? $10 million? $20 million?

No, a New Mexico jury awarded the plaintiff just shy of $2.9 million when McDonald's gave her hot coffee, exactly what she ordered. This award broke down to approximately $160,000 in compensatory damages for her medical expenses and $2.7 million in punitive damages. The jury assigned 20% of the fault to the plaintiff for spilling the coffee.

Important disclaimer: the plaintiff in this case was seriously injured. She suffered third-degree burns when the coffee spilled in her lap, requiring skin grafts and seven days of hospitalization.[2] The plaintiff was injured, and we believe injured plaintiffs should be made whole, fully and fairly. It was reported the fast-food giant only offered $800[3] and opted not to settle the case. Plaintiff's attorney "suggested penalizing McDonald's the equivalent of one to two days of companywide coffee sales, which he estimated at $1.35 million per day."[4]

But remember what an impact this case made? Everyday Americans were outraged. The verdict caused many to question the efficacy of our civil justice system. It spurred tort reform. National media called the case "the poster child of excessive lawsuits"[5] in 2007.

So, what has happened over the last 30 years? "Same as it ever was[?]"[6] No. Things are much, much worse.

In March 2025, a Los Angeles jury decided a case very similar to the McDonald's case, where a delivery driver was burned by hot tea from Starbucks that spilled in his lap. The verdict? $50 million. The jury awarded the entire verdict for the delivery driver's pain and suffering damages; no medical expenses, no lost wages, no punitive damages.

---

2 Andrea Gerlin, *Spilled coffee worth $2.9 million*, TAMPA BAY TIMES (Sept. 2, 1994), https://www.tampabay.com/archive/1994/09/02/spilled-coffee-worth-2-9-million/ (on file with the Apex Defense Consulting library).

3 *Id.*

4 *Id.*

5 Lauren Pearle, *'I'm Being Sued for WHAT?'*, ABC NEWS (May 2, 2007), https://abcnews.go.com/TheLaw/story?id=3121086 [http://web.archive.org/web/20150327160920/http:/abcnews.go.com:80/TheLaw/story?id=3121086] (on file with the Apex Defense Consulting library).

6 TALKING HEADS, *Once in a Lifetime*, *on* REMAIN IN LIGHT (DELUXE VERSION) (Apple Music, Sire Recs. Oct. 8, 1980).

Why? What has changed in the last 30 years? Why are American juries more willing than ever to award outsized verdicts? Are plaintiffs getting injured more often or more severely? Have state laws changed to grant plaintiffs more money than in the past? Have state supreme courts ruled that verdicts are just not high enough, instructing juries to award even more?

No. Put quite simply: the plaintiffs' bar has changed. Plaintiffs' attorneys are better than ever before at persuading our neighbors to award large sums of money, often generational wealth. It is now time for the defense to respond in kind. It is time for The Apex.

WHAT ARE NUCLEAR VERDICTS?

A Nuclear Verdict is simply defined as an outsized jury verdict of $10 million or more. The more exact definition examines the relationship between economic and noneconomic damages to determine whether the label applies. Specifically, a Nuclear Verdict is any case where the jury awards noneconomic damages, typically referred to as pain and suffering, disproportionate to the economic damages in the case.

Nuclear Verdicts are unjust and unfair. "They are 'nuclear' in the sense that such a verdict can have devastating impacts on business, entire industries, and society at large," even when the excessive award is later overturned or reduced by a judge.[7] Nuclear Verdicts no longer only happen in big cities that traditionally have a more plaintiff-friendly jury pool. These outsized awards are occurring more often and for larger amounts in almost every state across the country.

In fact, in 2018, our country saw the first ever single plaintiff $1 billion verdict in Georgia. Juries often award Nuclear Verdicts in cases involving catastrophic, life-changing injuries or death, such as the Georgia case. Despite these gut-wrenching losses, a verdict of tens or hundreds of millions, even billions of dollars, often goes far beyond just compensating the plaintiff like

---

7 Cary Silverman & Christopher E. Appel, *Nuclear Verdicts: An Update on Trends, Causes, and Solutions*, U.S. Chamber of Com. Inst. for Legal Reform 2 (May 30, 2024), https://instituteforlegalreform.com/wp-content/uploads/2024/05/ILR-May-2024-Nuclear-Verdicts-Study.pdf (on file with the Apex Defense Consulting library).

the law requires. Awarding someone generational wealth, even in the most significant cases, is not the purpose of our American civil justice system.

Sir Isaac Newton taught us that, "For every action there is an equal and opposite reaction." We wish this applied to the impact of Nuclear Verdicts. For every Nuclear Verdict (action), we see an unequal, disproportionate ripple effect (reaction) throughout American society and economy. The frequency and severity of Nuclear Verdicts has risen to the point that folk are starting to take notice.

Enter: social inflation.

THE BIGGER PROBLEM: SOCIAL INFLATION

Nuclear Verdicts are one of the primary drivers of social inflation in the United States.[8] "Social inflation" is a term coined by Warren Buffett in a letter to Berkshire Hathaway's shareholders in 1977, where he described it as, "a broadening definition by society and juries of what is covered by insurance policies."[9] The United States liability insurance market is in a state of social inflation today, where the increased costs of insured liability claims are outpacing economic inflation.[10] Specifically, the net costs of liability claims were at a 20-year high of 7% in 2023[11] and rising much faster than the average rate of economic inflation of 3.6%.[12] The result? The cost of insurance policies is also going up and rising at a faster clip than economic inflation.

---

8 Martin Boerlin, James Finucane, Thomas Holzheu, Roman Lechner, Arnauld Vanolli, Shuyang Wu & John Zhu, *sigma No 4: Litigation costs drive claims inflation: indexing liability loss trends*, SWISS RE: INST. 2 (2024), https://www.swissre.com/dam/jcr:6bc7d3b7-0f42-4209-a01a-e22787b98685/sri-sigma4-2024-litigation-costs-claims-inflation-final.pdf ("Liability claims severity has trended significantly higher than economic factors due mostly to a rising number of very large verdicts against commercial defendants.") (on file with the Apex Defense Consulting library). *See also Regulator Insight: Social Inflation*, NAT'L ASS'N OF INS. COMM'RS: CTR. FOR INS. POL'Y AND RSCH. (Jan. 2023), https://content.naic.org/sites/default/files/cipr-report-social-inflation.pdf (discussing social inflation in more depth) (on file with the Apex Defense Consulting library).

9 *Regulator Insight: Social Inflation supra* note 8, at 2.

10 *Litigation costs drive US liability claims by 57% over past decade, reveals Swiss Re Institute*, SWISS RE (Sept. 7, 2024), https://www.swissre.com/press-release/Litigation-costs-drive-US-liability-claims-by-57-over-past-decade-reveals-Swiss-Re-Institute/0b538159-9648-47da-a152-4550a7640d35 (on file with the Apex Defense Consulting library).

11 *Id.* at 2.

12 *Id.* at 7.

The United States liability risk pool is the largest in the world and is highly susceptible to social inflation. Since 2015, the U.S. has seen a sharp increase in Nuclear Verdicts, particularly in bodily injury cases.[13] Anyone who scrolls news headlines or drives by those catchy billboards has seen it firsthand—we are experiencing a "rising frequency of large single-claimant events, often based on ballooning…[pain and suffering]…damages."[14]

Comparing the McDonald's hot coffee case to the Starbucks hot tea case is a powerful case study. The 1994 McDonald's verdict of $2.9 million has the same buying power as about $6.2 million in 2025.[15] Yet, the 2025 Starbucks verdict for $50 million was a 1,700% larger verdict than the jury's verdict in 1994. Additionally, the entire Starbucks jury award was for pain and suffering damages, while 93% of the McDonald's verdict was for punitive damages. Personal injury jury trials of today (1) carry much higher financial stakes and (2) are heavily, if not exclusively, focused on pain and suffering.

Social Inflation: The Cause

Over the past 20 years, the plaintiffs' bar has dramatically changed the way they work up and try cases. They now deploy applied psychology to jury trials and test their tactics on mock juries in order to increase the likelihood that a jury will decide a case more on emotion than fact.[16] Through the "use of psychology-based strategies"[17] plaintiffs' attorneys effectively "manipulate juror behavior" and "inflate damages[,]"[18] especially in personal injury cases. We fully dive into these psychological tactics throughout this book. Outside the courtroom, plaintiffs' attorney advertising, the rise of social media and news coverage around these excessive jury awards, changes in jurors' attitudes

---

13 *Id.* at 2-3.

14 *Id.* at 9.

15 *CPI Inflation Calculator*, U.S. Bureau of Lab. Stat., https://www.bls.gov/data/inflation_calculator.htm (input "2,900,000.00" into the first box, "August" into the second, "1994" into the third, "May" into the fourth, and "2025" into the fifth, or insert the current month and year into the fourth and fifth boxes for a more updated figure) (on file with the Apex Defense Consulting library) (last visited June 16, 2025).

16 Boerlin et al., *supra* note 8, at 15.

17 *Id.* at 2.

18 Silverman & Appel, *supra* note 7, at 5.

toward social injustices, and rising anti-corporate sentiment all feed the problem of Nuclear Verdicts.

The dirty little secret of the plaintiffs' bar (maybe one of many) is that the injured plaintiffs are not receiving most of the money awarded by juries in their cases. Instead, the plaintiffs' lawyers take 40% to 50% of these verdicts as a contingency fee. Then, expert witnesses, who are used over and over again by the plaintiffs' bar, are paid handsomely for the outcome. Other litigation expenses are also deducted. Well, you would think that leaves at least 30% of these verdicts for the injured plaintiffs, right? Wrong.

There is a growing, "trending" cause of these outsized awards that seriously harms the plaintiff and contributes to social inflation. In many cases, a litigation finance company, often called a Third-Party Litigation Funder or "TPLF," bankrolls the litigation. These finance companies give both plaintiffs and their lawyers loans on their lawsuit and then expect to be paid back many times over on their money.

Litigation Funding is basically an investment by a third party otherwise uninterested in the lawsuit that leaves the aggrieved plaintiff relatively, if not actually, very little money at all. A recent report by Swiss Re found the amount of money a plaintiff recovers "decreases by 21%" when TPLF is involved.[19] Of course, there is little to no disclosure required of TPLF involvement, so these predatory agreements continue without any oversight or intervention. The U.S. Chamber of Commerce Institute for Legal Reform tracks and publishes papers regarding the industry and its impact, and its resources are invaluable for continued reading.

Why does all this happen? You guessed it. This line of "finance" is highly lucrative for the "investor" and the plaintiffs' attorneys.

Despite all the big headlines about multimillion dollar verdicts, very little of it makes it to the plaintiff. Jurors who think they are making a plaintiff's life measurably better have no clue they have just funded the wealthy lifestyle of

19 Irina Fan, James Finucane, Anja Grujovic-Vischer, Thomas Holzheu, Dale Predmore & Ayush Uchil, *US litigation funding and social inflation: The rising costs of legal liability*, SWISS RE: INST. 3 (Dec. 2021), https://www.swissre.com/dam/jcr:7435a896-5f4b-463b-a1e6-7d4ec17db556/swiss-re-institute-expertise-publication-us-litigation-funding-and-social-inflation (on file with the Apex Defense Consulting library).

lawyers (many of whom travel via private jet or yacht), doctors, and funding corporations instead.

Social Inflation: The Effect

Nuclear Verdicts harm society. Outsized awards are increasing in frequency and severity across almost every jurisdiction and line of commercial insurance business in the country. "When excluding the pandemic years, the data shows an upward trend in the frequency of reported [N]uclear [V]erdicts at all levels" between 2013 and 2022.[20] Verdict award amounts are also increasing. Nuclear Verdicts in excess of $100 million have given rise to the new term "Mega"[21] Nuclear Verdicts and "Thermonuclear"[22] Verdicts. Experts predict that while economic inflation seems to be cooling, social inflation in the United States continues to increase and is likely to spread across Europe.

We often hear the feedback that Nuclear Verdicts are not a big problem because the plaintiff does not actually recover the full verdict amount that the jury awarded at the end of the day or because the awards are often reduced or overturned on appeal. While this may sometimes be true, the fact that juries across the country are awarding outsized verdicts remains a very real problem that has very real (and detrimental) impact. These verdicts embolden plaintiffs and their attorneys and drive up the value of claims. Nuclear Verdicts drag out the lifespan of a civil case and drive up the cost of defense because they very often involve an appeal after the verdict is rendered, bringing bonds and post-judgment interest into play. Everyday Americans begin to believe that verdicts in the hundreds of millions of dollars are the norm and are justified, so the next trial has an even higher likelihood of going nuclear.

Liability insurance carriers exposed to bodily injury claims have experienced a cumulative underwriting loss of $143 billion between 2018-2023, leading to significantly reduced capacity, reduced limits, and increased

20 *Id.* at 2.

21 *Id.* at 3.

22 *Corporate Verdicts Go Thermonuclear*, Marathon Strategies (2024), https://marathon-strategies.com/wp-content/uploads/2024/05/Marathon-Strategies_Corporate-Verdicts-Go-Thermonuclear-2024.pdf (on file with the Apex Defense Consulting library).

premium costs in the business insurance marketplace.[23] The risk of Nuclear Verdicts makes it more difficult for insurance carriers and defense counsel to resolve claims. Nuclear Verdicts also threaten the "viability of a business or the availability of a needed product, or create insurability problems for an entire industry."[24]

Courtroom or Cashroom?

Plaintiffs' attorneys have run away with the American civil legal system. Our legal system was not intended to create generational wealth. The civil justice system was intended to right wrongs, make injured people whole, and deliver justice for all. Instead, courtrooms have become cash registers. Our court system is being manipulated as a for-profit machine.

Nuclear Verdicts cost Americans their jobs, their businesses, and raise the prices of goods and insurance for all of us. The insurance industry, businesses of all sizes, and ultimately, consumers are paying the price through the trickle-down increased costs of goods and services. Every one of us suffers from these unjust verdicts.

The trend must stop. "If left to develop along their current trajectory, [N]uclear [V]erdicts promise to become further entrenched and to continue threatening livelihoods and raising costs across the economy."[25]

The good news? We have a solution. All we need to do is look in the mirror.

---

23 Boerlin et al., *supra* note 8, at 2.

24 Silverman & Appel, *supra* note 7, at 5.

25 Cary Silverman & Christopher E. Appel, *Research: Nuclear Verdicts: An Update on Trends, Causes, and Solutions*, U.S. Chamber of Com. Inst. for Legal Reform (May 30, 2024), https://instituteforlegalreform.com/research/nuclear-verdicts-an-update-on-trends-causes-and-solutions/ (on file with the Apex Defense Consulting library).

WE ARE THE SOLUTION

"You must be the change you wish to see in the world."
—Mahatma Gandhi

The leading research institutions in the country have published suggested solutions to stopping Nuclear Verdicts and social inflation. These include instituting more tort reform (such as laws to bifurcate cases, limit noneconomic damages, strengthen expert opinion evidence based on sound science, prevent forum shopping, and institute more damages caps); regulating plaintiffs' lawyer advertising; ending or requiring transparency around third-party litigation funding; increasing corporate loss mitigation; and rejecting legislation to extend statutes of limitations and damages caps.[26] These are all outstanding solutions. Let us do them all. Everyone should write their Congressperson, right now. Let us know how that works. We know many of us have been trying this for over 30 years.

In the meantime, want to stop Nuclear Verdicts now? Well, here lies the value in this book:

We are the immediate solution to the problem of Nuclear Verdicts.

Where do Nuclear Verdicts happen? In courtrooms. Who is on the front line in courtrooms every single day, defending against Nuclear Verdicts? We are.

We are the solution.

Our civil justice system is not broken; we are.

We defense lawyers are getting outlawyered. Plaintiffs' lawyers are not better trial lawyers than we are, but they are using better trial techniques. It is time for us to adapt. We must defend and try our cases differently today to stop Nuclear Verdicts from the trenches of the courtroom battlefield. We must protect our clients—individuals and businesses of all sizes—from these exaggerated awards. We can stop Nuclear Verdicts, one case at a time. This book provides the tools to do so.

26 Silverman & Appel, *supra* note 7, at 54-60; Boerlin et al., *supra* note 8, at 38-40.

Experts have classified Nuclear Verdicts as "fundamentally unpredictable."[27] We disagree. While these verdicts may be difficult to predict from an underwriting perspective, we believe these verdicts can be predicted at the claims stage, especially with the use of AI-driven software advancements.[28] We also believe defense attorneys have the power to prevent these outcomes because plaintiffs' attorneys follow a formula to obtain Nuclear Verdicts. What can YOU do today to stop Nuclear Verdicts?

THE DEFENSE PLAYBOOK, SUPPORTED BY DATA: THE APEX

Nuclear Verdicts: Defending Justice for All ("*Nuclear Verdicts*")[29] drew upon Bob Tyson's and Tyson & Mendes' trial experience to show how to execute innovative defense strategies to defuse juror anger and avoid a Nuclear Verdict. Since we published *Nuclear Verdicts* in 2020, we continued our study of Nuclear Verdicts in further pursuit of Justice for All. We tracked Nuclear Verdicts as they hit the media. We also pulled trial transcripts to study what is happening in the courtroom to drive these outrageous results. Our research and analysis led to the book you hold in your hand.

This book examines the quantitative and qualitative data behind Nuclear Verdicts. In 2022, we began collecting trial transcripts from 100 Nuclear Verdicts across the country. We read these transcripts and analyzed the arguments presented by the plaintiff and defense attorneys word-for-word to determine the tactics, strategies, and methods advanced by each side.

Break the Nuclear Verdicts Pattern with The Apex

Spoiler Alert: Nuclear Verdicts follow a pattern.

This book not only shares the Nuclear Verdict pattern we discovered, but it also lays out the defense playbook and data supporting it to give you the tools to stop a nuclear result in your next trial. This book shares the plaintiffs'

27 Silverman & Appel, *supra* note 7, at 2.

28 Schaefer City Techs., schaefercity.ai (on file with the Apex Defense Consulting library) (last visited June 16, 2025).

29 Robert F. Tyson, Jr., Nuclear Verdicts: Defending Justice for All (2020).

bar's formula for trial, allowing the defense to predict how the plaintiffs' bar is going to position and manipulate their next case in front of a jury.

Our research also proves what we at Tyson & Mendes have known all along: the trial strategies presented by Bob Tyson in *Nuclear Verdicts* are not piecemeal methods to pick and choose to deploy at trial. These strategies to prevent a Nuclear Verdict are a complete, holistic approach to defending cases. Our comprehensive defense approach is now "**The Apex**."

The Roadmap

PART I

The Apex will transform the way you analyze and defend your cases, and we cannot wait to present it to you in Part I. Part I also provides an overview of our analysis of 100 Nuclear Verdicts and provides the framework for our following deep-dive sections that explore each element of the Core Four.

PARTS II, III, IV, AND V

Parts II-V examine each element of the Core Four: *Personalize the Defendant* (Part II), *Accept Responsibility* (Part III), *Give a Number* (Part IV), and *Argue Pain and Suffering* (Part V). Each section is comprised of three chapters. Within each section, we take a deep dive into a different case study across civil practice areas that resulted in a Nuclear Verdict to examine plain-tiff 's story and the psychological techniques used by the plaintiffs' lawyers to get the jury angry. We next explore the psychological research in support of the element of the Core Four and present our data about the element's impact on Nuclear Verdicts. Finally, we present a hypothetical, alternative Apex defense approach to the original case study, explaining how the defense could apply the element of the Core Four in that case.

How We Tell These Stories and Why

As co-authors, we (Bob and Cayce) tell personal stories throughout the book. When necessary, we name the storyteller for your ease of reading. We hope you enjoy!

We also introduce each case study from a real Nuclear Verdict with a narrative story from plaintiff's perspective, drawn from publicly available documents including trial and other transcripts, court filings, and news articles about the cases. We editorialize at times to paint a vivid picture for you, our reader. Our Nuclear Verdict narratives advance the arguments made by plaintiffs' counsel, including the judgments, characterizations, and word choices to incite and fuel juror anger. We have also changed the names of parties and witnesses in our Nuclear Verdict case studies to respect those involved. Any similarity in name to real entities or individuals is coincidental.

This book is not a criticism of specific defense attorneys. While the defense bar has not adapted, it is not our fault alone. First, the insurance industry, one of the oldest financial institutions in the world, often does not allow us to adapt. The industry, by nature, is risk averse and fundamentally conservative. Insurance companies have also put significant hurdles in place to prevent us from acting outside the box to make their costs predictable. Litigation billing guidelines do not promote creativity.

Second, hindsight is almost always 20/20. Our analysis is based on limited available data. This book is not intended to Monday-morning quarterback a case based on our document review and analysis. Defense teams live and breathe cases for years. There is no way for us to know all the elements that caused a defense lawyer to take a particular approach in a case. Nevertheless, we believe this analysis is necessary and meaningful for our industry. We must reflect on our losses. We must draw conclusions. We must look forward. We must learn and grow in order to better defend our clients and stop Nuclear Verdicts.

Based on the records available, we conclude Nuclear Verdicts fit a pattern. Our review of these cases gives us data from which we can learn and appropriately respond. We cannot change the past, but we can change the future, through different choices and a different defense strategy. Our intent in this book was to show how an alternative defense approach to these cases through The Apex mitigates a nuclear result and helps achieve a just result for both parties—not just plaintiffs and their attorneys. Our purpose was to give the insurance defense industry the most actionable information to change the course of history. We have created resources to complement the findings and tools offered in this book. We invite you to join our Apex Defense Community for continued growth.

Please visit www.apexdefenseconsulting.com.

So, are you ready for it?

PART I:
THE APEX

CHAPTER 1

JUROR ANGER FUELS NUCLEAR VERDICTS

"It is your duty to find the facts from all the evidence in the case. To those facts you will apply the law as I give it to you. You must follow the law as I give it to you whether you agree with it or not. And you must not be influenced by any personal likes or dislikes, opinions, prejudices[,] or sympathy. That means that you must decide the case solely on the evidence before you. You will recall that you took an oath to do so."

—Ninth Circuit Civil Jury Instructions (emphasis added)

CAYCE'S TRIAL CALL AT "THE VAULT"

THE MOOD IN THE HALLWAY outside the courtroom was tense. As a young associate, naturally, my stomach was full of knots at the reality of having to enter the courtroom and sit at the defense table in mere minutes. We were assigned to the courtroom at the very end of the long marble hallway of the Downtown Los Angeles Superior Court, also known as "the Bank" or "the Vault," largely in recognition of the venue's propensity for Nuclear Verdicts.

Our defense team huddled together in the corner and tried to look calm, confident, and commanding. My supervising partner, Mina Miserlis, sat on the wooden bench to my right. She was polished and ready to welcome potential jurors into the courtroom. Just after arguing motions *in limine* (pre-trial motions), that is. She quietly flipped the pages of our motions, soaking in the case citations one last time, and took steady breaths.

Mina and I bonded over the course of the last month working up this case in which Tyson & Mendes was hired to represent the defendant just weeks before trial, what we call a "parachute case." We worked long days and late nights getting up to speed on the case and developing our trial strategy to avoid a Nuclear Verdict. I now knew Mina well enough to sense that while on the surface she looked calm if not outright serene, under the water her little duck feet were paddling away, ready to go. While the fear of the unknown fueled some of my anxiety, Mina had been in this situation many times before. Her energy was one of overpreparation and eagerness—confidence.

In the corner just past Mina, our co-counsel also sat, quietly scrolling his phone. The whole defense team held an intense meeting the night before in a cramped Marriott hotel room to finalize our defense strategy. Under a popcorn ceiling, we huddled to discuss the same approach Mina and I had recommended for the last three weeks leading up to trial call, but our co-counsel still would not agree to our unorthodox method.

The excess carrier brought our firm into the case in the eleventh hour because they feared the verdict would hit their layer of insurance, which began at $2 million. Our co-counsel, a team led by an experienced trial attorney at a big firm in Los Angeles, had defended the high net worth insured since day one under the primary policy—a personal auto policy. The excess carrier believed in our creative approach to trial and asked us to join the defense trial team to implement these strategies and protect the insured and both carriers from an outsized jury award.

As one might imagine, our co-counsel did not exactly want us involved. Though Mina and I played nice, he did not appreciate our input. The primary carrier never offered their policy limits to settle the case, so it retained control of the defense. Our co-counsel was lead in this trial, and he let us know it in so many words.

In our meeting the night before, we had a heated discussion about how to apply the four strategies Mina and I believed would defuse juror anger and avoid an outsized jury award. Co-counsel agreed that he would *Personalize the Defendant*—we represented a physician who had a powerful story to tell about overcoming adversity to earn his medical degree and help others. Co-counsel also agreed to *Accept Responsibility* (to a limited extent) at trial because this was an admitted liability case. Specifically, counsel planned to tell the jury our client "stipulated to liability" in jury selection and opening statement. He declined, however, to apply either of the two remaining strategies; he would not *Give a Number* nor *Argue Pain and Suffering* to the jury.

I heard a "click, click," and turned to find the court clerk unlocking the doors to the courtroom. Co-counsel jumped up and moved toward the door, signaling his intent to be first to the defense table. I took a breath and said a silent prayer for him, "Please show the jury you are a good human today."

THE APEX: DEFUSE JUROR ANGER

The Apex is a framework of litigation and trial strategies for the defense to address and stop the number one driver of social inflation: outsized and unjust Nuclear Verdicts. Developed by Nuclear Verdict experts and trial lawyers from our law firm, Tyson & Mendes, the defense approach consists of four levels of skills and strategies that build upon one another and work together toward the ultimate goal and apex: **defuse juror anger**. Each tool included in the pyramid is intentional, strategic, data-backed, and necessary. The Apex provides the framework for the defense to take back control of the thing that the law prohibits from entering the deliberation room but is inevitably always there: emotion.

Juror Emotion Drives Nuclear Verdicts

"Men, as well as women, are much oftener led by their hearts than by their understandings."
—Earl of Chesterfield, Philip Dormer Stanhope, 1694-1773

The plaintiffs' bar has dramatically changed the way they try cases over the last 20 years, based on human psychology. Plaintiffs' lawyers have studied the way humans process information and the impact of emotions on decision-making. What they learned makes sense: emotions "powerfully, predictably, and pervasively" drive almost every decision we make.[1] Despite jury instructions to the contrary, personal beliefs and emotion affect jury verdicts.

"[J]urors' emotions and moods can affect their judgments in various ways: by influencing the type of information processing in which they engage, by inclining them to construe evidence in a direction consistent with their moods, and by providing informational cues about the appropriate verdict."[2] "Despite instructions to remain impartial, jurors bring their own life experiences and moral perspectives into the deliberation room."[3] It bears noting that while studies confirm these truths, one need only look at a typical approach to selecting a jury for trial to see the universal acknowledgment that humans are guided by life experience and feeling in jury service. Counsel on both sides typically aim to do three things in jury selection: (1) educate the jury about the case and why they should win; (2) identify jurors who cannot

---

1 Jennifer S. Lerner, Ye Li, Piercarlo Valdesolo & Karim S. Kassam, *Emotion and Decision Making*, 66 Ann. Rev. Psych. 799, 802 (2015), https://www.annualreviews.org/content/journals/10.1146/annurev-psych-010213-115043?originator=useradmin&identity=5131&timestamp=20991231000000&signature=f2fc615517c25fcbcc1950705c210b26 (on file with the Apex Defense Consulting library).

2 Brian H. Bornstein & Edie Greene, *Jury Decision Making: Implications For and From Psychology*, 20 Curr. Dir. Psych. Sci. 63, 65 (2011) (citing Neal Feigenson, *Emotional Influences on Judgments of Legal Blame: How They Happen, Whether They Should, and What to Do About It*, 56 Nebraska Symposium on Motivation: Emotion and the Law: Psychological Perspectives 45 (Brian Bornstein and Richard Wiener, eds. 2009)), https://www.law.nyu.edu/sites/default/files/upload_documents/Jury-Decision-Making.pdf (on file with the Apex Defense Consulting library).

3 *Behind Closed Doors: Exploring Jury Decision-Making Dynamics*, LITILI Litig. Legal Insight, https://litiligroup.com/jury-decision/ (on file with the Apex Defense Consulting library) (last visited June 17, 2025).

be fair due to their personal experiences and biases; and (3) get jurors to like them.

Inherent in our jury system is the reality that humans, complete with their biases and fallibility, serve as our finders of fact. Juror biases influence their interpretation of evidence, testimony, and the law, potentially leading to unjust outcomes. The legal system strives to mitigate jury bias through jury instructions and the deliberation process, but the presumption or belief that any juror can enter the deliberation room without their humanity, life experience, and lens on the world intact is unrealistic. The difference between the plaintiffs' bar and the defense bar is that plaintiffs' lawyers, through their study of human psychology and collaboration, have harnessed the power of this truth while the defense bar has largely failed to adapt.

Jurors Award Nuclear Verdicts When They Are Angry

One particular emotion drives human behavior more than others: **anger.** "[A]nger is an emotion that we feel when something gets in the way of a desired outcome or *when we believe there's a violation of the way things should be.*"[4] Angry humans think and act irrationally. Anger "activates our nervous system and can hijack our thoughts and behaviors."[5] Anger is not conducive to logical and rational decision-making. Perhaps unsurprisingly, it is this emotion that drives disproportionate jury verdicts more than any other.[6] While there has been recent debate surrounding the role of anger in Nuclear Verdicts, multiple studies, our trial experience, and the study of nuclear trial transcripts confirm its power. As you will see through the examples we reference throughout the rest of this book, the language that plaintiffs' lawyers use in trial is intentional, powerful, and clearly targeted at generating anger.

The plaintiffs' bar embraces the concept that "[w]hen we feel anger, we believe that someone or something else is to blame for an unfair or unjust

4 Brené Brown, Atlas of the Heart: Mapping Meaningful Connection and the Language of Human Experience 220 (2021) (emphasis added).

5 *Id.* at 220.

6 Julie H. Goldberg, Jennifer S. Lerner & Philip E. Tetlock, *Rage and reason: the psychology of the intuitive prosecutor*, 29 Eur. J. Soc. Psych. 781 (1999), https://jenniferlerner.com/wp-content/uploads/2017/07/37.Rage-and-Reason.pdf (on file with the Apex Defense Consulting library).

situation, *and that something can be done to resolve the problem*."[7] Someone who is angry is also likely to feel certain, and this may be in part because anger is a means of re-establishing control. "When an individual feels certain, this tells him or her that the information he or she currently has is correct and complete, thus eliminating the need to search for more information."[8] Feeling anger is also "related to lower quality information processing," meaning anger can stop the human brain from receiving and accurately processing additional information.[9]

Anger is also a powerful catalyst that can spark action. Anger motivates jurors "to blame and punish the accused."[10] One study concluded that anger leads to more punitive jury verdicts in the criminal setting.[11] This makes sense: humans do not like feelings of vulnerability (likely an evolutionary holdover), and anger acts to restore control through subsequent behavior. Plaintiffs' counsel often empower an angry jury to "send a message" with their verdict, leading jurors to believe they have the power to prevent this kind of accident or incident from happening again to someone else. In the civil arena, angry jurors believe the larger the dollar amount of their verdict, the more the defendant is punished and the less likely this kind of harm will recur. In other words, jurors believe the amount of their verdict is directly proportional to their ability to protect the safety of their community; higher Nuclear Verdict = safer community.

Anger arises when we see harm caused by someone who had the ability to control whether the harm occurred and then leads us to assign blame to the perpetrator.[12] In criminal trials, "angry jurors are more likely to sen-

7 Brené Brown, *supra* note 4, at 220 (emphasis added).

8 Victoria Estrada-Reynolds, Kimberly A. Scheitzer & Narina Nuñez, *Emotions in the Courtroom: How Sadness, Fear, Anger, and Disgust Affect Jurors' Decisions*, 16 Wyo. L. Rev. 343, 350 (2016), https://scholarship.law.uwyo.edu/cgi/viewcontent.cgi?article=1365&context=wlr (on file with the Apex Defense Consulting library).

9 *Id.* at 351.

10 *Id.*

11 *Id.*

12 Jennifer S. Lerner, Julie H. Goldberg & Philip E. Tetlock, *Sober Second Thought: The Effects of Accountability, Anger, and Authoritarianism on Attributions of Responsibility*, 24 Pers. & Soc. Psych. Bull. 563 (1998), https://scholar.harvard.edu/files/jenniferlerner/files/www.jenniferlerner.com__7.pdf (on file with the Apex Defense Consulting library).

tence defendants to death and argue that the prosecution was stronger than the defense."[13] One psychological study found that "people who saw an anger-inducing video of a boy being bullied were then more punitive toward defendants in a series of unrelated fictional tort cases involving negligence and injury than were people who had seen a neutral video[.]"[14] Psycho-legal scholars have consistently concluded that anger affects juror decision-making.[15] This has proven to be disastrous for the defense.

Up until about 20 years ago, the number one emotion the plaintiffs' bar tried to elicit from jurors was sympathy. The pivot toward anger was advanced by the publication of *Reptile: The 2009 Manual of the Plaintiff's Revolution* ("*Reptile*") (since rebranded as "The Edge"), which was the result of years of jury research specific to how the reptilian brain drives jury decision-making. And while the book urges readers to believe its aim is *not* the manipulation of juror emotion, an introductory chapter to the book called "The Reptile Speaks" is revelatory. Here, a person's reptilian brain "speaks" to him: "*I want to kill whatever threatener wakes me... I do not get angry.* ***I make you angry so you will do what I want you to.***"[16]

Today's plaintiffs' bar uses specific tactics to make jurors feel this emotion—anger—to drive a Nuclear Verdict. These changes in their approach to trial have resulted in higher jury verdicts occurring more frequently across almost every jurisdiction in the country, regardless of case type or injury severity. To arrive at an outsized jury award, jurors must, at a primitive and deeply-felt level, be angry at the defendants for something they did or failed to do.

To enrage a jury, effective plaintiffs' attorneys focus their arguments on the conduct of the defense and its potential for further, speculative harm

---

13 Estrada-Reynolds et al., *supra* note 8, at 350.

14 Jennifer S. Lerner & Katherine Shonk, *How Anger Poisons Decision Making*, Harv. Bus. Rev. (Sept. 2010), https://hbr.org/2010/09/how-anger-poisons-decision-making (on file with the Apex Defense Consulting library).

15 Estrada-Reynolds et al., *supra* note 9, at 350.

16 David Ball & Don Keenan, Reptile: The 2009 Manual of the Plaintiff's Revolution 21-22 (2009).

(what *Reptile* calls "tentacles of danger")[17] instead of the plaintiff's actions or the incident giving rise to the lawsuit. For example, in a trucking accident trial, instead of focusing only on the subject accident, persuasive plaintiffs' attorneys will focus the jury on the defense's hiring and training practices and larger safety record. Focusing on the defendant, not sympathy for the plaintiff, is a radical change in trial strategy.

When defense counsel stands to deliver opening statements, she is, at best, inheriting a jury at the threshold of anger. At worst, she is inheriting jurors already feeling rage, even *before any evidence is presented.* Thus begs the question: how is the defense to respond when faced with such an uphill battle, littered with landmines meticulously laid out by a plaintiffs' bar equipped with psychological tools and traps? How can the defense defuse juror anger?

Enter: The Apex.

17 *Id.*

CHAPTER 2

THE APEX

THE APEX DEFUSES JUROR ANGER AND PREVENTS NUCLEAR VERDICTS

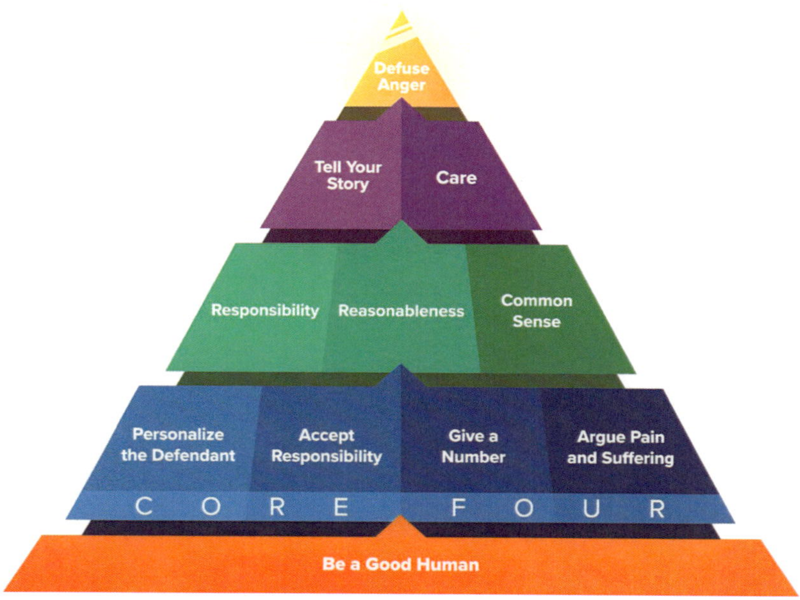

THE APEX PROVIDES A STRUCTURED, strategic approach to developing and presenting the defense's case to the jury. The Apex gives us the tools to combat plaintiff's psychological tricks in the courtroom by embracing humanity at every step of our defense. This methodical approach to our defense (and ultimately trial) empowers us not only to ethically influence juror emotion, but it goes further to tackle the primary emotion driving Nuclear Verdicts: (you guessed it) anger.

The purpose of The Apex is to defuse juror anger. That is why it occupies the top of the pyramid (the apex), and why the name of the method itself reminds us in moments of doubt or struggle, to look *up*. This method, when delivered by the defense from a place of authentic empathy, effectively disarms any rage felt by a jury. It vanquishes the *Reptile*, the Edge, or any other cleverly branded plaintiffs' tactic aimed at manipulating jurors. By defusing juror anger, The Apex leaves the jury space to deliberate a case based on common sense, logic, and reason (three characteristics the defense and the law itself appreciate in jurors, but that plaintiffs' counsel abhors). This approach educates, equips, and empowers a jury to reach a verdict that is fair and reasonable to all parties involved, not just plaintiffs and their lawyers (who stand to gain 40% or more of whatever verdict the jury returns).

WHY THE APEX?

In response to (and despite) the psychological truth that anger is a better motivator than sympathy, the defense bar has largely remained loyal to the decades-old approach to defending cases: poke holes in plaintiff's arguments, fight liability at all costs, admit nothing, and avoid discussing money with the jury. This traditional defense approach plays right into plaintiffs' attorneys' hands. It makes the defense appear cold, heartless, sneaky, and greedy. It fuels juror anger. And, in turn, it leads to Nuclear Verdicts. We contend, and the data in this book confirms, that when the defense does not adapt, we are complicit in the nuclear result we receive.

We developed The Apex for avoiding a Nuclear Verdict through trial (pun intended), study, and research. Frankly, we developed this method based on our courtroom and trial experience. Our attorneys go up against the best plaintiffs' attorneys in the country every single day across the United States. We have seen them in action. We have beaten them in action. We know what they are up to, we are ready for them, and we want *you* to be ready, too. Our clients deserve it, and justice demands it.

We also developed The Apex through our research and study, the apex of which (again, pun intended) you hold in your hand. We are not ashamed to admit we took a cue from the plaintiffs' bar here. The same psychological studies and principles available for plaintiffs are available for the defense. After all, there is no such thing as "plaintiffs' bar psychology" and "defense bar psychology." There is just "human psychology." Jurors are humans. We must use arguments and framing that are effective when persuading humans serving jury duty.

The Apex taps into human psychology in a compelling and useful way, but you must understand the following: The Apex is genuinely aimed at justice and fairness. It is not based in gimmicks. It is not a trick or a tactic. It does not make defense attorneys look "slick." The Apex shows the jury that the defense *truly is* the most reasonable party in the courtroom, *not simply acting* like the most reasonable party in the courtroom. And, it will make you uncomfortable. Good—that is where growth happens.

The skills and strategies that make up each component of The Apex are meant to build upon one another from the ground up. The defense team must enter The Apex at its foundation and work up through each strategy to reach the "apex" and defuse juror anger. In sum, The Apex demonstrates the humanity of the defendant while embracing the humanity of the plaintiff and the jurors, positions the defense as the most reasonable party in the room, defuses juror anger, and empowers the jury to deliver justice—for *all*.

THE APEX FOUNDATION: *BE A GOOD HUMAN*

Lawyers, especially defense lawyers, must show the jury their humanity at trial. Good trial lawyers understand their vulnerability is a superpower rather than a weakness. We must demonstrate genuine empathy in trial. We must be good humans in the way we defend our cases, approach our facts, and negotiate with plaintiffs.

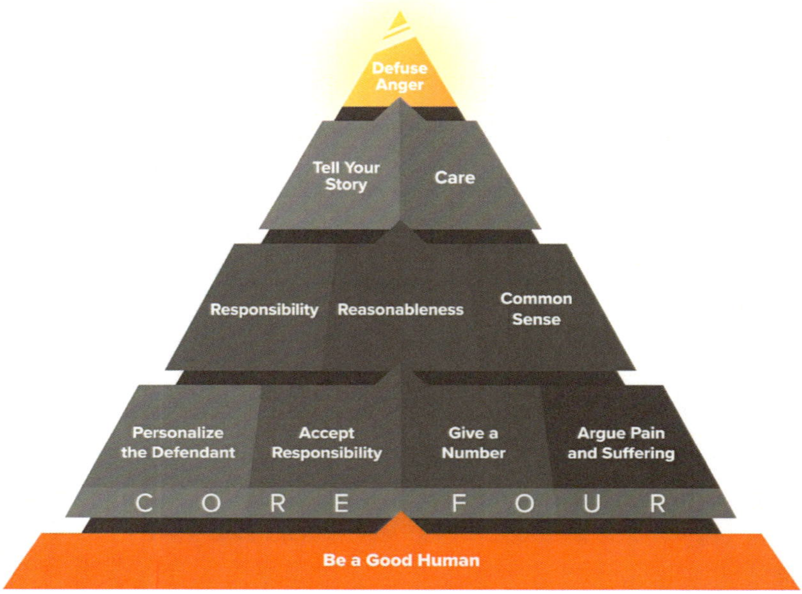

We are not jerks. We care about justice and fairness. We care about people, including the plaintiff. We must continue to show up as the good, caring people we are, even in the midst of an adversarial process.

Lawyers, especially trial lawyers, like to win. It is easy to be so focused on "winning" that we fail to see the forest for the trees. On the other side of the courtroom, seated at plaintiff's table, are humans. The plaintiff is a human who may have suffered a real and painful loss. How would we encounter an injured or suffering person outside the courtroom? Would we not show compassion, empathy, and understanding? Of course we would.

Human suffering is a devastating and unavoidable part of life. Empathy is a true measure of comfort to human suffering. We cannot allow ourselves to be so focused on the "win" that we lose sight of who we are. Sometimes we defense lawyers focus so hard on vigorously defending our client that we forget about empathy.

The result? Our traditional trial approach makes plaintiff's suffering worse, not better. We look like total jerks to the jury: out of touch, robotic, and cold. Is that who we are? Is that who our clients deserve? No.

We cannot check our humanity at the courthouse steps, just like jurors cannot leave their common sense behind when they show up for jury service. We must intentionally bring the whole of who we are when we stand before jurors. Our partner, Jim Sell, describes the foundation of The Apex, *Be a Good Human*, as "Be the Person Your Mother Raised You to Be." We are sons, daughters, siblings, spouses, parents, leaders, friends, and community members. We are bright, vibrant, awkward, delightful, layered *humans*. Who could not love us if they truly knew us?

We must talk to jurors like we talk to our neighbors. We must share true stories about our life as it relates to the case and the decision the jurors face. We must validate the plaintiff's feelings, not only because it is the kind and decent thing to do, but because jurors are likely to feel the same. We must show empathy in our word choice, tone, and phrasing of questions.

The Apex is not only effective at trial when defense counsel (and the defendant, as discussed later in this book) allow themselves to be fully, genuinely, imperfectly, and empathetically human. Our humanity, our empathy is the foundation of The Apex. Without it, justice will not be served.

THE APEX LEVEL TWO: THE CORE FOUR

The Core Four forms the second tier of The Apex. Our research presented in this book focuses almost exclusively on the Core Four. We examined whether and to what extent the defense is engaging these four strategies when the jury awards a Nuclear Verdict. We present our analysis and conclusions about the efficacy of the Core Four in the pages you are about to read.

As discussed in Bob Tyson's first book, *Nuclear Verdicts*, the defense must develop and implement the Core Four at trial to defuse juror anger and secure a reasonable verdict:

1. *Personalize the Defendant*
2. *Accept Responsibility*
3. *Give a Number*
4. *Argue Pain and Suffering*

The Core Four are built upon the foundation of *Be a Good Human*. Without fully embracing our humanity and using all four strategies, we are not equipped to move up toward the apex, defuse juror anger, and avoid a Nuclear Verdict.

Personalize the Defendant

"Engrave this upon your heart: there isn't anyone you couldn't love once you've heard their story."

—Mary Lou Kownacki

The Apex calls defense counsel to *Personalize the Defendant*—whether an individual or an entity—at trial.[1] Companies are made up of people. The law across the fifty states requires the jury to treat the corporate defendant (i.e., companies) as it would an individual defendant (i.e., a person). But, left to their own devices (thanks to corporate identity effect) and with the help of the plaintiffs' bar, jurors rarely do this.

It is much easier for jurors to be angry at a faceless (and therefore presumed "evil" or "greedy") corporation (with "deep pockets") than it is to be angry at the empathetic people who founded, built, staff, grow, and keep a company. A faceless corporation plays right into plaintiffs' attorneys' tactics and themes.

---

1 *See* Robert F. Tyson, Jr., Nuclear Verdicts: Defending Justice for All 112-125 (2020) (providing a full discussion of personalizing the corporate defendant).

The same is true for a faceless individual defendant. While Nuclear Verdicts against single, individual defendants are rare, we must personalize our individual clients for the jury, as well.

DEHUMANIZATION

The plaintiffs' bar aims to dehumanize the defense in the eyes of the jury—both the defendant itself and even defense counsel as its representative. Dehumanization is "the psychological process of demonizing the enemy, making them seem less than human and hence not worthy of humane treatment."[2] Dr. Brené Brown has called dehumanization "one of the greatest threats to humanity."[3] We argue it is also one of the greatest threats to our civil and criminal justice systems.

When deployed on a large scale, dehumanization is at the root of unspeakable atrocities and human rights violations around the globe. On a very small scale in civil courtrooms across the United States, a dehumanized corporate defendant is an easy target for an outsized, punitive verdict even when punitive damages are not at play. This tactic, coupled with the fact that corporate mistrust is at an all-time high post-pandemic,[4] creates a nuclear volcano ready to erupt.

HUMANIZE AND PERSONALIZE

Defense counsel must combat this by not only humanizing our corporate client, but by also personalizing our client for the jury. We should "humanize" the defendant by showing that people make up the company and then go further to "personalize" the corporate client by showing the jury *who* the people are behind the company. While we refer to "corporations"

---

2 Michelle Maiese, *Dehumanization*, Beyond Intractability (modified by Heidi Burgess, June 2020), https://www.beyondintractability.org/essay/dehumanization (on file with the Apex Defense Consulting library).

3 Brené Brown, Atlas of the Heart: Mapping Meaningful Connection and the Language of Human Experience 233 (2021).

4 *Juror Attitudes in a Polarized Society*, Orrick, Herrington & Sutcliffe LLP, https://www.orrick.com/en/Insights/Groundbreaking-Jury-Research-Reveals-US-Jury-Attitudes-in-a-Polarized-Society (on file with the Apex Defense Consulting library) (last visited February 15, 2025); *Confidence in Institutions*, Gallup®, https://news.gallup.com/poll/1597/confidence-institutions.aspx (on file with the Apex Defense Consulting library) (last visited February 15, 2025).

and "companies," this strategy is just as critical for other entity defendants, including municipalities, school districts, and others.

Defense counsel must *Personalize the Defendant* through storytelling. These stories defuse juror anger by building human connections even the *Reptile* cannot sever. Counsel must uncover and then share the origin story of the company, why the business was founded, and the good the company does. The jury should come to know the positive impact the company has on the lives of its employees, as well as what drives it. Every superhero has an origin story, so why not a corporate defendant?

Counsel must also personalize the entity through the corporate representative who attends trial every day. This person may also testify at trial, ideally telling a personal story of their experience working for the company. The corporate representative who attends trial demonstrates the humanity of the defendant and shows that the defendant cares about the plaintiff.

Accept Responsibility

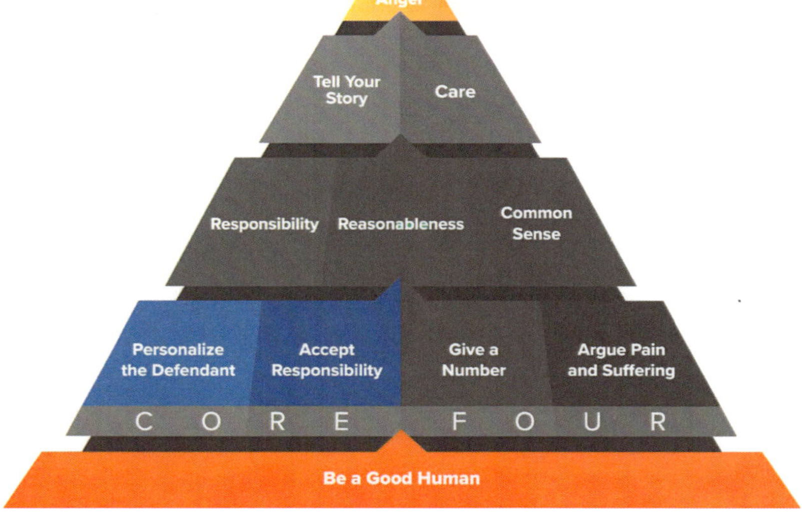

The Apex requires the defense to *Accept Responsibility* for *something* in every single trial, even when the defense is seeking a defense verdict.[5] Yes, the defense can (and must!) *Accept Responsibility* and still obtain a defense verdict.

Psychology tells us the most effective way to defuse anger is to validate it. At trial, the most effective way for the defense to validate is to *Accept Responsibility* for something. *How* defense counsel should *Accept Responsibility* varies based on the facts of each case and the strength of our liability arguments. But the defense must *Accept Responsibility* for something in every single case regardless of our liability position. Refusing to *Accept Responsibility* equips plaintiff's attorney with the powerful narrative that the defense does not care and is not listening, which only fuels more juror anger.

Defense teams—defense counsel, defendant(s), and insurance carrier(s)—very often resist accepting responsibility for a host of reasons, primarily because they believe that accepting responsibility means admitting liability. Here lies the core concept of this strategy:

Responsibility is not the same as fault.

We will say it again for the people in the back:

Responsibility ≠ Fault

"[Here is] one way to think about the distinction between the two concepts. Fault is past tense. Responsibility is present tense. Fault results from choices that have already been made. Responsibility results from choices [we are] currently making, every second of every day."[6] Conflating the two concepts is what Mark Manson calls the "responsibility/fault fallacy," and we see it in our defense practice time and again.

Accepting responsibility validates plaintiff's, and likely the jury's, feelings. It de-escalates feelings of annoyance, irritation, and anger. It demonstrates the reasonableness of both the defendant and the defense's arguments. Once the jury's anger is addressed (defused), the jury is able to listen and

5 *See* TYSON, *supra* note 1, at 14-32 (providing a full discussion of accepting responsibility).

6 MARK MANSON, THE SUBTLE ART OF NOT GIVING A F*CK: A COUNTERINTUITIVE APPROACH TO LIVING A GOOD LIFE 95 (2016).

process the defense's evidence and arguments. A jury who feels emotions other than anger can still reach a logical verdict based on reason.

Give a Number

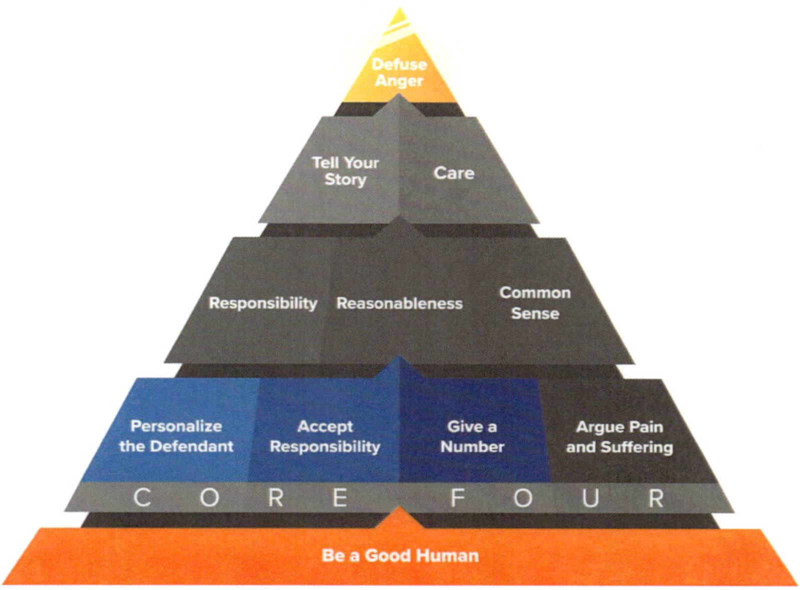

Plaintiffs' attorneys have come to understand there is a simple but powerful way to get a Nuclear Verdict from the jury: just ask for it. Using the psychological tactic of anchoring, plaintiffs' attorneys condition jurors to accept the reasonableness of a verdict of tens or hundreds of millions of dollars, even before the jury has heard any evidence. Anchoring is the "cognitive bias that describes the common human tendency to rely too heavily on the first piece of information offered (the 'anchor') when making decisions."[7]

The plaintiffs' bar methodically approaches discussing money with the jury to get bigger and bigger verdicts. Specifically, plaintiffs' attorneys talk to jurors about a number as early as possible in the trial, as early as jury

7 *The Anchoring Effect and How it Can Impact Your Negotiation*, HARV. L. SCH.: PROGRAM ON NEGOT. (Mar. 5, 2025), https://www.pon.harvard.edu/daily/negotiation-skills-daily/the-drawbacks-of-goals/ (on file with the Apex Defense Consulting library).

selection in jurisdictions where permitted. This is called priming. Plaintiffs' counsel also repeat their number(s) to jurors throughout the course of trial. This is called desensitizing. Finally, plaintiffs' counsel conclude closing arguments by justifying their number with creative tactics. This is called recency. When combined, these psychological tactics condition jurors to award a Nuclear Verdict.

In order to combat these anchoring effects at trial, The Apex instructs the defense to also *Give A Number* in every single case.[8] When plaintiff's counsel sponsors a number for the jury at trial, the defense can ignore it, identify it, provide a counter-anchor, or attack plaintiff's number. Yes, of course, we can fight whether plaintiff's counsel should be allowed to discuss numbers with a jury in pretrial motions and other objections. But, as the traditional adage says, "If you can't beat 'em, join 'em."

Studies have shown that the most effective way for the defense to combat the cognitive bias created by plaintiff's anchor is to provide a counter-anchor at trial.[9] This is true even when we argue that there is no liability and the jury should award a full defense verdict. In fact, one study shows the defense is *even more likely* to get a defense verdict when we sponsor a counter-anchor.[10] Yes, not only can you give a number and still get a defense verdict, but giving a number actually increases the likelihood you will obtain a defense verdict. Now that is change!

The Apex lays out several parameters for giving a defense number, all tied to overcoming the cognitive bias of plaintiff's anchoring. We must (1) give the number early, (2) repeat the number often, (3) never increase the number, and (4) the number must be reasonable. These parameters ensure the defense's valuation is memorable, trusted, and reasonable to the jury at the time of deliberation.

---

8 *See* Tyson, *supra* note 1, at 33-49 (providing a full discussion of giving a number).

9 John Campbell, Bernard Chao, Christopher Robertson & David V. Yokum, *Countering the Plaintiff's Anchor: Jury Simulations to Evaluate Damages Arguments*, 101 Iowa L. Rev. 543 (2016), https://ilr.law.uiowa.edu/sites/ilr.law.uiowa.edu/files/2023-02/ILR-101-2-Campbell.pdf (on file with the Apex Defense Consulting library).

10 *Id.*

Argue Pain and Suffering

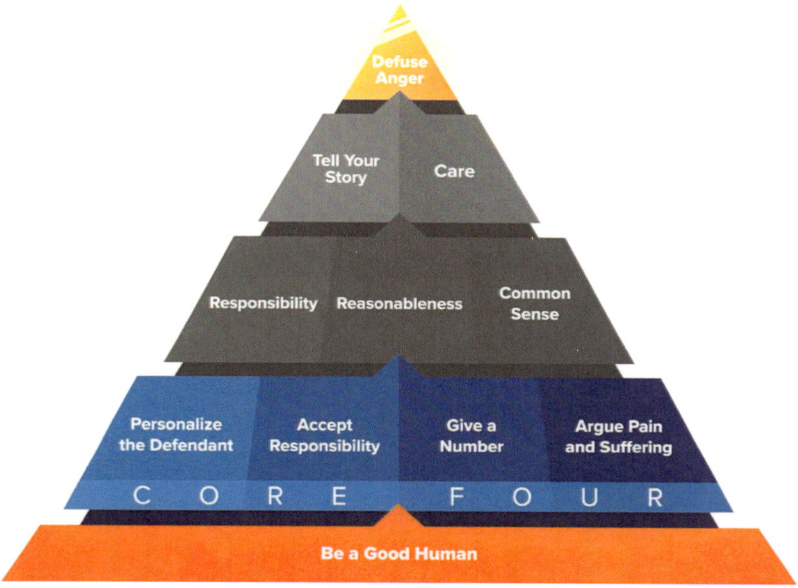

Noneconomic damages, also known as general damages or pain and suffering damages, make up the largest damages component in most Nuclear Verdicts. This is no accident: this category of damages is nebulous and intangible, and the law specifically offers little guidance nor formula. It is also the most "human" category. Noneconomic damages are meant to compensate for the loss of emotional connectors: love, joy, hope, and future.

The plaintiffs' bar has developed a series of powerful narratives to support their requests for tens and hundreds of millions of dollars from a jury for pain and suffering. Juries who award Nuclear Verdicts are not only angry, but they also agree with plaintiffs' counsel that the "human losses" are the most significant harm plaintiffs have suffered. We created a glossary of plaintiffs' attorneys' most common and effective pain and suffering arguments, included as Appendix A.[11]

11 *See also* TYSON, *supra* note 1, at 64-84 (providing a more in-depth discussion of many of plaintiffs' attorneys' common pain and suffering arguments).

Effectively arguing pain and suffering is perhaps the most important element of the Core Four. The defense must argue to a jury why our number is fair and reasonable and is going to make the plaintiff (this specific human plaintiff) whole. Our pain and suffering arguments educate jurors and equip them with the reasoning to align with our client when it is time to deliberate. It also provides the jury with a reasonable counter-narrative to plaintiffs' counsel's incredulous and manipulative pain and suffering arguments.

The Apex directs defense counsel to *Argue Pain and Suffering* in every single case, even when seeking a defense verdict. In most Nuclear Verdicts, the defense does not argue pain and suffering at all in closing argument. When defense counsel declines to argue pain and suffering, the jury deliberates with only one narrative about the human losses in the case: plaintiff's counsel's narrative. Defense counsel who choose to remain silent on pain and suffering lose a critical opportunity to connect with the jury on a human level, and instead play into the plaintiff's anger-driving narrative.

The Apex provides a two-pronged approach to arguing pain and suffering: defense counsel must argue (1) the impact of the accident on plaintiff's life and (2) the impact of money on plaintiff's life.[12] Delivering both prongs of this method in closing argument requires us to strategically develop the evidence to determine and support the defense's number in discovery. It also requires empathy, creativity, and storytelling.

ALL OR NOTHING

We introduce the higher levels of The Apex as we conclude this book. For now, we must emphasize The Apex is an all-or-nothing strategy. To defuse anger and avoid a Nuclear Verdict, the defense team must fully engage with every single component of The Apex. We often hear from defense attorneys, defendants, and claims professionals that these unconventional skills and strategies only apply to "some" cases or in the "right" case. We disagree.

12 *See id.* at 14-32 (providing an in-depth discussion of how the defense should argue pain and suffering).

Every single element of The Apex is intentional and necessary. The Apex is not a buffet. Counsel cannot pick and choose which strategies to apply in a particular case. Each level builds upon the others to elevate the defense toward achieving the goal of defusing juror anger. Only when every element of the pyramid is engaged will the defense rise to the apex and prevent a Nuclear Verdict.

CHAPTER 3

100 NUCLEAR VERDICTS: THE PATTERN OF INJUSTICE

"Turning data into action is the foundational key to success."
—Billy Beane

THE 100 NUCLEAR VERDICTS ANALYZED

"I WENT TO LAW SCHOOL because I couldn't kick it in math and science courses in college." If you know or work with lawyers, you might have heard this phrase a time or two. We are lawyers, not statisticians. That said, we now know there is no better teacher than writing a book about data and numbers. If it takes 10,000 hours to become an expert at something, we might be closing in on the finish line of true expertise.

Our goal in conducting this analysis and writing this book was to find and present a clear picture of what universal threads exist in Nuclear Verdicts across every case type, injury severity, and jurisdiction. We wanted to answer: "What is actually happening in trial when a jury awards a Nuclear Verdict?" What better way to find out than to go to the source: the courtrooms themselves?

We decided to obtain the closing argument transcripts from 100 Nuclear Verdicts across the country to closely examine the closing arguments advanced by both the plaintiff and defense. The closing argument phase is a valuable capsule of what happened over the course of the trial. In closing argument, attorneys recap the best parts of their case, the worst parts of their opponent's case, and argue to the jury why they should decide in favor of their client. Plus, closing arguments are generally available to the public if you know where to look.

When we first began the project of reading transcripts from 100 real Nuclear Verdicts, we set out with hypotheses of what we expected to find, as well as a general idea of the data points we wanted to track. After we analyzed a couple dozen cases, we noticed trends, patterns, and common arguments we did not initially set out to track. So, with this new knowledge, we started our work again from the beginning.

We share this so you know a couple of things: first, we attempted (as much as possible) to apply consistent standards for tracking and analyzing the data at the heart of this book. Second, even *we* were surprised by some of what we found. We are confident the final 60+ data points we analyzed in every single trial represent the most comprehensive and complete set of data points available for analysis. Third, we relied not only on our experience as trial lawyers in finding, contextualizing, tracking, and analyzing this data, but also on the information the data itself provided.

"Nuclear" Results

When we began our analysis in 2022, the only criteria for whether we included a case was the case had to be "nuclear." In our final data set, most (but not all!) verdicts are over $10 million, aligning with the traditional threshold of a Nuclear Verdict. However, a case that falls short of that $10 million definition may still be nuclear if the award (particularly the pain and suffering damages) is disproportionate to the facts and injuries of the case. So, included in our final set of 100 verdicts is a small handful (three, to be exact) of cases where the verdicts were below $10 million but the noneconomic damages were disproportionate to the economic damages.

Get the Transcripts

Beyond the requirement that cases be "nuclear," our next requirement was we had to actually get the trial transcripts. This was surprisingly difficult in some cases. Most often, we had to find the court reporter who covered the trial and purchase the transcript directly from them or their company.

The court reporting landscape has changed dramatically in the last 10 years. Human court reporters are highly in demand. It was difficult to track down the real court reporter for each trial. Many court reporters were incredibly helpful—thank you! In one instance, we called the court reporter on her personal cell phone—we apologize! At the end of the day, we found the transcripts despite many roadblocks, and you now hold this book in your hand.

A Decade of Nuclear Verdicts

Beginning our analysis a second time offered us a chance also to ensure the cases included were fresh enough to be helpful. We culled from our list any cases older than 2015. This gave us a solid 10 years of cases to analyze.

We did not set out to obtain more cases from known plaintiff-friendly jurisdictions, sometimes called "Judicial Hellholes®", but as you will see, there was a greater percentage of those jurisdictions included in our 100 verdicts, consistent with other studies which have identified these "top" states. We did not include in our universe of cases any class actions (in large part because a $20 million verdict in a class action would not actually be nuclear if the class consisted of 5,000), nor did we seek out specific types of cases. Our selection process was intended to produce a randomized, representative sample of outsized jury awards. We believe it did just that.

Analysis by Human

Humans analyzed all the data that went into this book. We say this to tell you that AI had no part in our analysis. We love what AI can do (identifying

Nuclear Verdicts before they happen, for example),[1] but we did not know of any generative artificial intelligence in 2022 that we trusted to take on this analysis for us. The accuracy of the data was just too important to us to take the risk. In hindsight, it sure would have been nice to have the technology we have now back then!

Instead, our small research team of mostly attorneys read these verdicts line-by-line. We tracked over 60 data points in each trial to figure out what psychology-based methods plaintiffs' lawyers are using to drive juries to Nuclear Verdicts and how defense attorneys are responding. Trial is dynamic, layered, and contextual. Words matter, so we focused our painstaking analysis on the exact words chosen by attorneys on each side of the case to show us what is and is not effective when persuading a jury.

This work required reading for context and applying reasoned judgment. Just as our jurors are (and must be) human, so too is our research team. The project of reading the hundreds of thousands of trial transcript pages necessary for a complete (and accurate) analysis of trends required a trained, focused *human* eye. We are forever grateful to our team of Nuclear Verdict experts who came together to make this book possible.

Our process was methodical, time-consuming, and deeply gratifying. The data was surprising, validating, and endlessly fascinating. We have tried to refrain from "geeking out" about the data too much in this book (you are welcome). Instead, you will find a solid introduction to the cases, our methodology in analyzing them, and the overarching trends we observed.

A Few Disclaimers

As lawyers, we must provide a few disclaimers about the data and analysis at the heart of this book. This data set is inherently limited to 100 out of thousands of Nuclear Verdicts throughout the course of history. Extrapolation and statistical significance is inherently limited (i.e., we cannot

1 *E.g.*, SCHAEFER CITY TECHS., schaefercity.ai (on file with the Apex Defense Consulting library) (last visited June 16, 2025).

run regression analysis on this data). Nevertheless, the data is powerful, accurate, and meaningful.

It might go without saying, but this data set is explicitly limited to Nuclear Verdicts. There are no defense verdicts represented within the set of 100 cases analyzed, nor are there any verdicts that are *not* nuclear. This analysis was conducted to determine what is happening in courtrooms where Nuclear Verdicts are delivered, so those are the only cases we considered. As you read about the impact of using the Core Four on overall verdict size, recall that we are dealing *only* with Nuclear Verdicts. We do not analyze in this book the frequency of defense verdicts when using the Core Four.

It is also important you know what information we did *not* have for this analysis. We did not have access to pretrial demands in any of the cases within our data set; our analysis is explicitly limited to what occurred in trial. We also did not know much (if anything) about the carrier involved in these cases, or policy limits or terms. We did not conduct interviews of jurors in these cases, nor did we interview counsel. We situated ourselves as closely as possible to the jurors who heard and ultimately decided these cases, free of extrajudicial information that might have unfairly impacted our analysis.

For consistency's sake, we tried to avoid comparing verdict sizes between cases, because the verdict in a multi-fatality wrongful death case is not truly comparable to the verdict in an employment law case. It would be unfair and inaccurate to draw conclusions from a larger verdict in a wrongful death case than from an employment law case, because the nature and extent of "injury" is so different.

Instead, we compared the final verdict amount the jury awarded to the amount plaintiff's counsel requested in damages at trial. We measured whether a particular trial method was effective based on the final jury's award compared to plaintiff's damages ask. If defense counsel used method A and it resulted in the jury awarding only 40% of plaintiff's requested damages and method B resulted in the jury awarding 110% of plaintiff's ask, we concluded that method A was more effective for the defense, even though the case resulted in a nuclear award. This provided a more uniform and consistent mechanism of evaluating trial methods.

Further Growth: Join Our Apex Defense Community

Believe it or not, this book provides the highest-level data, analysis, conclusions, and recommendations on preventing Nuclear Verdicts with The Apex. Yes, we have even more information to share. For more insight, expertise, discussion, and collaboration (including more data!), we created Apex Defense Consulting, a space dedicated to moving the insurance defense industry forward through unparalleled community and expert-led education and consulting. Join our Apex Defense Community for more![2]

So, are you ready to meet the 100 Nuclear Verdicts we analyzed? Let's go!

THE PATTERN REVEALED

We provide the 30,000-foot overview of the Nuclear Verdicts we analyzed below. Keep in mind, this data does not represent all Nuclear Verdicts from 2015 to 2024. Rather, this data represents the relevant Nuclear Verdicts we were able to obtain and chose to examine. The U.S. Chamber of Commerce Institute for Legal Reform publishes outstanding research and analysis on the holistic problem of Nuclear Verdicts, considering a more complete list of jury awards.

Plaintiff-Friendly Jurisdictions are Hotter than Ever

There is a known list of plaintiff-friendly jurisdictions prone to delivering Nuclear Verdicts. The U.S. Chamber of Commerce Institute for Legal Reform has identified the top 10 states by cumulative Nuclear Verdicts between 2013 and 2022 to be: California, Florida, New York, Texas, Georgia, Illinois, Pennsylvania, Washington, Missouri, and Ohio.[3] While we did not seek

---

2 Visit www.apexdefenseconsulting.com to learn more.

3 Cary Silverman & Christopher E. Appel, *Nuclear Verdicts: An Update on Trends, Causes, and Solutions*, U.S. Chamber of Com. Inst. for Legal Reform (May 30, 2024), https://instituteforlegalreform.com/wp-content/uploads/2024/05/ILR-May-2024-Nuclear-Verdicts-Study.pdf (on file with the Apex Defense Consulting library).

out cases from these jurisdictions, the top states represented in our data set mirrors that list pretty closely.

California topped our list as the state hosting the highest number of Nuclear Verdicts, at 30%. Number two was Georgia, at 11%. Florida and Texas tied at 7%, and Pennsylvania came in at 5%.

Top Five States for Nuclear Verdicts

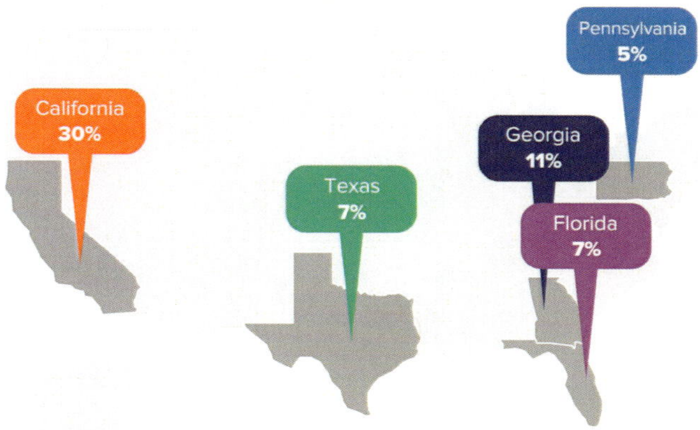

However, the list shakes up when we look at the average verdict amount in each state.

Missouri takes the cake there, where the average of only three cases was $1.8 billion. Next comes Texas, with the average verdict amount of $236,872,500. Third up was Pennsylvania, where the average verdict was $212,220,000, and then Georgia, with an average verdict of $210,782,241. After those top three, there was a steep drop-off to reach California, with an average verdict amount of $83,251,635, and then Florida came in at number six with an average verdict of $57,918,077.

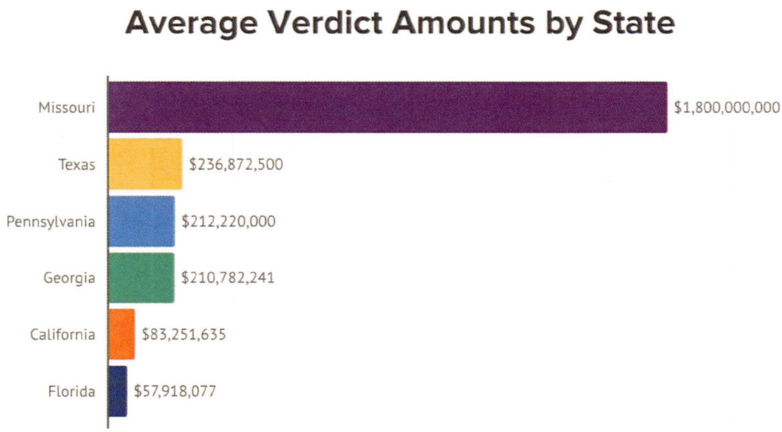

The average verdict for all 100 Nuclear Verdicts was $166.5 million, including the whopping average of $1.8 billion represented in Missouri. Removing that outlier, the average for all other states was $92 million.

Personal Injury and Wrongful Death Cases Make Up the Largest Percentage of Nuclear Verdicts

As mentioned, we surveyed broad types of Nuclear Verdicts for inclusion in our analysis. The resulting list of case types, therefore, is incredibly broad both in terms of case type and injury severity. Represented among our 100 Nuclear Verdict analyses are the following case types:

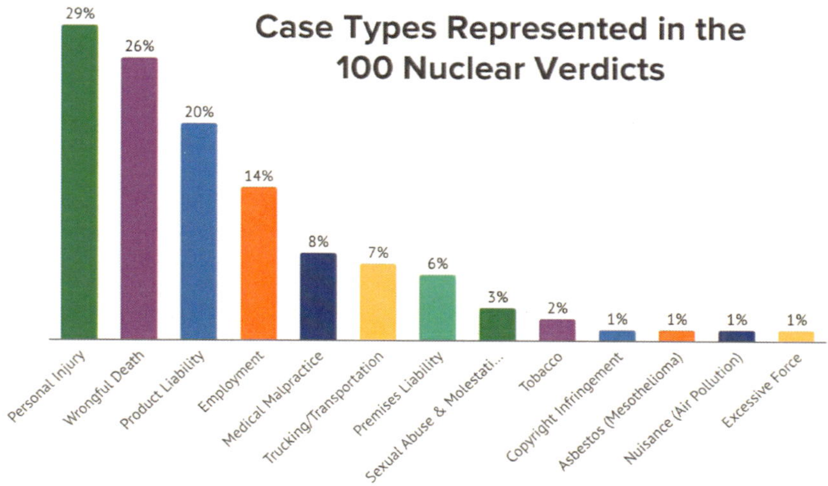

Of course, there is overlap between these categories. For example, "personal injury" or "wrongful death" may also include "trucking/transportation" and "medical malpractice" cases.

2021 and 2022 Saw Frequent Nuclear Verdicts

The 100 Nuclear Verdicts spanned from 2015 to 2024. Below is a chart demonstrating the percentage of cases from each year, in chronological order:

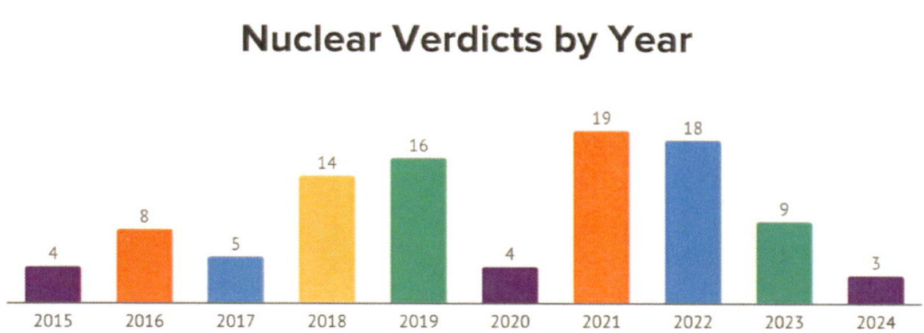

Unsurprisingly, we saw 2020 had the lowest average verdict amount, with only four Nuclear Verdicts coming in with an average of $25 million. In the aftermath of pandemic-related court closures, we collected a significant number of Nuclear Verdicts from 2021 and 2022. The year with the highest average verdict amount was 2018, at $36.6 million.

Repeat Players Get Nuclear Verdicts

We also tracked plaintiff's counsel and defense counsel in each of the 100 Nuclear Verdicts, and we saw repeat players in both columns. Surprisingly, it is often the most well-known and experienced defense counsel whose names appear in our list. Yes, big lawyers try big cases. But we believe this speaks to the need for a fresh approach and a willingness to adapt, try new things, take risks, and get creative. The same strategy that worked 20 years ago simply does not work now, and the recurrence of experienced counsel speaks volumes to that point.

THE CORE FOUR: HIGH-LEVEL TAKEAWAYS

As we dug into 100 closing arguments to learn what is happening in courtrooms when juries award Nuclear Verdicts, we focused on the specific approaches, strategies, and tactics used by both the plaintiff and the defense. Specifically, we focused on whether the defense utilized any aspect of the Core Four: *Personalize the Defendant*, *Accept Responsibility*, *Give a Number*, and *Argue Pain and Suffering*. We analyzed the frequency with which the defense used any of these strategies, as well as the impact of the element on overall verdict awards. Each of the following Parts of this book dive into an element of the Core Four, explaining how we considered whether a defense attorney "applied" the element at trial and to what effect, with conclusions and recommendations.

Some Good News

When looking at the Core Four level of The Apex as a whole, we found some good news. We noticed that the use of elements of the Core Four increased as time progressed. That is, the defense in the 2015 cases was substantially less likely to use any of the Core Four than the defense in 2024 cases. Again, while our analysis only surveyed nuclear results, we think this is good news for our industry. Since the publication of *Nuclear Verdicts*, we have spoken to thousands of claims professionals and their counsel about the strategies we use in trial to defuse juror anger and prevent Nuclear Verdicts. For a while, we thought the plaintiffs' bar had read our first book more often than defense counsel did. Seeing the progression of defense counsel using the Core Four is very encouraging!

No Nuclear Verdict Used the Complete Core Four

Our next finding is the thesis of this book: we have yet to find a single Nuclear Verdict where the defense employed all four elements of the Core Four as required by The Apex. As you will see in the pages that follow, the defense still routinely fails to use the Core Four and never uses all four when a Nuclear Verdict results.

The defense correctly used all four of the Core Four in 0% of cases, and used none of the Core Four in 31% of cases. As we discuss in Chapter 14, we were exceedingly generous in counting a defense discussion of noneconomic damages as having "argued" pain and suffering, so this percentage is significantly higher if we applied the more accurate, stringent definition.

Of the remaining 69% of cases where the defense used one or more of the Core Four, the defense was less likely to apply multiple strategies at once. The defense used one of the Core Four strategies in 38% of cases, two of the Core Four strategies in 21% of cases, and three of the Core Four strategies in 8% of cases. The combination of the strategies used varied, and is detailed in the chapters that follow.

To our surprise, the defense was the most likely to *Give a Number* than use any of the other Core Four strategies. The defense utilized *Give a Number* in 46% of cases, followed by *Argue Pain and Suffering* (meaning that they addressed noneconomic damages at all) in 31% of cases. The defense chose to *Personalize the Defendant* 22% of the time and agreed to *Accept Responsibility* in only 15% of cases. We expected to see a greater willingness to *Personalize the Defendant* than any other strategy, given that it is so easy to do and has no perceived bearing on liability, but the data shows this to be one of the least-used strategies in Nuclear Verdicts.

Frequency of Use of Each of the Core Four

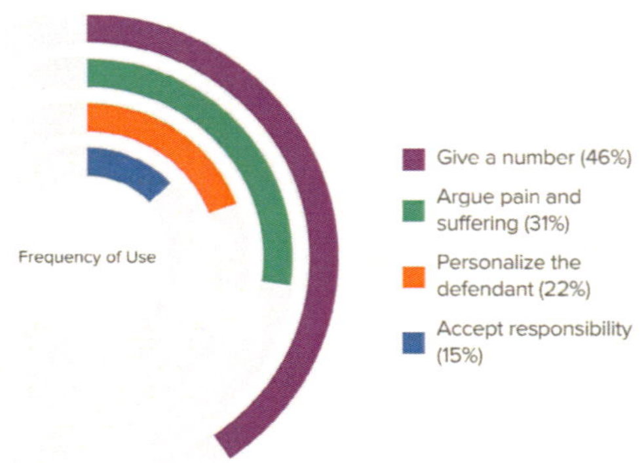

And, as you will see when we discuss it in greater depth in Chapter 14, even though the defense is more willing to address pain and suffering in *some* way than the other Core Four strategies, in only 2% of cases did the defense argue both Apex elements of pain and suffering, but zero cases fully and effectively delivered on these elements as demonstrated later in this book. Interestingly, there were three cases that came dangerously close to using all four of the Core Four strategies, and they are discussed in greater detail below.

The Prime Example Case

There was one case that emerged as a prime example of The Apex working to *stop* a Nuclear Verdict, even in our set of 100 Nuclear Verdicts. We know—that sounds contradictory! In this case, there were three named defendants: one individual, one small corporation, and one large corporation. The individual and the small corporation shared counsel, while the large corporation had separate counsel. The defense counsel for the individual and small corporation executed a near-perfect use of The Apex: they chose to *Accept Responsibility* (verbatim, even in a partial liability case!), *Personalize the Defendant*, *Give a Number*, and *Argue Pain and Suffering*. The counsel for the large corporation, however, did not use the Core Four. So, how did each party fare?

The defense counsel for the small corporation and the individual defendant delivered justice—for all. The combined verdicts against those two defendants was *under* $300,000! By contrast, the large corporation got hit for a whopping $30 million. In short: this case serves as a perfect example of what The Apex can do to avoid a Nuclear Verdict in a case that has all the markings of an outsized and unjust award. Bravo to this defense counsel!

The Close but No Cigar Cases

We identified two cases where the defense almost fully executed The Apex, but fell short when it came to pain and suffering. In those two cases, the defense agreed to *Accept Responsibility*, *Personalize the Defendant*, and *Give a Number* (though neither gave a number in the manner The Apex requires, as set forth in Chapter 11). And, they at least *discussed* pain and suffering, but in neither case did the defense use both elements of *Argue Pain and Suffering* as required by The Apex and set forth in Chapter 14. Instead, defense counsel either argued any noneconomic damages must be "fair and reasonable," or they argued the impact of the accident/incident, but *not* impact of money.

Here, even an imperfect application of The Apex made a huge difference in the final jury verdict! These verdicts averaged 39.5% of plaintiff's ask, compared to the 148.6% of plaintiff's ask where the defense failed to use any of the Core Four.

THE APEX PREVENTS NUCLEAR VERDICTS

It is here that we pause, take a breath, and say with bold confidence:

The Core Four Prevent Nuclear Verdicts.

We know this to be true. Now, the data supports it. Yes, we essentially proved a negative here. But the data is clear: we cannot find a Nuclear Verdict where the defense used the complete Core Four, meaning all four elements as taught in this book.

We have the solution to Nuclear Verdicts. All it takes is us being willing to try cases differently. We must fully and completely embrace The Apex, including the Core Four. When we do, we prevent Nuclear Verdicts and prevent social inflation.

We acknowledge these are bold statements. We stand behind them. Read on to learn how the plaintiffs' bar is securing Nuclear Verdicts, the psychology behind each element of the Core Four, and concrete examples of how you can choose to implement the complete Core Four in your next trial.

PART II:
PERSONALIZE THE DEFENDANT

CHAPTER 4

THE CASE OF (MIS)INFORMED CONSENT

Trigger Warning: The following case involves teenage pregnancy, abortion, and birth trauma.

AN IMMIGRANT TEEN NEEDS WORLD-LEADING PRENATAL CARE

Lydia Immigrates to the United States as a Teenager

LYDIA PRESCOTT WAS 16 YEARS old and pregnant when she left her home country of Liberia to immigrate to the United States. Lydia lived through the civil war in Liberia and fled the country at the height of the Ebola crisis. Lydia traveled halfway around the world by herself, alone and scared, where she was adopted by Julie and Jake Prescott, an American couple who wanted to help a child in need from the war-torn country.

On a crisp fall morning in mid-October, Lydia, who had been in the United States for only a few months, went with Julie to the doctor for a prenatal checkup. She had not received prenatal care prior to arriving in the States, so she was understandably excited and nervous about the appointment.

After routine weight and vital sign checks with the nurse, the doctor arrived in the examination room. Sitting on her swiveling stool, the doctor explained to Lydia that her blood pressure was elevated. The doctor wanted her to be examined further at Southern New England Hospital, where they had better facilities to treat her symptoms.

Doctor Refers Lydia to Southern New England Hospital

Later that day at Southern New England Hospital, another doctor examined Lydia and quickly diagnosed her with preeclampsia, a not uncommon but potentially fatal condition where a woman develops high blood pressure after twenty weeks of pregnancy. The Southern New England doctor explained to Lydia and Julie that, if left untreated, preeclampsia can lead to serious complications, including death, for the pregnant mother and the baby, and that the baby would need to be delivered early.

The doctor also explained to Lydia and Julie the need to transfer Lydia to Calloway Research Hospital, which had a Level III Neonatal Intensive Care Unit (NICU) equipped to care for premature babies and to treat preeclampsia in pregnancy. The move would provide Lydia a higher level of care, and her baby would benefit from their state-of-the-art NICU. The doctor asked both Lydia and Julie to sign a consent form for the transfer, which they signed, confident the doctor was advising them what was best for mother and baby.

Southern New England Hospital Transfers Lydia to State-of-the-Art Calloway Research Hospital

Accompanied by Julie, Lydia traveled to Calloway Research Hospital by helicopter. Lydia had never been in a helicopter before. As she flew over the city, she held Julie's hand, took deep breaths, and thought about her baby to try to calm her fears.

Once in her room, Lydia and Julie signed a general consent form authorizing the hospital to provide treatment for labor and delivery. The consent form noted the reason for treatment was preeclampsia and stated the benefit of receiving treatment was maternal/fetal well-being. It also indicated the probability of success was "fair."

An ultrasound soon followed. Doctors estimated the baby's weight was 644 grams, or about 1.4 pounds. Lydia's membranes had not yet ruptured, which happens when a woman is ready to deliver, leading the doctors to conclude Lydia was not in labor. The doctors at Calloway Research Hospital also had access to Lydia's medical history from Southern New England Hospital, which indicated the baby appeared otherwise healthy.

After assessing all the data at hand, Resident Dr. Smith reviewed the information with Lydia and Julie. Dr. Smith explained she anticipated Lydia would likely need to deliver early and require a Cesarean section (C-section), which was the best course of action for maternal and fetal well-being. She explained the major risks, benefits, and possible side effects to Lydia and the baby, including possible injury or death for the infant or the mother if she did not proceed with a C-section delivery.

After all Lydia and Julie's questions were answered, Lydia, Julie, and Dr. Smith signed the informed consent form. With their signatures, Lydia and Julie agreed Calloway Research Hospital would manage Lydia's labor and a vaginal delivery if one were possible, and Calloway Research Hospital could perform a C-section for any purpose it deemed necessary for the health of Lydia or the baby. As Lydia understood it, there were complications that needed to be managed, but she was confident she was in good hands at Calloway Research Hospital.

And then everything changed.

Calloway Research Hospital Provides Inaccurate Information Regarding Baby's Condition

The following morning, Calloway Research Hospital conducted an official ultrasound and estimated the baby's gestational age at 25 weeks and 4 days, over halfway to a full-term pregnancy. The scan also revealed the level of amniotic fluid in Lydia's uterus was well below normal. The baby measured at a size consistent with a gestational age of 23 weeks and 5 days–suggesting significant developmental delay. These findings were grim.

Later that afternoon, members of the NICU and obstetrical teams stood around Lydia's hospital bed and told her there was zero chance the baby's brain would develop normally. They also explained there was a high likelihood of death or a developmental disability for the baby. For the sake of Lydia's health, she needed to deliver the baby soon due to her high blood pressure.

The medical team recommended Lydia permit them to perform a C-section. Doctors cautioned a C-section carried risks of impacting her ability to carry future children. Based on her and her baby's condition, doctors would need to perform a classical C-section (with a north-south incision). Lydia was also told a C-section could cause her uterus to "explode" in the future. Nevertheless, doctors still recommended a C-section as the best course of action for Lydia and the baby.

Lydia had a decision to make. She and Julie expressed they wanted the opportunity to consider the information and discuss their options between inducing vaginal labor or going ahead with the recommended C-section. During that time, the doctors told them repeatedly the baby would most likely die either in utero or shortly following birth in either case. They said the NICU team would not be present at the delivery because the hospital would not resuscitate a baby in such condition.

The OB/GYN assigned to Lydia's case, Dr. Jones, then stepped in and offered to terminate the pregnancy because measurements taken by ultrasound indicated the gestational age was 23 weeks and 5 days. Abortion had never been discussed before. Lydia was shocked. She recalled doctors previously told her she was further along into her pregnancy. Calloway Research Hospital's policy allowed a parent to terminate a pregnancy or decline full resuscitative effort after delivery if a baby had a gestational age of *24 weeks* or less. According to Dr. Jones, at 23 weeks and 5 days based on the baby's size, Lydia could opt to terminate the pregnancy, induce labor for vaginal delivery, or choose to deliver by C-section.

Lydia is Faced with an Impossible Choice

Lydia faced an impossible and gut-wrenching choice for any mother-to-be, let alone a 16-year-old who was far from her home country. A C-section offered the best option if the baby was to live, but everything indicated it would not. A vaginal delivery was the safest option for Lydia's future health.

Lydia sat in her hospital bed and cried. Based on the initial diagnoses, Lydia had agreed to a C-section. But, given everything she now knew—that the baby would likely die no matter what she did, and the C-section would cause her pain and future difficulty delivering a healthy baby—Lydia changed her mind and chose to induce vaginal labor.

Within hours, nurses turned off the fetal monitor, which had continuously monitored the baby's heart rate and condition since arriving at Calloway Research Hospital. The constant "beeps" and "clicks" communicating the baby's condition fell silent. The hospital was no longer tracking the baby's position, condition, or health.

Doctors Scramble to Cover Their Mistakes

The following morning, Dr. Abbott, head of Labor and Delivery, learned that Lydia's fetal heart rate monitor had been turned off the night before, that termination had been offered to Lydia, and that Lydia was told the NICU would not be present to take care of the baby at birth. Dr. Abbott knew Lydia should not have been offered termination as an option because the baby was, in fact, over 24 weeks of gestational age. Dr. Abbott went to see Dr. Langley, chair of Obstetrics and Gynecology, to discuss all that had happened in the previous 48 hours. Together, the two doctors determined offering termination was wrong and, to cover the error, the NICU needed to be present at delivery.

Lydia sat in her hospital bed with her adoptive parents nearby when the NICU team visited her, along with Drs. Abbott, Smith, and Jones. This team surrounded the teenage mother, counseling her and her adoptive mother about her worsening preeclampsia and liver function test results. Dr. Abbott laid out the options for Lydia again, this time without offering the option to terminate the pregnancy: she could undergo a C-section for fetal indications or induce labor for a vaginal delivery.

Doctors Continue to Inform Lydia Her Baby Will Not Survive, So Lydia Again Declines a C-Section

After weighing her options and discussing the new developments with her adoptive mother, Lydia again chose an induced vaginal delivery. Approximately three and a half days after her initial prenatal doctor visit, under doctors' orders, a nurse administered medication to begin inducing labor.

Just 45 minutes later, Dr. Aldridge came on shift and began performing rounds to get up to speed on each obstetrics patient's condition. Reading Lydia's chart, Dr. Aldridge quickly noticed Drs. Abbott, Smith, and Jones had neglected to obtain Lydia or Julie's signatures on an informed consent form for the induction. This oversight could be costly in the event something went wrong with this already very complicated delivery.

To cover the hospital's tracks, Dr. Aldridge decided to create a post-induction informed consent form. It stated that: (1) Lydia declined a C-section for fetal indications with the understanding that induction of labor would impose additional stress to the fetus and could result in fetal loss or extreme compromise resulting in permanent disability, and (2) that Lydia understood the infant would have a better chance of intact survival if the C-section were performed instead of an induction of labor. Pleased he had covered their bases and saved the hospital from potential risk, Dr. Aldridge then presented the consent form to Lydia twice over the next few hours while she labored in her hospital bed alone, as Julie had stepped away for a break during the slow hours of early labor. Both times, the frightened and confused teenager refused to sign it, saying she needed her parent to be there with her. Lydia and Julie did not sign the new consent form until the following day, more than 15 hours after labor was induced.

Baby Amara is Born with Severe Birth Defects

Almost 24 hours later, Lydia's baby girl was born prematurely at 26 weeks' gestational age.[1] She named her Amara Prescott. Amara was limp, apneic, and weighed about 1.47 pounds. At the time of birth, the fetal monitor had been off for 63 hours and 15 minutes, during which time any medical issues Lydia's doctors could have addressed were not seen. Amara was whisked away to the NICU almost immediately. She had no heart rate and was intubated at four minutes old. The NICU specialists began compressions on her tiny body. Finally, at five minutes old, Amara's heart began to beat.

Amara was hooked up to monitors that regulated her breathing, heart rate, and all other vital signs. She was kept warm under lights and by a tiny, knitted cap on her head. Lydia visited her daily.

Amara remained in the Calloway Research Hospital NICU for nearly two months until, finally, it was determined she was stable enough to move to another hospital for longer-term care. She was discharged from Calloway Research Hospital and transferred to a nearby pediatric hospital.

Amara would live, but Lydia worried about what kind of life she would have. Lydia was stricken with grief and guilt. Looking back, she questioned her decision to opt for a vaginal delivery over a C-section because the doctors at Calloway Research Hospital told her the baby would die.

As a child, Amara has severe cerebral palsy. She suffers from brain damage and developmental delays. Amara is unable to walk or speak and requires constant care and attention. She cannot eat on her own and is fed with a feeding tube. She cannot experience life the way others do, and she will need care for the rest of her life, requiring hours of skilled nursing attention each day.

Lydia knows Amara is worth it, but it is too much for her to handle on her own. Amara now lives in a foster home. Just a young adult herself, Lydia is unable to provide the care Amara needs to live.

1 A full-term pregnancy is considered 39 weeks' gestational age.

THE POWERFUL, HEARTLESS CORPORATE DEFENDANT

On behalf of herself and Amara, Lydia sued Calloway Research Hospital, claiming the hospital violated her right to informed consent and provided negligent treatment. Lydia asserted she chose to deliver Amara vaginally rather than via C-section because her doctors at Calloway Research Hospital gave her inaccurate predictions for the baby's likelihood of survival. Lydia understood a C-section would involve a painful recovery and could impact any future pregnancies, but she persuasively claimed the doctors led her to believe the baby would not survive after birth, regardless of the delivery method.

Thus, she chose the least risky delivery method for herself: vaginal birth. If she had known the baby was in fact viable, Lydia claimed she would have agreed to a C-section despite the pain and risk to herself, in order to save Amara from birth injuries and disability. Ultimately, Lydia asserted she made a misinformed decision to forgo a C-section at the time of delivery based on negligent and false information from her doctors, and because of the misinformation provided to her, she never actually gave informed consent.

After just under three hours of deliberation, a jury found in favor of Lydia and Amara on all counts and awarded damages in the amount of $229,640,000. Not only did this jury award exceed the amount plaintiffs requested at trial, but it was also the largest medical malpractice verdict in United States' history. The jury award broke down as follows:

- $3,620,000 for past medical expenses
- $200,000,000 for future medical expenses
- $1,020,000 for loss of earnings
- $25,000,000 for noneconomic damages.[2]

At trial, Lydia's lawyers successfully portrayed Calloway Research Hospital as a self-interested corporation, focused more on its own public image and profits than on patient safety and health. In short: counsel

2 The noneconomic damages award was later reduced to $740,000 to comply with the state's statutory cap on noneconomic damages for medical malpractice claims.

villainized the corporate defendant in the eyes of the jury to fuel anger, and in turn, deliver the Nuclear Verdict.

The Imbalance of Power

To cultivate juror anger towards Calloway Research Hospital, plaintiffs' counsel employed a powerful "imbalance of power" theme—exposing the stark differences in power between a 16-year-old pregnant, immigrant patient and a widely-regarded and sophisticated hospital system. Expanding the theme from the personal to the universal, counsel explained, "There is an imbalance of power, an imbalance of knowledge, that puts patients at the mercy of their physicians." Counsel argued, "If someone is in a car accident and they've been t-boned by a driver running through a red light, the person who is injured knows that something has gone wrong. But in the doctor/patient setting, the patient is at the mercy of the doctor to tell them that."

In this case, the doctors had a duty to two patients: Lydia and her unborn baby, Amara. Not only was there an imbalance of power between Lydia and Calloway Research Hospital, but at the polar opposite ends of the spectrum of power also lay baby Amara and the hospital system. Calloway Research Hospital failed to protect their unborn patient, the weakest of the weak in this case. The doctors knew the best way to protect baby Amara was to perform a C-section, and they failed to perform the necessary operation.

Amara was born prematurely at 26 weeks' gestation at the hospital renowned for taking care of premature babies. Yet these expert doctors did not provide the care Amara needed to reduce the likelihood of permanent disabilities.

CALLOWAY RESEARCH HOSPITAL FAILED TO OWN ITS NUMEROUS MISTAKES

Lydia and Amara were at the mercy of Calloway Research Hospital and its physicians. Tragically, the doctors at Calloway Research Hospital made three primary mistakes in Lydia and Amara's care: (1) a doctor provided inaccurate information to Lydia about Amara's medical condition and likelihood of survival; (2) a doctor improperly offered Lydia an abortion against hospital policy; and (3) after Lydia declined a C-section, doctors turned off Amara's fetal monitor. Throughout trial, plaintiffs' counsel effectively argued that had the hospital and its staff at any moment before Amara's birth owned their mistakes and reversed course, Lydia and her baby would have been able to live normal lives.

CALLOWAY RESEARCH HOSPITAL GAVE WRONG INFORMATION REGARDING BABY'S CONDITION AND LIKELIHOOD OF SURVIVAL

Head of Labor and Delivery, Dr. Abbott, recognized Lydia had received inaccurate information regarding Amara's size, gestational age, and prognosis, but did not correct it. When Lydia was told the probability of a successful outcome for her and Amara was "fair," she consented to a C-section. It was only after doctors provided incorrect information about Amara's condition and likelihood of survival that Lydia changed her mind and elected for induction and a vaginal delivery.

Lydia was admitted to the hospital with the foremost experts on treating premature babies. Yet Calloway Research Hospital told Lydia the NICU would not be present when her baby was born, her baby had zero chance of coming into this world with a normal brain, and her baby would likely die. Essentially, the doctors said, "We're going to wrap [your baby] in a blanket and give it to you, because that's all we can do for you. And you can hold your baby til [sic] it dies."

Calloway Research Hospital had all the power to tell Lydia they made a mistake by providing inaccurate information regarding Amara's condition and likelihood of survival. Doctors could have corrected course before inducing the vaginal delivery and causing irreversible damage to Amara. This argument proved critical to plaintiffs' counsel at trial, not only because it effectively dismantled any argument for comparative negligence as to Lydia Prescott, but because it invited and fanned the flames of juror anger.

The *Reptile* calls plaintiffs' attorney to maximize the jury's impression of the defendant's hypocrisy because hypocrisy generates anger and motivates jurors toward a disproportionate award. The hypocrisy of a world-class hospital giving wrong (and damaging) medical information and then failing to correct it, was ripe for exploitation. Plaintiffs' counsel did so masterfully.

CALLOWAY RESEARCH HOSPITAL IMPROPERLY OFFERED LYDIA THE OPTION TO TERMINATE THE BABY

Dr. Abbott also recognized Lydia should not have been offered the option to terminate her pregnancy. When Calloway Research Hospital offered termination to a "clearly viable fetus," it reinforced the message to Lydia that the baby would not survive. Yet the doctors were wrong. Counsel asked the jury to consider, how hard would it have been for Dr. Abbott to go to Lydia's bedside and say, "We've made a mistake"?:

> They can't even admit their mistake now. They certainly couldn't admit it back then. How hard would it have been to just go in and say; [sic] look, we've given you wrong information, we think we've sent you down the wrong path, we want to make it right. It would have taken some courage, it would have taken some dignity, and it would have taken about 10 whole minutes of [Dr. Abbott]'s day. But no, they were too concerned about a public relations crisis. But it wasn't [Lydia Prescott] they were concerned about. They weren't concerned about 16-year-old [Lydia Prescott].

Plaintiffs' counsel employed a secondary theme: "words matter." And this theme resonated considering the words the hospital and its doctors used when discussing the baby's likelihood for survival and Lydia's future. Plaintiffs' counsel was effective in using the words the hospital used against it to land a key anger-generating message: this horrific outcome was avoidable, and the defendant chose not to avoid it.

DOCTORS NEGLIGENTLY TURNED OFF THE BABY'S FETAL MONITOR

Finally, once Lydia changed her mind and declined the C-section, doctors turned off Amara's fetal monitor. By turning off the monitor, the doctors no longer had any information about Amara's condition when it came to counseling Lydia about her treatment options. Once Amara was off the monitor, she "was done for." Calloway Research Hospital turned off the fetal monitor and "gave up on a viable baby with a biophysical profile of 10 out of 10 and a reassuring fetal heart rate tracing." At this point, Lydia's doctors sealed Amara's fate because they would never own "up to their own negligence" and perform the necessary C-section to save Amara.

CALLOWAY RESEARCH HOSPITAL ATTEMPTED TO FORCE LYDIA'S WRITTEN CONSENT TO COVER UP ITS MISTAKES

Instead of owning up to their mistakes, the doctors offered Lydia a dangerous vaginal induction. Lydia's physicians began the induction in violation of hospital policy without obtaining her signature or the signature of her legal guardian on a consent form. To cover their bases after the fact, Calloway Research Hospital attempted to wield its power over Lydia in order to protect itself. Specifically, Dr. Aldridge prepared a new consent form and presented it to Lydia while she was in labor and without her adoptive mother present.

Plaintiffs' counsel argued the retroactive consent form was the smoking gun in the case—"dripping with their guilt" and an attempt to "sign away their own incompetence." Counsel also argued the retroactive consent form was the prime example of the imbalance of power. Calloway Research Hospital imposed its power upon a 16-year-old girl in the throes of labor when her adult guardian was not present. This clear abuse of power signaled not only Calloway Research Hospital's negligence, but also the malintent of the hospital and its physicians.

The Hospital Was Only Concerned for Its Reputation

Plaintiffs' counsel argued the doctors at Calloway Research Hospital knew full well they provided inaccurate information to Lydia about Amara's condition, leading Lydia to decline a C-section and risking Amara's life and health. Yet these doctors did not go back to correct their mistakes with Lydia because they "put the corporation ahead of the patient."

To drive home this point, plaintiffs' counsel discussed the controversy and error surrounding the Hospital's offer to Lydia to terminate her pregnancy. Calloway Research Hospital's offer to terminate the baby was against hospital policy and illegal in the state. When Dr. Abbott found out termination had been wrongfully offered, she called the Calloway Research Hospital chairs and the chiefs of obstetrics to run it "all the way up the flagpole." She felt they had a right to know and weigh in on the mistake. Dr. Abbott's concern, in her own words, was controlling "media and hospital-wide attention." She admitted to the jury that "termination is a hot button, controversial, political issue that . . . had the potential to explode[.]"

The facts made clear Dr. Abbott was worried about possible media exposure and chose to report the issue to her bosses instead of informing the impacted patient, Lydia, that the hospital gave her wrong information. Counsel asked the jury to consider, "Did [Dr. Abbott], for one minute, think about instead of picking up the phone and calling her bosses, and worrying about a possible media explosion, did she ever think it might be the right thing to do in compliance with the standard of care? To go in and tell the mom that she had been given wrong information?"

Counsel argued that admitting the Hospital's mistakes would have raised questions from Lydia's adoptive family. Plaintiffs' counsel argued, had Calloway Research Hospital's doctors admitted to their mistakes, the questions raised by Lydia's parents would have resulted in a "public relations crisis." Counsel argued, "[Calloway Research Hospital] has a reputation to... protect. And they weren't about to have that reputation harmed because of a 16-year-old [Lydia Prescott.]"

Calloway Research Hospital Doctors Villainized Through Inflammatory Narrative

Finally, plaintiffs' counsel effectively villainized the doctors and hospital system in closing argument by using inflammatory language. Counsel chose words intended to cause intense feelings of anger toward the hospital, its doctors, and its lawyers. Counsel levied the following accusations against Calloway Research Hospital and the medical team:

- "They want to blame a 16-year-old girl from [sic] changing her mind after being told terribly wrong information to which I have yet to hear an explanation for. A 16-year-old. I think it's a new low."

- "...doctors have the audacity..."
- "Taking the imbalance of power and trying to impose it on a 16-year-old girl without her parents there when she wanted her parents there. And I'm sorry, I think it's despicable. And I think it's indefensible."
- "...I submit to you, ladies and gentlemen, that the consent form is the smoking gun in this case. It is dripping with their guilt."
- "I'll let you come to your own conclusions, ladies and gentlemen, about [what] a warm and fuzzy person [Dr. Jones] was."
- "They are absolutely blaming [Lydia] for what happened to her baby. And look at who they're using to do that... Oh, my God. Look at his CV. Because the one award you won't find is one for compassion, because it doesn't exist."

Additionally, plaintiffs' counsel also attacked the defense attorneys in closing argument. Counsel argued:

- "What do you do when you got [sic] conduct that's ... indefensible and you don't want to take responsibility for your actions? Hire expensive medical experts to fly to trial and make up medical diagnoses."
- "You saw [Amara Prescott] in this courtroom. You saw her with your own eyes. You know that she needs a lot more than just an extra set of hands. It's offensive."
- "– it's disgusting. To say to a little girl who clearly needs care, as a child neurologist, to come in here and say that she just needs an extra pair of hands so that [Calloway Research Hospital] doesn't have to pay $47 an hour, they only have to pay $10. And who cares if she doesn't get fed correctly, or get her medications, or chokes. Hey, just needs a pair of hands. What's the big deal. [sic] Oh, and by the way, she doesn't need anybody overnight. Just cram all that food down her throat before she goes to bed and then you won't have to worry about those overnight feedings."

By the time the jury was charged with deliberating its verdict, plaintiffs' counsel's tactics successfully accumulated to paint the corporate defendant, Calloway Research Hospital, as a heartless, greedy corporation, more dedicated to its own self-interest than the health of its patients. The jury's nuclear award demonstrates just how angry the jury was with Calloway Research Hospital.

Plaintiffs' Counsel Slammed the Hospital for Failing to Personalize

Plaintiffs' counsel also took advantage of the defense's choice not to call many witnesses to testify. It appears only four doctors testified for the defense. Counsel asked the jury in closing argument: "And when we want to talk about bringing people in to talk about their actions, where are all of the treaters? They're nowhere to be found." Plaintiffs' counsel effectively played to the jury's desire to know about and hear from critical parties and players in the case.

PLAINTIFFS' COUNSEL'S OTHER EFFECTIVE TRIAL TECHNIQUES

In addition to villainizing the corporate defendant, plaintiffs' counsel used other successful methods often seen in closing arguments leading to a Nuclear Verdict.

Plaintiffs' Counsel Blamed Calloway Research Hospital for Failing to Accept Responsibility

Plaintiffs' counsel also blamed the hospital system for failing to take responsibility for its actions. As discussed above, plaintiffs' counsel drilled home the accusation that Calloway Research Hospital would not own up to (i.e., accept responsibility for) its many mistakes, leading to Amara's birth and resulting birth defects.

Counsel argued, "And it doesn't mean anything to tell us you were wrong. But they refused, they refused to say they were wrong, they refused to acknowledge what that means to a mom." Counsel argued the doctors "didn't admit" when they were wrong in the days they treated Lydia and Amara, nor did they admit their mistakes in the courtroom. To the contrary, instead of accepting responsibility, plaintiffs' attorney argued the defendants tried to cover up their mistakes by presenting Lydia with a new consent form hours into her labor. It appears Calloway Research Hospital's failure to *Accept Responsibility* resonated with the jury, as evidenced by its verdict.

Plaintiffs' Counsel Gave a Number (In Part) but Did Not Argue Pain and Suffering

Plaintiffs' counsel uniquely addressed the issue of a damages award at trial, departing from traditional patterns seen in resulting Nuclear Verdicts.

PLAINTIFFS' ATTORNEYS SPONSORED A NUMBER, BUT ONLY ONCE, AND ONLY FOR ECONOMIC DAMAGES

Lydia's lawyers asked the jury to ensure Amara was "taken care of for the rest of her life" and would receive the best care possible. Counsel did not sponsor a damages number in opening statement but explained Amara would need 24/7 care for the rest of her life. Counsel stated, "And what you're going to hear is that's expensive, but I think at the end what you're going to hear is she's worth it."

In closing, plaintiffs' counsel urged the jury to award between $29 and $36 million dollars for future medical expenses depending on Amara's life expectancy. Between plaintiffs' counsel's closing and rebuttal arguments, he only mentioned these numbers once.

Notably, plaintiffs' counsel did not sponsor a number in closing for pain and suffering damages. Counsel stated, "And honestly, for the rest, I don't really care. I just want to make sure that Amara is taken care of for the rest of her life. For non-economic [sic] damages, you can give a dollar. I just want to make sure that Amara is taken care of for the rest of her life."

PLAINTIFFS' COUNSEL DID NOT ARGUE PAIN AND SUFFERING

Not only did plaintiffs' counsel decline to sponsor a number for a noneconomic damages award at trial, but they also declined to make any traditional arguments outlined in Appendix A to support an award for noneconomic damages. Nevertheless, the jury awarded $25,000,000 for pain and suffering to Amara.

While the jury's noneconomic damages award was later reduced to comply with the state's statutory cap on noneconomic damages in medical malpractice cases, counsel's trial arguments and techniques effectively drove an angry jury to a Nuclear Verdict. Plaintiffs' counsel was able to aggravate the facts alone in this case to drive the outsized economic damages award, rendering the typical pain and suffering arguments unnecessary. This tactic is highly effective in jurisdictions with noneconomic damages caps in medical malpractice cases, such as this case.

THIS NUCLEAR VERDICT DEPARTS FROM TRADITIONAL RATIOS OF ELEMENTS OF DAMAGES FOUND IN NUCLEAR VERDICTS

Of additional note, this jury verdict is comprised of different ratios of elements of damages than what we typically see in a Nuclear Verdict. Specifically, astronomical noneconomic damages awards typically make up the majority of Nuclear Verdicts, where pain and suffering awards are 10 or 20 times the value of economic damages. In this case, future medical expenses comprised almost the entire verdict, with pain and suffering totaling only 12.5% of the total award. The award breakdown is an anomaly; so, what caused it?

As mentioned, state law in this case caps noneconomic damage awards at $750,000 in medical malpractice cases. First, this motivated plaintiffs' counsel to focus entirely on the economic damages and avoid a reduction of a potentially massive noneconomic damages award. Accordingly, plaintiffs' counsel was able to pull off only asking for a $1 pain and suffering award. It appears they rightly banked on the angry jury providing a large economic damages award. A final verdict of $200,000,000 for pain and suffering instead of future medical care would have been reduced to only

$750,000, per the statutory damages cap. And, asking for only a $1 pain and suffering award likely bolstered their credibility in asking for such a large future medical number.

Second, the damages cap required plaintiffs' counsel to craft creative, powerful themes related to liability and economic damages. Without the viability of a nuclear pain and suffering award in the state, the traditional plaintiff pain and suffering arguments became almost irrelevant. To replace these compelling pain and suffering narratives, counsel delivered powerful, inflammatory arguments to fuel juror anger while empowering the jury to ensure the final verdict provided all of Amara's future medical and care needs. Counsel's creative arguments and themes discussed earlier in this chapter were quite effective.

Other Notable Trial Techniques

PLAINTIFFS' COUNSEL UNDERSTOOD WORDS MATTER

Plaintiffs' counsel used the theme "words matter" throughout closing. Counsel opened his closing argument with this powerful phrase, and explained:

> Words matter. They matter at home, they matter at work, they matter with our loved ones, . . . they matter in this courthouse. And they will matter in your deliberations. And this isn't some new or novel concept. This is something that is embedded in the fabric of who we are as human beings as we communicate with one another. Words matter.

Plaintiffs' lawyer effectively used this theme as he walked the jury through his allegations of Calloway Research Hospital's many mistakes. For example, counsel argued words did not matter to Calloway Research Hospital when it came to Lydia and Amara's care except for one phrase: "patient declines Cesarean section for fetal indications."

However, when reflecting on the totality of plaintiffs' counsel's closing argument, it becomes apparent that "words mattered" to the attorneys crafting plaintiffs' case. Counsel was deliberate in the words chosen and delivered to the jury. One can almost hear the tone in counsel's voice when merely reading the closing transcript because the words chosen were so powerfully inflammatory. "New low." "The audacity." "Despicable." "Indefensible." These words were strategically chosen to incite juror anger and fuel a Nuclear Verdict.

REPTILE BUZZ PHRASES

Plaintiffs' counsel empowered the jury tasked with rendering its verdict in a nod to the *Reptile*. Counsel argued:

> For me, I feel like we live in a world that is sometimes turbulent and sometimes pretty crazy. And the frustration that I feel when I watch the news is that I am powerless to make change. I just feel that way. I love my job, I love doing what I do. But in a grand global sense, I just feel powerless. And the power that you are going to have in this case is immense. You are going to wield a power that you may never wield again. The power to make a difference in a little girl's life for the negligent acts of [Calloway Research Hospital]. This is her only swing at this. And I hope and I pray that you hit it out of the park, so [Calloway Research Hospital] knows words matter.

Plaintiffs' counsel used another classic *Reptile* trope: he effectively argued the hospital "put the corporation ahead of the patient." In a post-pandemic America, jurors are craving control over something in their lives. "Rising costs and uncertainty of the future" drive increased jury verdicts.[3] While this closing argument was delivered prior to the COVID-19 pandemic, we predict more plaintiffs' counsel will employ this juror empowerment theme, especially as more Americans than ever before struggle with reported feelings of anxiety and depression.[4]

PLAINTIFFS' APPEARANCE AT TRIAL

Lydia appeared at trial but did not testify. Lydia's parents also did not testify, and it seems based on the transcripts that they did not appear at trial.

---

3 *How the Pandemic Affects Juror Perspectives*, Magna Legal Servs. (June 2021), https://magnals.com/newsletter/magnafyi-june-2021/how-the-pandemic-affects-juror-perspectives (on file with the Apex Defense Consulting library).

4 *Stress in America 2023*, Am. Psych. Ass'n (Nov. 2023), https://www.apa.org/news/press/releases/stress/2023/collective-trauma-recovery (on file with the Apex Defense Consulting library).

It also seems Amara made an appearance for the jury to observe her. Instead of using these traditional witnesses, plaintiffs' counsel presented their case through the testimony of expert witnesses.

CONCLUSION

Plaintiffs' counsel's powerful narrative maligning the defendant successfully fueled juror anger and resulted in a Nuclear Verdict. When anger toward the defendant is unchecked by the defense, it is easy for a jury to award astronomical damages. Not only did the jury award a Nuclear Verdict in this case, but the verdict award was also over five times higher than the damages number plaintiffs' counsel sought.

How could the defense have defused juror anger? In the face of plaintiffs' permanent injuries, was this an unwinnable battle for the defense? Is there any way the jury could have come back with a defense verdict or even a more reasonable damages award considering plaintiffs' counsel's effective presentation? Despite plaintiffs' powerful arguments and evidence, we believe this verdict may have been avoided.

EPILOGUE: THE APPEAL

After the jury rendered this Nuclear Verdict over $225 million, the defendant hospital filed a Motion for Judgment Not Withstanding the Verdict, which the Trial Court denied. The defendants then appealed the judgment, arguing plaintiff did not offer sufficient evidence to support the jury's finding of failure to provide informed consent or negligence. About 19 months after the jury gave its verdict, the Appellate Court agreed with the defendant hospital and overturned the verdict.

Regardless of this successful appeal, this Nuclear Verdict shows the significant role juror anger plays in driving up damages. By applying the Core Four of The Apex and personalizing the defendant, the defense is better equipped to win at trial, avoiding a costly appeal.

CHAPTER 5

THE HUMAN STORY: *PERSONALIZE THE DEFENDANT*

JURORS DO NOT FOLLOW THE LAW WHEN A CORPORATION IS AT THE DEFENSE TABLE

"[A CORPORATION] IS ENTITLED TO the same fair and impartial treatment that you would give to an individual. You must decide this case with the same fairness that you would use if you were deciding the case between individuals."[1] Judges give this instruction, or some version of it, every day in courtrooms across the country. But even though the law says jurors must afford corporations and individuals the same treatment, the reality of jury decision-making is bleak for corporate defendants who let juror anger go unchecked. The impact of the "corporate identity effect"—the phenomenon where corporate defendants are viewed as more liable and more owing of

1 Judicial Council of California Advisory Committee on Civil Jury Instructions, *Judicial Council of California Civil Jury Instructions: CACI*, Cal. Cts.: Jud. Branch of Cal. 18 (2024), https://courts.ca.gov/system/files/file/judicial_council_of_california_civil_jury_instructions_2025.pdf (on file with the Apex Defense Consulting library).

higher damages than individual defendants[2]—is well-documented and unsurprising but largely still unaddressed by corporate defendants in trial. With anti-corporate bias doubling since the 2020 pandemic[3] and the plaintiffs' bar more creative and collaborative than ever before, corporate defendants are at greater risk for nuclear results if they do not adapt.

The Corporate Identity Effect Infiltrates the Jury Deliberation Room

Multiple studies dating back to the 1980s have observed the corporate identity effect.[4] In both historical analyses of actual jury verdicts and studies involving mock jurors, liability determinations and ultimate verdict awards have been identified as being higher against corporations than individuals, even in studies where individual human defendants engaged in the same hypothetical conduct as corporate defendants.[5] Mock jurors are quicker to identify a corporate defendant's behavior as negligent, and more likely to assume causation—that is, that the identified negligence caused the plaintiff's injuries.[6] Translation? Jurors hold corporate defendants to higher standards than individual defendants, even despite the instruction you read at the start of this chapter.

Early studies contemplated whether the reason for this disparate treatment stems from a perception of corporations as having "deep pockets," but later studies debunked the hypothesis, finding that jurors' verdicts were

---

2 Kelly R. Rebeck, *Understanding the Corporate Identity Effect: An Examination of How Legal Standards are Applied to the Behavior of Corporate versus Individual Defendants in a Civil Lawsuit Scenario* (2012) (M.A. paper, University of Chicago), https://papers.ssrn.com/sol3/Delivery.cfm/SSRN_ID2163246_code1915288.pdf?abstractid=2163246&mirid=1&type=2 (on file with the Apex Defense Consulting library).

3 *Juror Attitudes in a Polarized Society*, Orrick, Herrington & Sutcliffe LLP, https://www.orrick.com/en/Insights/Groundbreaking-Jury-Research-Reveals-US-Jury-Attitudes-in-a-Polarized-Society (on file with the Apex Defense Consulting library) (last visited February 15, 2025).

4 Audrey Chin & Mark A. Peterson, Deep Pockets, Empty Pockets: Who Wins in Cook County Jury Trials (1985), https://www.rand.org/content/dam/rand/pubs/reports/2007/R3249.pdf (on file with the Apex Defense Consulting library).

5 Valerie P. Hans & M. David Ermann, *Responses to Corporate Versus Individual Wrongdoing*, 13 Law & Hum. Behav. 151 (1989), https://scholarship.law.cornell.edu/cgi/viewcontent.cgi?article=1466&context=facpub (on file with the Apex Defense Consulting library);
Rebeck, *supra* note 2.

6 *Id.*

unaffected by perceived defendant wealth, even as corporations were still treated more harshly than individual defendants.[7] This study identified three possible alternative reasons for the consistent unfair treatment of corporate defendants: "distrust of commercial actors"; "alternative standards" due to potential for greater harm; and "the impersonal nature of corporations."[8]

Corporate Distrust: Jurors Do Not Like or Trust Us

"Anti-corporate sentiment has doubled from 27% pre-pandemic to 45%" in 2024.[9] Americans reporting very little or no confidence in big business jumped from 25% in 1999 to 42% in 2024.[10] The seminal studies on corporate identity effect and its causes were written in the 1980s, a time when Americans felt more financially secure and did not evince a general distrust or dislike for corporations. It is highly likely we would observe an even more pronounced difference in treatment between individual and corporate defendants if these studies were conducted today. In the era of "fake news" and "being canceled," society views corporate defendants as both untrustworthy and worthy of punishment. These views permeate courtrooms and civil jury trials every day across the country.

Tentacles of Danger: Why the *Reptile* Works

The second possible explanation for the corporate identity effect stems from the general perception that corporations, due to their size and reach, are capable of causing significantly greater harm than individuals. This belief makes sense: a company with hundreds of employees, manufacturing thousands of products that reach millions of people, has greater impact (for better or worse) than a single human. In this view, some argue that corporations should be more policed due to the potentially great harm they can cause

---

7 Robert J. MacCoun, *Differential Treatment of Corporate Defendants by Juries: An Examination of the "Deep-Pockets" Hypothesis*, 30 Law & Soc'y Rev. 121 (1996), https://lawcat.berkeley.edu/record/1115734/files/fulltext.pdf (on file with the Apex Defense Consulting library).

8 *Id.* at 141-42.

9 *Juror Attitudes in a Polarized Society, supra* note 3.

10 *Confidence in Institutions*, Gallup®, https://news.gallup.com/poll/1597/confidence-institutions.aspx (on file with the Apex Defense Consulting library) (last visited February 15, 2025).

and their breadth of influence. Similarly, those who perceive corporations as more dangerous tend to also believe that corporations should be held to higher standards than individuals in order to keep communities safe. The focus here is less on the specific *conduct* of a perceived corporate bad actor and more on the *standard* to which they are held.[11]

If this sounds familiar, it should. This belief is at the center of *Reptile*, which refers to the philosophy as defendants having "Tentacles of Danger." *Reptile* works by tapping into and exploiting this worry, inviting jurors to speculate about just how dangerous the defendant's behavior *could* have been and then activating them to *do something* about the perceived danger in order to protect the greater community. Modern society primes jurors for this *Reptile* tactic: 62% of jurors today think it is an "important function" of juries to "send messages to corporations to improve their behavior."[12]

"Tentacles of Danger" invites jurors to do three things the law specifically precludes them from doing: speculating, considering irrelevant information, and deciding based on emotion. There is a reason the law precludes these things. When a juror's decision is based on (1) unfounded speculation, (2) evidence not vetted by the Rules of Evidence, or (3) their emotions, the jury's ultimate decision is inherently unfair and unjust, often resulting in a Nuclear Verdict. This is exactly why the plaintiffs' bar loves the "Tentacles of Danger" scheme.

In sum, American jurors are primed to deliver unjust verdicts rooted in the corporate identity effect due to existing negative attitudes toward corporations. Their tendency to rely on latent anti-corporate bias is ratcheted up when they are angry. Angry jurors are also more likely to rely on stereotyping when making decisions.[13]

---

11 MacCoun, *supra* note 7.

12 *Juror Attitudes in a Polarized Society*, *supra* note 3.

13 Galen V. Bodenhausen, Lori A. Sheppard & Geoffrey P. Kramer, *Negative Affect and Social Judgment: The Differential Impact of Anger and Sadness*, 24 Eur. J. Soc. Psych. 45 (1994), https://www.researchgate.net/profile/Galen_Bodenhausen/publication/227638728_Negative_Affect_and_Social_Judgment_The_Differential_Impact_of_Anger_and_Sadness/links/5a7edb304585154d57d5f13f/Negative-Affect-and-Social-Judgment-The-Differential-Impact-of-Anger-and-Sadness.pdf (on file with the Apex Defense Consulting library).

Some Good News: We Can Personalize to Defuse Juror Anger

We cannot control a vast number of things when we enter the courtroom. We cannot control whether a third-party litigation funder is pulling strings behind the scenes, whether our legislature has rolled back caps on damages, or whether our judge will issue damaging and incorrect rulings. We cannot control whether plaintiff's counsel uses *Reptile* traps or if the plaintiff even shows up to trial. But we can control the story the jury receives about the defendant, and we can control how much anger is present in the deliberation room. That is good news, because studies have confirmed that a personalized corporate defendant is less apt to suffer from corporate identity effect.[14]

In a 2012 study conducted at the University of Chicago using a Cook County mock jury pool, total damage awards tended to be the highest against a "faceless" corporation lacking any personalization, followed by the personalized corporation and individual human defendant, respectively.[15] And, in that same study, mock jurors assessing liability against the faceless corporation were quicker to define a behavior as negligent than respondents in the other two conditions. The personalized corporate defendant and the individual human defendant received similar treatment to one another, while the faceless corporate defendant was on the receiving end of greater liability findings and higher verdicts overall (though the study noted these findings were not statistically significant, and the scenario may have been "unintentionally biased").[16] The takeaway: personalizing a corporate defendant mitigates anti-corporate bias, the corporate identity effect, and, we believe, juror anger.

Personalizing Develops Connection

Humans have a deep need for belonging. Psychologists and others have studied "belongingness" or "community" extensively since the 1940s and Maslow's Motivational Hierarchy. Some believe we seek out commonality and

---

14 Rebeck, *supra* note 2.

15 *Id.*

16 *Id.*

community as an evolutionary response predicated on survival.[17] One of the most frequently cited articles on the theory of belonging urges that "...belongingness can be almost as compelling a need as food and that human culture is significantly conditioned by the pressure to provide belongingness."[18]

The need to belong does not evaporate when a panel of potential jurors enters the courtroom to begin jury selection, and it certainly does not decline as the trial progresses. While group dynamics and belongingness impact jurors' deliberations, these same principles also impact the way jurors receive evidence, perceive the parties involved, and ultimately, how they *feel*. Put another way: jurors are humans who innately crave connection with other humans. If the only "human" party they see in the courtroom is the plaintiff, that connection will color the way they evaluate evidence, assess credibility, and ultimately decide the case.

The reason we are taught to share personal details with a kidnapper or assailant is the same reason we must *Personalize the Defendant* in litigation and trial: perceived similarity and connection make it harder to inflict punishment or harm. Studies have concluded empathy occurs when a subject moves from viewing another as an "object" to viewing them as a "subject," i.e., a human with whom they share perceived similarity.[19] Empathy is a powerful tool for defendants as well as plaintiffs, though plaintiffs' lawyers are often the only party making use of it in trial.

As you will see shortly, our data confirms that plaintiffs' counsel personalize their client all the time. By the time you are done reading the closing argument from a Nuclear Verdict, you almost always know everything about

---

17 Stephen Braren, *The Evolution of Social Connection as a Basic Human Need*, SOC. CREATURES, https://www.thesocialcreatures.org/thecreaturetimes/evolution-of-social-connection (on file with the Apex Defense Consulting library) (last visited June 18, 2025).

18 Roy F. Baumeister & Mark R. Leary, *The Need to Belong: Desire for Interpersonal Attachments as a Fundamental Human Motivation*, 117 PSYCH. BULL. 497, 498 (1995), https://www.researchgate.net/profile/Mark-Leary-2/publication/15420847_The_Need_to_Belong_Desire_for_Interpersonal_Attachments_as_a_Fundamental_Human_Motivation/links/5b647053aca272e3b6af9211/The-Need-to-Belong-Desire-for-Interpersonal-Attachments-as-a-Fundamental-Human-Motivation.pdf (on file with the Apex Defense Consulting library).

19 Jakob Håkansson, *Exploring the phenomenon of empathy* (2003) (Ph.D. dissertation, Stockholm University), https://www.atu.dk/sites/default/files/aktiviteter/empathy_dissertation.pdf (on file with the Apex Defense Consulting library).

the plaintiff. You know what the plaintiff was like leading up to the accident, where she went to school, what she liked to do for fun, even what she was like growing up.

In the big *Howell v. Hamilton Meats* case Bob won at trial and at the California Supreme Court, the plaintiff was in her mid-forties. Not only did the trial judge allow, over Bob's objection, multiple friends and family to tell the jury how she was doing before the accident, they testified about how strong a girl she was growing up. In fact, the jury was allowed to hear from the plaintiff's high school soccer coach when she was growing up. That was 30 years earlier!

Why on earth would plaintiff's lawyer want a jury to hear stories about what the plaintiff was like 30 years ago when the trial was about an accident that occurred only three years ago? Plaintiffs' lawyers are doing it for the same reason they do everything else they do in a jury trial: to maximize the jury verdict. Plaintiffs' lawyers know if they can form a connection between their client and the jury, the jury will be more likely to rule in the plaintiff's favor and, in turn, also more likely to return a large award. They believe the more a jury knows about and likes the plaintiff, the better the outcome will be.

The Liking Principle

So, what do you think? Does this strategy work? Does it work in your own lives? Do you look more favorably upon people you know and like? Or do you prefer to do favors for people you do not know or do not care about? I think we would all agree: if we have something in common with someone and like them, we tend to look more favorably upon them. It is just basic human nature.

It is also a real scientific phenomenon called "The Liking Principle." This is one of the principles of persuasion explained by Dr. Robert Cialdini in his authoritative best-selling book, *Influence: The Psychology of Persuasion.*[20] The Liking Principle states just what you would expect: people tend to agree with

20 Robert B. Cialdini, Influence, New and Expanded: The Psychology of Persuasion (rev. ed. 2021).

people they like. We are more likely to be persuaded by people we like or with whom we have a connection. Dr. Cialdini proposes The Liking Principle is much more than just a friendly feeling; it is also a powerful tool of influence.

Finding common ground is a big part of likability. Getting to know someone, their interests and passions, their friends and family, is all important for likability and, ultimately, persuading people. It takes time and effort to create this bond, but it works. It is not only common sense, but also science.

Does this all sound strangely like what plaintiffs' lawyers do and try to do in a jury trial? They are *always* trying to get more and more family members and friends to testify during the trial, on topics that have nothing to do with the accident or subject of the trial. Why on earth would plaintiffs' lawyers want to spend all this effort to just waste the jury's time about things that have nothing to do with the trial? Oh yes, because they want to win! They want to persuade the jury to vote their way. And plaintiffs' lawyers do not believe they are wasting the jury's time at all. In fact, they know The Liking Principle is so strong that this may be the most important evidence for them in the whole trial!

That evidence and principle is ours for the taking, too. Why should the jury only know or care about the plaintiff? Nothing in the law says a corporate or entity defendant is precluded from sharing their story. In fact, as you have seen, the law says exactly the opposite: corporate defendants are to be afforded the same fairness and equal treatment as individuals. So, let us do it! Let us share our story, too!

Personalizing the Defendant Feeds Our Need for Story

When humans enter unknown environments or receive new stimuli, our brains search for patterns to make sense of the information and determine how we should respond. Our brains are good at pattern recognition because the neocortex (the outermost layer of the brain) is organized around groups of 300 million neurons literally called "pattern recognizers"![21] When

21 Robert C. Barkman, *Why the Human Brain Is So Good at Detecting Patterns*, Psych. Today (May 19, 2021), https://www.psychologytoday.com/us/blog/singular-perspective/202105/why-the-human-brain-is-so-good-detecting-patterns (on file with the Apex Defense Consulting library).

we identify a pattern, we get a burst of dopamine, the so-called "happy hormone."[22] Identifying patterns not only keeps us safe by offering context for new information, but it also feels good.

What do patterns have to do with stories? Stories are the most basic patterns that exist: they organize information into a coherent, predictable sequence, allowing recipients to derive meaning, interpret stimuli, and act accordingly. Interestingly, our brains cannot even tell the difference between a good story and a lived experience. Brain imaging studies have revealed that "hearing vivid sensory details activates the same regions [in the brain] that would light up if actually experiencing the event firsthand."[23]

Unsurprisingly, jurors assemble evidence into stories, and those stories in turn guide their decision-making in trial. There is a reason that the higher levels of The Apex include an entire strategy centered around telling our story. **Sharing human stories builds critical connection, cultivates empathy, assists the jury in understanding, counteracts the corporate identity effect, and ultimately, defuses juror anger.**

False Barriers to Personalizing

Of the Core Four, *Personalize the Defendant* is arguably the easiest for defense teams to agree with and to implement. It resonates with people because it is common sense. Again, it is not just common sense to form a connection between your client and the jury; it is science. If it works for plaintiffs' attorneys, it will work for the defense.

Personalize the Defendant does not carry the perceived risks associated with *Accept Responsibility*, *Give a Number*, or *Argue Pain and Suffering*. There is virtually no risk associated with sharing the human story behind the corporate defendant. So why then is there little effort by defense lawyers

---

22 Robert A. Burton, *Our Brains Tell Stories So We Can Live*, NAUTILUS (Aug. 6, 2019), https://nautil.us/our-brains-tell-stories-so-we-can-live-237501/ (on file with the Apex Defense Consulting library).

23 Jonathan H. Westover, *The Power of Storytelling: How Our Brains Are Wired for Narratives*, HUM. CAP. INNOVATIONS (Jan. 11, 2024), https://www.innovativehumancapital.com/article/the-power-of-storytelling-how-our-brains-are-wired-for-narratives (on file with the Apex Defense Consulting library).

to make their own clients likable to a jury? What is holding back defense lawyers from using this powerful psychological tool?

The defense fails to personalize our clients for several reasons. In a way, it all boils down to fear. The defense is afraid that telling the jury about the defendant is not relevant and, therefore, objectionable. The fear looks like this: Who the defendant is or why the company exists arguably has nothing to do with the accident. Even worse, such an objection by plaintiff's counsel to this evidence might be sustained, and that would be just terrible. A judge, who has no vote on the outcome of our jury trial, ruling against us on an evidentiary objection. Untenable!

What do the high school days and athletic prowess of a teenage girl have to do with a 45-year-old plaintiff who was in a trucking accident? Absolutely nothing! And despite the fact all of this history that has nothing to do with the case comes into evidence at the urging of plaintiff's counsel, the defense in a typical case does not even ask the defendant on the stand if they have any family, does not even ask what the client likes about his work, how he feels about this accident, where he is from, or really anything that might form a deeper connection with the jury deciding his fate!

Hmm... that does not seem right. It does not seem fair. And we all just want a fair trial, right?

When we speak to carriers and counsel across the country regarding the Core Four, this is the element on which we receive the least pushback, though defense counsel are often concerned about how to argue the relevance of this information. It is here we must pause and remind you of three things: (1) objections are a part of trial, and we must not be afraid of them; (2) appeasing the judge is not our goal, persuading the jury is; and (3) so long as you have a good-faith basis for your argument or line of questioning, use your fouls!

Information about the named defendant is *absolutely relevant* for the jury's consideration, especially when the plaintiff has put at issue their actions, inactions, policies, knowledge, or wealth. The plaintiffs' bar knows the power of personalization. Why else would they spend such a long time in trial explaining in detail their client's hopes, dreams, fears, loves, wants, wishes, and loss?

Do not allow yourself to be fooled into complacency here by believing plaintiffs' lawyers just have it *easier*. Yes, establishing causation and damages is the plaintiff's burden of proof. And yes, plaintiffs are typically individual humans compared to corporations. However, remember the instruction you read at the very start of this chapter: corporations are to be afforded the same impartiality and fairness as individuals. The law knows something we know, but that our jurors are tricked into forgetting: behind every corporation is just another *human*.

How to *Personalize the Defendant*

"Life shrinks or expands in proportion to one's courage."
—Anaïs Nin

JUST TRY!

So, what can we do? How can the defense personalize their client during trial? Well, it is pretty simple: Just try!

Please, just do something. Start somewhere, anywhere, and tell your jury about your client. It just is not happening in courtrooms across America. The defense is not doing anything to form a connection between their client and the jury in most Nuclear Verdicts.

When we go to trial, we should try to do what plaintiff's counsel does. Think about what we want this jury to know about our client and tell them. Tell them in opening statement, and then tell them through evidence. Ask not only questions of our client that will help him connect with the jury; ask questions of other witnesses about our client. Have others tell our client's story, convey his likability factors and traits. Ask random doctors or economists or experts or eyewitnesses about our client to elicit favorable testimony. This is what the plaintiff does.

There is much discussion about the most effective way to personalize your client in front of a jury. We could debate it here too, what works and what does not work with juries. But we would say this: just do something, anything, please.

The likability of the defendant is such a powerful persuasion tool, it cannot continue to go unused by defense teams and, quite frankly, abused by the plaintiffs' bar. Stop debating and start doing. Start thinking about what we like about the defendant and how we want to convey that to the jury, and then do it.

MAKE IT PERSONAL

How do we really personalize any entity? We make it personal. Every entity is made up of people. We must tell a people story. Tell the jury things about our people that they would want to know.

Who are our people? What do they do? Are they parents? Are they coaches? Do they volunteer? Are they good citizens? Do they read? Do they have a passion? Who *are* they? Why did they join this hospital? Why did they become a healthcare provider? The answer to that question may be very powerful. We want our jurors to hear it, right?

When we do any or all of the above, we are light years ahead of what the defense has been doing. But really, this is all just a good start. What we need to do is to take this to the next level. Take it to the level that plaintiff lawyers have taken it. We need to share with the jury exactly what plaintiff's counsel would share with them. What is that?

We need to tell the jury what impact this incident has had upon our client. Yes, just like plaintiff counsel spends hours, days, and even weeks talking about the impact of this tragic incident upon his client, we have to spend just a little time talking about the impact on the other party in this case, our client. How do we do that? Let us give you an example.

Share the real stories of the people that make up our client's organization. Tell the impact this incident had on our people. In this scenario, tell the impact this tragedy had on the doctors, the nurses, the administrators, the staff, the maintenance workers, everyone. They are our client. Their stories are just as important as any other party in this litigation. Get their testimony in front of the jury. Put a face on the faceless entity that is the hospital.

To personalize any defendant entity, we must get personal. We must tell a people story, and it must be a personal one. Get to know the people who make up our defendant entity and tell their story, their personal story. Who are they and how did this incident impact them? Tell that to the jury and get them to care about our people.

"BUT NONE OF THIS IS ADMISSIBLE"

Now, some of you defense lawyers may be thinking: how is any of this relevant? How is telling the impact of a tragic event on the defendant relevant to our case? The defense cannot take it to the next level. The defense cannot make it personal like the plaintiff does. The plaintiff has to tell how she feels because it is her injury, her termination from her job, her loss, her tragedy. She went through all of this, and she has to share it with the jury so she can get paid. It is part of her damages. The defense has no damages, so none of this is relevant or admissible for the defense.

Really? How do we know that? Have we ever tried to get this testimony by our client into evidence? Our data on Nuclear Verdicts shows we probably have not tried. We probably have never asked our client on the stand:

"How did you feel when you heard about
this tragic accident with the plaintiff?"

"What did you do when you heard about this incident?"

"Ms. Defendant, you seem upset today; why are you upset right now?"

"When you heard about this tragedy, did you care?"

"How has this accident impacted your company?"

"What did you think when you saw/heard about this accident?"

"Has this accident impacted you or your company in any way?"

"Ms. Defendant, did you want this to happen, or was it an accident?"

"Ms. Defendant, do you care the plaintiff was injured in this accident?"

"Ms. Defendant, are you sorry this accident happened?"

Have we ever asked any of these questions? Probably not! Are the answers admissible? Are our client's answers relevant? Absolutely!

Our client is a party to the lawsuit just like the plaintiff. All of the emotion we are letting come out on the stand when plaintiff and her friends and family are on the stand is not compensable. Those emotions are not part of recoverable damages. They are, therefore, not relevant or admissible. But we are letting it come into evidence! Even worse, we are not even trying to get that same testimony into evidence for our client. This is unacceptable.

Stop worrying about objections or what a jury will think if we lose an objection. Our client deserves to have his story told, just like the plaintiff. They are both parties to this case and our client's story is just as important. We need to fight to get the defendant's story in front of the jury. Justice demands it.

CASE STUDY OVERVIEW: *PERSONALIZE THE DEFENDANT*

The plaintiffs' bar continues to use science, namely psychology, to beat the defense and to obtain Nuclear Verdicts. The science behind personalizing our client, the defendant, is clear and straightforward. Most defense lawyers understand The Liking Principle and believe in it, along with the other psychological principles we have discussed in this chapter. Yet in most Nuclear Verdicts, defense teams are not personalizing the defendant for the jury. The effect? The defendant is a faceless, greedy corporation in the eyes of deliberating jurors. The defendant is a sitting duck for a Nuclear Verdict.

Methodology

In our analysis of 100 closing arguments from Nuclear Verdicts, we set standard parameters for assessing whether the defense personalized the defendant. We did *not* accept mere reference to safety records as "personalization." Instead, we read with a close eye for *any* reference to a company's origin story, corporate representative, involvement in the community, relationship with employees, purpose, or any other information regarding the humans behind the corporation or entity. Understanding that personalizing the defendant occurs primarily through testimony and evidence, we were extraordinarily lenient in quantifying whether the defendant personalized in closing arguments and counted any reference to the corporate story as a successful utilization.

Ideally, the defense identifies a corporate representative to serve as the human face of the company and attend trial every single day. Because there would be no consistent way to determine from transcripts if a corporate representative were present unless they testified, we were unable to track this.

Hypotheses

Our hypothesis was twofold: first, in the majority of Nuclear Verdicts, defense counsel does not *Personalize the Defendant*. Second, in the majority of Nuclear Verdicts, plaintiffs' counsel personalizes the plaintiff.

Results

Our case study analysis supported both hypotheses. In the majority of Nuclear Verdicts, the defense failed to employ the easiest aspect of the Core Four and offered no personalization of the defendant at all. Conversely, plaintiffs' counsel did personalize the plaintiff in most Nuclear Verdicts. Our results also confirmed that personalizing the defendant is truly only effective at reducing damages when used in tandem with the other Core Four.

PLAINTIFFS' COUNSEL UNDERSTANDS THE POWER OF PERSONALIZING WHILE THE DEFENSE FALLS SHORT

The plaintiffs' bar has long known the power of both storytelling and personalizing their client, and our trial experience led us to believe we would see a greater number of plaintiffs' counsel personalizing their client than the defense. However, we also know how simple it is for the defense to personalize, so we were not prepared for the stark difference we found between each party implementing this approach.

Plaintiffs' counsel personalized their client (by sharing biographical details beyond just the moment of impact/accident or its effects) **87% of**

the time. The defense, however, only personalized the defendant **22% of the time**.

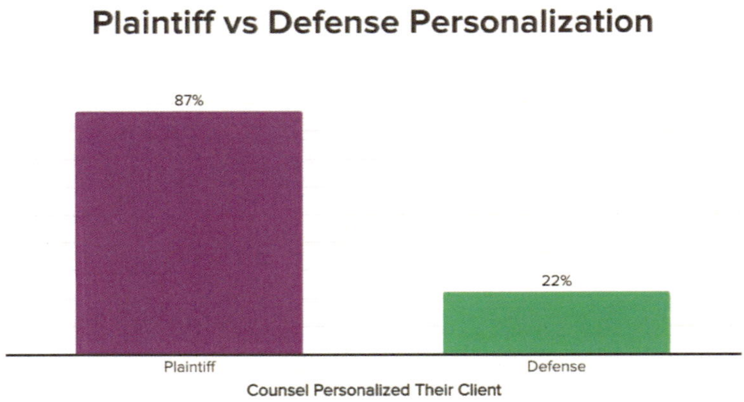

So, in **78% of Nuclear Verdicts, the defense failed to *Personalize the Defendant* in any way in closing argument**. The defense gave a number (arguably one of the most controversial of the Core Four) *more than double* the number of times the defense personalized the defendant! This statistic is somewhat demoralizing, but it gets even worse.

The Defense is Even Less Likely to Personalize in Stipulated Liability Cases

In stipulated liability cases, where the only thing at issue is how much money the defendant will pay, the defense only personalized the defendant **10% of the time.** This is particularly problematic considering the increased rates of anti-corporate bias and the belief that corporations should be "punished." Liability in these cases had already been determined; the only question for the jury to answer was to what extent the corporate defendant should pay damages. Absent the benefits bestowed by personalization, a corporate defendant facing stipulated liability will suffer—the jury has effectively been handed a blank check.

Where the defense stipulated to liability and personalized the defendant, the verdict averaged approximately 39% of plaintiff's ask, compared to 65% of plaintiff's ask in cases where the defense stipulated to liability but did *not Personalize the Defendant*. Put another way: **failing to *Personalize the Defendant* in stipulated liability cases was correlated with a greater percentage of plaintiff's ask ultimately awarded.**

But what impact did personalizing have on verdicts overall?

Personalizing the Defendant Alone Has Little to No Impact on Ultimate Verdict

Of the 22 cases where the defense personalized the defendant, there was not a single case where the defense also used all three of the other Core Four strategies. Noting the limited nature of our data set, we were curious about the impact personalizing the defendant had on the Nuclear Verdict amount returned compared to plaintiff's attorney's request of the jury. For each case, we measured what percentage the verdict was of plaintiff's ask and then averaged those percentages across each condition to compare. However, this analysis shrank the data pool even further.

In 13 of the 22 cases where the defense personalized, plaintiffs' counsel did not clearly ask for a specific dollar amount from the jury in closing argument. Put another way, we could only compare the final verdict award to plaintiff's ask in nine cases where the defense personalized the defendant. In one of the nine cases where the defense personalized the defendant and we were able to compare the verdict to the plaintiff's ask, the verdict was a whopping 637.9% of plaintiff's ask. This specific case is analyzed and used as an Apex detailed example in Chapters 4 and 6. This percentage is the greatest outlier in the whole of our 100 Nuclear Verdicts.

When we removed the 637.9% case as an outlier, the average Nuclear Verdict award compared to plaintiff's ask was 81.3% in cases where the defense personalized the defendant. This finding does not parallel the power we know personalizing the defendant has on a jury based on our experience, but the data still shows that when the defense chooses to engage this element of The Apex, the final jury award is less than plaintiff's ask!

Out of the remaining 78 cases where the defense did *not Personalize the Defendant*, we had sufficient data to calculate a percentage of the final Nuclear Verdict award compared to plaintiffs' attorneys' ask in 50 of them. The average percentage of verdict compared to plaintiff's ask in that condition was 83.9%.

Put most simply: **personalizing the defendant at trial without engaging the other elements of the Core Four resulted in an almost 3% reduction in Nuclear Verdict award amount compared to plaintiffs' attorneys' requested verdict from the jury.** So, how often did the defense *Personalize the Defendant* in conjunction with any of the other Core Four, and what impact was observed on those verdict awards?

Personalizing is Most Effective When Combined with the Other Core Four

As discussed, psychological truths and our trial experience inform our conclusion that the defense must *Personalize the Defendant* to avoid a Nuclear Verdict. Our detailed analysis of the closing arguments from 100 Nuclear Verdicts reveals that personalizing the corporate client is most effective when used in conjunction with other elements of the Core Four. While we maintain the defense must use all four strategies articulated as the Core Four, we examine the efficacy of personalizing the defendant in scenarios where the defense did not do so.

DEFENSE USED ONLY ONE ELEMENT OF THE CORE FOUR: *PERSONALIZE THE DEFENDANT*

Of the 100 Nuclear Verdicts analyzed, the defense chose to use a singular aspect of the Core Four in eight cases: *Personalize the Defendant*. Of these eight cases, in only one did the closing argument contain sufficient data to measure the final verdict as a percentage of plaintiffs' attorneys' ask. **In that one case, the verdict was 53.2% of the plaintiff's ask.**

That case also contained one of the most poignant examples of a corporate representative backfiring. In that case, while the defense designated a corporate representative, he could not remember the plaintiff's name when he testified. You can imagine how well that played with the jury, and the plaintiff's counsel capitalized, telling them: "[The corporate representative] didn't know her name. Make sure he never forgets it." The lesson to be learned here: prepare your corporate representatives to testify honestly, authentically, and empathetically.

DEFENSE USED TWO ELEMENTS OF THE CORE FOUR

The defense chose to both *Personalize the Defendant* and *Accept Responsibility* 4% of the time. **Personalizing the defendant and accepting responsibility at trial dropped the final Nuclear Verdict to 39.5% of plaintiff's attorney's ask.**

Personalize the Defendant
+ Accept Responsibility
= Verdict 60.5% Less than Plaintiff's Ask

The combination of accepting responsibility while telling a human story had a measurable impact on the verdict awarded. This makes sense: the tandem use of these two strategies works to show the defense to be not only reasonable but also *human* and worthy of connection and empathy.

Combining *Personalize the Defendant* and *Give a Number* resulted in a measurable benefit for the defense. Where the defense used both of these elements of the Core Four, the average Nuclear Verdict amount compared to plaintiff's lawyer's request was 69.6%.

Personalize the Defendant
+ Give a Number
= Verdict 30.4% Less than Plaintiff's Ask

The defense's deployment of these two Core Four strategies resulted in a lower final Nuclear Verdict award than when the defense chose to only *Personalize the Defendant*. However, the use of *Personalize the Defendant* and *Give a Number* was not as beneficial for the defense as choosing to *Personalize the Defendant* and *Accept Responsibility*.

We discuss in detail the psychological concepts supporting *Give a Number* in Chapter 11. They differ in many ways from the psychological frameworks for both *Personalize the Defendant* and *Accept Responsibility*.

Primacy, recency, and desensitization are at the heart of the effectiveness of giving a number, and they relate primarily to the ways in which humans gauge, remember, and trust numerical value. Connection, community, empathy, and validation serve as the psychological bases for both accepting responsibility and personalizing the defendant, and it would make sense for these psychological phenomena to have greater impact when used together.

Of the 100 Nuclear Verdicts analyzed, the defense never chose to both *Personalize the Defendant* and *Argue Pain and Suffering.*

DEFENSE USED THREE ELEMENTS OF THE CORE FOUR

The defense chose to use three aspects of the Core Four in two cases. In these cases, the defense chose to *Personalize the Defendant*, *Accept Responsibility*, and *Give a Number*. Between those two cases, the average percentage of plaintiff's ask was 43.7%.

Personalize the Defendant
+ Accept Responsibility
+ Give a Number
= Verdict 56.3% Less than Plaintiff's Ask

The most impactful combination of the Core Four we observed was *Personalize the Defendant* and *Accept Responsibility.* However, the difference between using three elements and employing two (*Personalize the Defendant* and *Accept Responsibility*) is negligible when examined as a percentage—56% less compared to 60% less.

This analysis is another example of The Apex serving as a single method, where every element therein builds upon one another and works together to avoid a Nuclear Verdict. We cannot treat The Apex like a buffet. We cannot pick and choose what elements to use in some cases and which to use in others. We must completely deploy The Apex strategy to avoid a Nuclear Verdict.

Attacking the Defendant is Effective for Plaintiffs

On the flipside, we also analyzed the impact of plaintiffs' counsel *dehumanizing* the defendant, either by attacking the defendant directly, or attacking defense counsel. We classified an "attack" as something beyond criticizing the defendant's action or inaction and instead looked for more inflammatory language that verged on personal. In other words, if we would have contemplated an objection to improper argument or denigration of counsel, we flagged it as an attack.

The average verdict was 128% of plaintiff's ask in cases where plaintiff's counsel attacked the defendant or defense counsel. In other words, the average verdict where plaintiff's counsel attacked or dehumanized the defendant *exceeded* plaintiff's ask by almost 30%. This is unsurprising given jurors' predisposition to distrust and their dislike of corporate defendants, and it speaks to the intentionality behind plaintiffs' counsel's chosen words and arguments. The most effective plaintiffs' lawyers are those who generate anger, and attacking a corporation in front of jurors who are primed to punish is the easiest way to do it.

THE DATA-BACKED CONCLUSION: PERSONALIZING THE DEFENDANT HELPS REDUCE JURY AWARDS, BUT IS MOST IMPACTFUL WHEN USED WITH THE OTHER CORE FOUR ELEMENTS

Where the defense did not use *any* element of the Core Four, juries awarded Nuclear Verdict amounts almost one and a half times (148.6%) the verdict amount plaintiffs' counsel requested in closing argument. This measure dropped to 81.3% where the defense personalized the defendant, to 69.6% where the defense personalized the defendant and gave a number, and even further to 43.7% where the defense personalized the defendant, gave a number, and accepted responsibility.

Average Verdict Where Defense Failed to Use Any of the Core Four vs Average Verdict Where Defense Personalized the Defendant

Verdict Amount as Percentage of Plaintiff's Ask

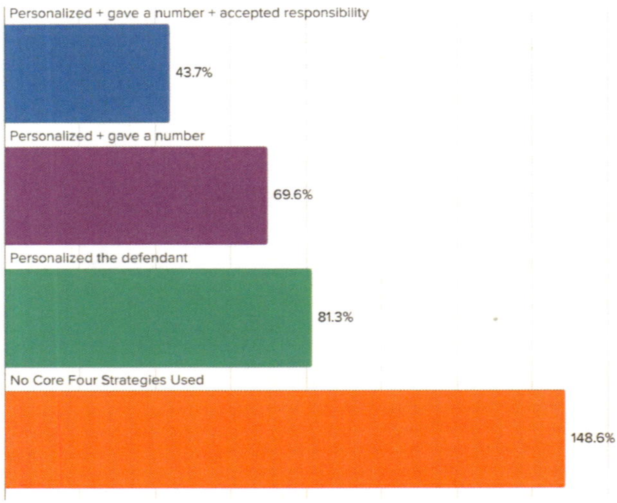

In the absence of being able to measure the effectiveness of personalizing the defendant while simultaneously engaging the three other elements of the Core Four, the most powerful use of personalizing the defendant in Nuclear Verdicts occurred when this element was used in combination with accepting responsibility. In these cases, the final Nuclear Verdict award was 39.5% of plaintiff's attorney's verdict request from the jury.

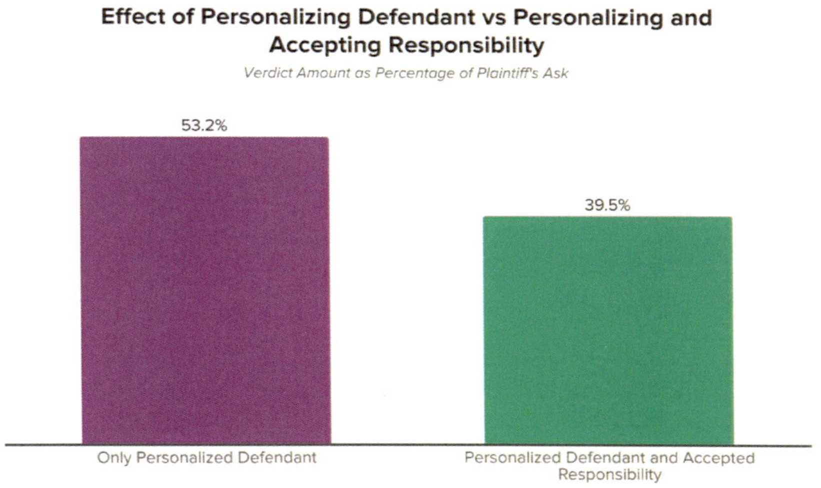

The data also confirms that we must be prepared for attack in trial. Plaintiffs' counsel know they effectively fuel juror anger when they dehumanize the defendant or defense counsel. Dehumanizing results in an average Nuclear Verdict award nine times higher than verdicts where the plaintiffs' attorney plays by the rules.

Our conclusion? Personalizing the defendant is helpful on its own but is most impactful when paired with the other strategies comprising the Core Four. Corporate defendants are entitled, under the law, to the same treatment as individual defendants. But our jury pools are not primed to follow that instruction, and existing biases are amplified by the manipulative tactics employed by the plaintiff's bar. It is up to us to ensure our clients are viewed as the humans they are: complex, beautiful, good, and worthy of empathy.

CHAPTER 6

THE PEOPLE MAKE THE COMPANY

BOB'S ALTERNATIVE, APEX CLOSING ARGUMENT

OUR DEFENSE THEMES

GOOD AFTERNOON. RESPONSIBILITY, REASONABLENESS, COMMON Sense. I told you a month ago that is what this case is about, and as I stand before you here today, I believe it was. Let's talk first about responsibility.

ACCEPT RESPONSIBILITY

[*Accept responsibility for something regardless of our liability stance, as discussed in Part III.*]

PERSONALIZE THE DEFENDANT

Who are we? What have you learned about us over the last few weeks? Well, first, Calloway Research Hospital is ranked not only among the best hospitals in the state, but in the entire country. Calloway Research Hospital is synonymous with superior care. This hospital provides high-quality, compassionate medical care to its patients. Our mission is to improve the health of the community and the world by setting the standard of excellence in medical education, research, and clinical care. It has a rich history rooted in philanthropy, diversity, inclusion, and a passion for innovation.

Over 130 years ago, a man named Peter Calloway decided to use his good fortune to establish a hospital that would provide the very best care to its patients and bring forth a new era for patient treatment. Calloway Research Hospital has made significant advancements that helped set a standard for other institutions and shaped the medical field into what it is today.

Calloway Research Hospital may be the best, but who are they really? It is not some faceless corporation. It is made up of doctors, nurses, and other healthcare providers, many of whom you have met in this trial. Who is Calloway Research Hospital really? Calloway Research Hospital is made up of people, people with family and friends in your community. Most importantly, Calloway Research Hospital is made up of people who care.

MAKE IT PERSONAL

The doctors you heard from became OB/GYNs because it was their calling. They wanted to be involved with primary care, enjoyed patient continuity, and appreciated the miracle of birth. They see patients, new and different, every day, deliver their babies, console the mothers when necessary, and build irreplaceable relationships with their clients. Some of them are mothers themselves and have personally experienced pregnancy and childbirth.

These doctors took time away from their current patients at the hospital to be here at trial. This is how much they accept responsibility for the medical care they provide, and this is how much they care: they show up. They wanted to speak to you directly because they know accepting responsibility matters. It matters out in the world, and it matters in this case.

You heard from Dr. Smith about the first birth she witnessed as a hospital volunteer during college. You heard how she described the intensity, the joy, and the vulnerability of the moment a baby is born. As she watched a woman bring life into the world, surrounded by a team of calm, focused, compassionate professionals, you heard her describe that something "cracked open" in her. She no longer wanted to be just a doctor. She wanted to be an OB/GYN so she could walk with women through some of the most transformative, sacred, and sometimes difficult moments of their lives.

You heard from Dr. Jones that becoming an OB/GYN felt like a calling. In medical school, she was drawn to the labor and delivery unit. Many of the patients she served were under-resourced, some battling substance use, chronic illness, or domestic violence. She witnessed deliveries where mothers were on the brink—physically, emotionally, and sometimes medically. There were moments when she wasn't sure if the mother, the baby, or both would survive, much like in this case. But in that chaos, she saw the power of what it means to truly show up for someone. As an OB/GYN, she considers herself a fighter—not just for lives, but for dignity.

Dr. Abbott testified that she has never wanted to shy away from the hard things in life, especially in her medical practice. She wants to be in the room when it matters most—when a life begins and when life hangs in the balance. This is one of the cases where it mattered most. Dr. Abbott testified that Amara's birth was one of the most difficult situations she has had to face. She remembers Lydia Prescott. She remembers baby Amara. She followed up on Amara's condition for months after Amara was born.

All of these doctors take immense pride in caring for people when they're most vulnerable. They do everything in their power to help save lives and follow a patient's wishes. Every doctor who testified in this trial explained to you that being a good OB/GYN doesn't mean always being in control. It means listening, respecting a patient's autonomy, and finding a way to support someone's wishes even when they don't align with your own. They have delivered babies in silence, in sobs, in joy, and in grief. And they stayed—to hold hands and explain the unfathomable. That kind of humility and trust is the heart of Calloway Research Hospital.

HIGHLIGHT THE CORPORATE REPRESENTATIVE

You also met a representative of Calloway Research Hospital, Mr. Schneider, who sat in court every day. He has been working for the hospital for over 30 years and testified that in his opinion, Calloway Research Hospital truly understands how critical each element is when operating a hospital.

He has witnessed Calloway Research Hospital direct its employees through ever-changing laws, while following all internal policies and procedures for excellence. You heard Mr. Schneider testify:

> We're a large hospital, yes—but we're also a collection of individuals: nurses who stay after their shifts to sit with patients who have no family, environmental services staff who know patients by name, and physicians who cry when outcomes don't go as hoped. We're not perfect—but we care deeply.

You heard from Mr. Schneider that Calloway Research Hospital has a culture of learning and accountability. When something goes wrong, they don't hide from it. Calloway Research Hospital has systems for reporting, reviewing, and learning—because patient safety and integrity aren't just priorities. Mr. Schneider described them as "our identity."

Mr. Schneider also described how the hospital believes in shared decision-making. Even when patients make choices they wouldn't advise, they listen. Calloway Research Hospital honors our patient's autonomy. This is the foundation of good and ethical medical care.

You also heard about the good things Calloway Research Hospital has done for Mr. Schneider and his co-workers. It is hard not to appreciate and understand the value Calloway Research Hospital provides to society. This hospital serves communities where access to medical care isn't guaranteed. You can just imagine the devastating impact an unreasonable award would have on the people of this hospital. An unreasonable award would affect many patients, doctors, staff, other employees, charities, and communities.

Each of these individuals has stepped forward and accepted responsibility for the care they provided to Lydia and Amara Prescott. These people who are the life and breath of this hospital care about these plaintiffs. Every single person who testified apologized to Amara, to Lydia Prescott, and to Lydia's parents. Every single witness is here for you to hold them accountable. The 130-year national reputation of this establishment is in your hands. It has truly been an honor to represent them.

WHY PERSONALIZE THE CORPORATE DEFENDANT? IT WORKS!!

We know in this Nuclear Verdict the defense did not *Personalize the Defendant* in closing argument.[1] The data also shows in the overwhelming majority of Nuclear Verdicts, when you are done reading the closing arguments of the defense, you will know almost nothing about the defendant. Nothing.

Does this mean you will automatically have a Nuclear Verdict if you fail to *Personalize the Defendant*? Of course not. But what else does the data show about the importance of personalizing your client? The data shows plaintiff's counsel does it in almost every single case!

So why personalize the corporate defendant? Because it works! It is not just common sense to form a connection between our client and the jury; it is science. Again, psychology is the study of human beings, not just plaintiff-friendly jurors. If it works for plaintiffs' attorneys, it will work for the defense.

The science behind personalizing your client is clear and straightforward. It resonates with people because it is common sense. Most defense lawyers understand The Liking Principle and believe in it. It is really just common sense for a trial lawyer. Most defense lawyers want to be liked themselves by a jury. We defense lawyers know the importance of a jury liking us to get jurors to rule in our client's favor. The likability of lawyers is critical to persuading a jury. We are always striving to be the most credible person, the most reasonable person, the most likable person in the courtroom. Plaintiffs' lawyers are always trying to make *their client* be likable to the jury, too.

When Did We Like Corporations?

There is a lot of discussion today about American juries not liking corporations. As you just read in Chapter 5, many experts say the anti-corporate sentiment has grown even worse since the pandemic. Jurors' attitudes

1 For more behind-the-scenes insight into Bob's thought process and the development of this Apex closing, join our Apex Defense Community at www.apexdefenseconsulting.com.

toward corporations are much more negative post-pandemic. Jurors distrust corporations; they do not believe them. They also are more prone to punish a corporation for their negligence, rather than just make the plaintiff whole. Jurors are eager to send a message on behalf of the community to a wrongdoing corporation. Recent surveys have shown that without knowing anything about a case, a potential juror is more likely to favor an individual over a corporation. Some of you may not like this, but those same surveys show jurors do not like the lawyers who represent corporations either!

Boy, the world really has changed. What has happened to the good ole days when everyone loved corporations? When no one ever complained about Corporate America and just felt warm and fuzzy for companies? But when was that exactly? When did we Americans love corporations?

Did we love corporations in the late 19th century when industrial oligarchs amassed large fortunes on the backs of inexpensive labor? Did we love corporations when they underpaid Chinese immigrants in the late 1800s and made them endure unimaginable working and living conditions to build our railroads? Or when they were overtly bribing government officials, prompting President Rutherford B. Hayes to say, "This is a government of the people, by the people, and for the people no longer. It is a government of corporations, by corporations, and for corporations." Lots of love!

How about in the 20th century when corporations allowed their factories to burn, killing innocent women and children working in sweatshops in the garment district in New York City? Or when they were exploiting our children, and the government needed to step in and enact child labor laws to protect the weakest among us from corporate abuse? Or how about when they caused thousands of Americans to lose their jobs and savings due to greed-driven scandals such as Enron, or the savings-and-loan failures in the 1980s, or the 2008 mortgage crisis with AIG and Lehman Brothers leading the way? Now those were the good old days when everyone loved corporate America!

We Do Not Like Corporations

So, you get our point: we Americans have never been big fans of corporations. This opinion goes back to the beginning of our Republic. Our Founding Fathers were creditors and small businessmen who were all in favor of the jury system for criminal trials, but not so much for the civil system. They were very concerned about how their companies would be treated by juries and about the integrity of the financial world if they could not receive fair and consistent rulings. We are still concerned about the treatment of businesses almost 250 years later!

So, the answer to the question of when did we ever really like corporations, is never. Is it worse now than before the pandemic? The reality is American jurors are made up of your neighbors. Are your neighbors a lot different now than before 2020? There are many jury consultants and psychologists who can opine this for you.

At the end of the day, it does not matter. Americans are not, and have never been, big fans of corporate America. Accept it.

The real issue is, what are we going to do? Americans do not like our clients and do not like us. That is a fact. We can complain about it and argue about whether juries used to like us and our clients back in the day, but this is our reality now. So, what are we going to do?

CONCLUSION

We have to do better. We have to tell our side of the story. We have to tell it through the eyes of our client, not of the plaintiff, her friends, and her hired experts. Our clients are real people, just like the plaintiff, who have been impacted by the events of this accident. These real people work in an organization that is a party to this lawsuit. Justice demands both sides of this story be told.

Plaintiffs' lawyers take personalizing their clients to an impermissible extreme all the time. They want the plaintiff to be liked by the jury. They study the psychology behind it; they know The Liking Principle. We know it, too. It is common sense. Use our common sense and personalize our client to a jury of their peers.

The pattern of Nuclear Verdicts reveals jurors are making no connection to the defendant. How could they when the jurors know nothing about them? It is time to break the pattern. Tell our client's story. It is relevant, it is real, and it is essential to avoiding a Nuclear Verdict. Justice demands we *Personalize the Defendant*. Please try.

PART III:
ACCEPT RESPONSIBILITY

CHAPTER 7

THE CASE OF THE UNHINGED HATCH

A LIGHTING TECHNICIAN'S EARLY MORNING

The sun just peeked over the horizon as Pancho pulled into the strip mall parking lot before 6:30 a.m. He sat in his bucket truck for a moment, savoring his last sips of coffee and thinking about the three-day car show he planned to attend with his dad that weekend. The sky to the east continued to brighten as he placed his empty 7-11 cup in the cupholder. He pulled out his map of Arendelle Center. Time for work.

Pancho loved being a commercial lighting technician. He was good at it. He loved working with his hands and the challenge of solving problems. At 35 years old, Pancho had over 13 years' experience. He was proud there was hardly ever a problem he could not solve or a job he could not tackle.

Pancho's body was strong enough to handle the manual work, and he loved it enough that he planned to retire from his current company, Aurora Systems. While it was still a mom-and-pop shop, Aurora was targeting big players in the area, securing new contracts, and growing rapidly.

This August morning, Pancho was a detective. He was assigned to conduct a lighting inspection around the strip mall and fix anything he noticed that was out of place. He had shopped in this strip mall many times before, and this was his third visit to the job site. Chain stores like Rite Aid, the 99 Cents Only Store, and Domino's Pizza, and a locally owned Cardenas Grocery lined the cream-and-terracotta stucco shopping center. Inspecting and servicing locations where he shopped was his favorite part of the job. It made him feel like he was making a difference.

The Inspection

Pancho started out his inspection by driving his truck around the strip mall, examining wall packs and pole lights, checking for any outages, and noting his findings on the map. Once his drive inspection was complete, Pancho parked his bucket truck and exited the cab. He swung his heavy toolbelt around his hips and secured it tightly. Pancho walked the storefronts, checked the recessed can light fixtures, and marked them on his map.

As he reached a particular section of the center called Pad A, he noticed the recessed lighting along the perimeter of the exterior building still burned brightly. These lights were supposed to turn off automatically in the daylight. Pancho figured there was either an issue with a time clock that timed the lights to the sunrise and sunset or a bad photocell sensor that automatically detected the sunlight to turn lights on and off. He continued to survey the building, searching for the device that controlled the lights. He did not find any, but he spotted a locked electrical room that likely housed a time clock or led to a rooftop photocell.

Pancho tracked down a security guard and asked her to open the electrical room so he could continue his search for the faulty photocell sensor. As the door opened to the small, dark electrical room, Pancho reached for the light switch. Click. Click. Click. Nothing. His eyes slowly adjusted to the dark-ness, aided by the light of the sun shining into the room. The room was small, perhaps 10 by 20 feet. He surveyed the perimeter and noted some meters on the wall, but no breakers labeled as "lighting" and no time clock box.

Pancho realized he needed to check the roofop for any photocells. To his right, he noticed an affixed access ladder on the wall leading about 16 feet high to a hatch door in the ceiling. "Perfect," he thought. "The sensor is likely out on the roof."

The Dangerous Hatch

Pancho climbed up the ladder as he had done so many times over the course of his career. The top of the ladder stopped short of the hatch door by about three feet. He clutched the top rung with his right hand and reached up to unlatch the hatch with his left. As he pushed the hatch door open, he noticed the door felt a little "off," heavier than it should be. He adapted instinctively, stepped up to the next rung on the ladder, pushed the door fully open, and latched the bar to hold the hatch open.

Pancho grabbed the right side of the hatch frame with both hands to pull himself onto the roof. He needed to clear the three-foot gap between the ladder and the hatch door. With the top half of his body through the hatch door, Pancho threw his right leg over the top of the hatch to exit onto the roof. As he moved his left leg to complete his exit, his toolbelt bumped the bar holding the hatch door open.

Pancho felt a little tug and heard a metal squeak. He knew instantly what was about to happen, but his awkward body position of one leg out the hatch prevented him from either quickly exiting the doorway or bracing himself for the impending impact of the hatch. Within two seconds, the weight of gravity gave the 60-pound door additional power and speed as it fell onto Pancho's spine, pinning him momentarily in the doorway.

Pancho had not had the wind knocked out of him this badly since Pee Wee football. He lay with his mid-back crushed beneath the hatch door and struggled to catch his breath. He clutched the hatch frame, fearing he would fall back through the hatch toward the ground. Within a few seconds, Pancho was able to shimmy out from underneath the door and roll onto the roof.

"Pull Yourself Together"

He was dazed. He was in pain. The sun beat down on him. He closed his eyes. "Shake it off," he thought to himself, "Take a few breaths." He was shaken by the blow and the fear of falling to the ground.

After he collected himself, Pancho pushed up to his feet. He noticed the immediate tingling in his arms. Soon the tingling reached his hands. Within a few moments, the tingling turned to numbness. His neck throbbed from being struck by the edge of the door.

Pancho fumbled to pull out his phone and called his supervisor. He realized this was an on-site accident that needed to be reported. He explained the incident, and his supervisor, Tom, asked if he needed an ambulance. Pancho declined, believing he had simply just taken a hard hit and that he would be able to work through the pain.

Tom asked Pancho if he felt well enough to take some pictures of the scene. Using his company cell phone, Pancho took pictures of the hatch. As he inspected the backside of the hatch, he held the door open with one hand and unlatched the locking mechanism. As soon as he did, the full weight of the door came crashing down again. There was no resistance on the door as there should have been. When working properly, these kinds of hatch doors include a spring mechanism that resists and buoys the weight of the door as a safety precaution, essentially holding resistance against the door so it does not slam closed, as it just did on Pancho's spine.

Pancho's only route off the roof was back through the broken hatch door, over the gap in the access ladder, and down the rungs along the wall of the electrical room. With his numb hands, he engaged the lock to hold the hatch door open. He lay on the ground and, through the pounding in his neck and head, shimmied his body carefully back through the hatch opening. He clutched as best as he could to the ladder without feeling in his hands, and he reached up to gingerly tap the locking mechanism with his fingertips to release it.

Slam. Pancho ducked as the hatch door came crashing closed once again. Pancho reached up to check that the door was secure one final time and cautiously moved down the ladder.

When Pancho had almost reached the floor, he noticed a worn handwritten sign taped to the wall that read:

"Hatch broken! Watch fingers and head. 😊"

"This isn't a joke," Pancho thought to himself. "What a lazy way of posting a warning."

New Reality for Pancho

Pancho returned to his truck and tried to continue with his work. He hoped to be able to work off the pain as the day went on. He just needed to take a little break. As he sat in his truck, breathing slowly, wondering what could be wrong and willing the pain to subside, he realized he needed a doctor. He contacted Tom again and informed him he needed to go to urgent care. Pancho located an urgent care clinic down the road. When Pancho entered the doctor's office, he did not suspect this would be the beginning of years of treatments, numerous surgeries, and hundreds of doctors' appointments to come. This had begun as an ordinary day on the job he loved most; he could never have known it was the beginning of a life-altering ordeal.

THE POWER OF RESPONSIBILITY

Francisco "Pancho" Medina filed a lawsuit against the shopping center's owner and property management company, claiming negligence and premises liability. Pancho claimed the defendants knew of a dangerous condition on the property, failed to warn him of the dangerous condition, and failed to repair the danger. At the time of trial, five years after Pancho's accident, he still had not fully recovered from his injuries.

The urgent care clinic originally diagnosed him with "sprain and strain" injury to his back. Later, the retained neurosurgeon explained Pancho had an undiagnosed degenerative condition in his spine, including disk bulges, at the time the accident happened. This degeneration caused narrowing of the center part of his spinal canal, which can jeopardize the spinal cord in certain circumstances.

Pancho ultimately underwent two spine surgeries: a cervical fusion surgery and a lumbar fusion. The surgeries eased Pancho's pain level, but did not eliminate it. Pancho's retained neurosurgeon testified he will likely suffer from neck and back pain the rest of his life. He also testified Pancho will likely need further surgeries on his neck, back, and possibly his shoulder. At the time of trial, Pancho had not returned to work due to his continued pain.

The Downtown Los Angeles jury found the owners and property managers of the shopping center negligent and awarded Pancho over $12.6 million, broken out as follows:

- $872,238.75 for Past Economic Loss
    - Lost Earnings: $266,000
    - Medical Expenses: $606,238.75;
- $1,950,000 for Future Economic Loss
    - Lost Earnings: $1,500,000
    - Medical Expenses: $450,000;
- $1,800,000 for Past Noneconomic Loss; and
- $8,000,000 for Future Noneconomic Loss.

How did plaintiff's counsel persuade the jury to award a Nuclear Verdict in this case? Simple. Plaintiff's counsel made the jury angry. How did plaintiff's counsel generate this anger? He made hay with the power of responsibility, and the defense's failure to accept any. In response, defense counsel did not defuse that anger.

The Jury Must Hold the Defendants Accountable

"Responsibility" was one of plaintiff's primary trial themes. He used the term "responsibility" 15 times in his closing argument alone. Like all good plaintiffs' attorneys, counsel was an effective storyteller. Plaintiff's counsel employed powerful language in his indictment of the defendants, language that was clearly designed to elicit the anger that ultimately went unchecked in the deliberation room. Numerous times throughout trial, he reminded the jury, "[Pancho Medina] had two seconds. The defendants had two years." This phrasing was particularly powerful for two reasons: it emphasized how quickly the plaintiff's life changed forever, and it cultivated anger toward the defendants, whose inaction over those two years ultimately cost plaintiff everything. Can we blame the jurors for their decision, when this is the only story the jury took into the deliberation room?

Jurors heard that almost *two years* before Pancho arrived at the strip mall that day, a roof repairman saw the broken spring assist—a spring that ensures the hatch door will open and close safely—and informed the property managers it needed to be fixed. The repair estimate for the spring was a mere $3,150. Property managers set aside the money for the repair and scheduled the repair for a year later. But one year stretched into two, and when Pancho arrived that August morning, the repair had still not been completed. Why had the defendants not repaired the condition for only $3,150? This question undoubtedly sat in the backs of jurors' minds as they heard testimony about not only the incident, but its impact on the plaintiff. And plaintiff's counsel capitalized.

Plaintiff's counsel argued defendants, whom he almost exclusively referred to as "the corporations," failed to accept any responsibility for the incident. He also accused "the corporations" of making disingenuous claims that they were accepting some responsibility in the case by arguing the hatch was an "open and obvious defect."[1]

1 Under applicable law, property owners who hire independent contractors cannot be liable for injuries to the contractor's employee. Of course, there are exceptions to this rule. Generally, when a property owner hires an independent contractor, the property owner may still be on the hook if the contractor hires an employee who is then injured. Whether the property owner is liable depends on the owner's control of the work and whether the injury was caused by a hidden hazard the contractor did not know about and could not have reasonably noticed. In essence, the defense would not be liable in this case if the jury found that the defect to the hatch was open and obvious.

The Defense Cried Crocodile Tears

During closing arguments, plaintiff's counsel slammed the defense for incredulously attempting to *Accept Responsibility* by admitting the danger of the hatch was open and obvious, while blaming Pancho for proceeding through the danger anyway. Plaintiff pointed the finger at the corporate defendants and accused them of "crocodile tears." Counsel explained to the jury the adage that when crocodiles eat their prey, something happens to their tear ducts that makes it look like they are crying. Yet, crocodiles are not sad for their prey.

Plaintiff's counsel used this adage to persuasively argue the defendants, just as crocodiles cry when devouring their prey, were "crying for show." The argument had the double impact of likening corporate defendants to vicious and predatory crocodiles while attacking them for being disingenuous. In short, it poured gasoline on the anger fire.

Too Little, Too Late

In a subtle nod to the *Reptile*, plaintiff's counsel also claimed defendants cared more about saving money than accepting responsibility, and stoked the anger fire he had ignited by implying the defendants did not believe his client even *deserved* care because of his station in life: "[H]e's just an electrician. That's really what they're saying if you think about it. That he doesn't deserve the best care. He doesn't deserve it. They want a discount. They don't want to accept responsibility."

Counsel also focused the jury on several "red herrings" the defendant corporations deployed as evidence of their failure to *Accept Responsibility*. "[I]t wasn't a good warning sign. It wasn't a warning sign. It wasn't up to OSHA. Simple. It's a red herring to avoid responsibility. That's why [the defense] keep[s] bringing it up."

Plaintiff's attorney then issued a challenge to the defense, baiting them to finally accept responsibility for *something*:

> We're here because they don't accept responsibility. I hope they finally do. And [I hope the defense] goes back on what

> [defense counsel] said in his opening statement where he asked for a defense verdict. I hope. I truly do. They still shouldn't get a discount because they've put us through this. But I hope they do finally accept responsibility for the whole thing.

Counsel urged the jury to hold the corporations fully accountable with their damages verdict, empowering the jury to do what the defendants would not do on their own: make them *Accept Responsibility*.

PLAINTIFF'S OTHER EFFECTIVE TRIAL TECHNIQUES

Plaintiff's counsel's closing argument shows he accepted his mission to get the jury angry at the defendant corporations to fuel the largest verdict possible. Counsel employed several techniques in addition to leveraging the theme of the "corporations" failing to *Accept Responsibility* to incite juror anger.

The Corporate Defendants Gambled with Pancho's Health and Safety

Plaintiff's attorney crafted the theme that the "corporations" gambled with Pancho's well-being to (1) focus the jury on the defendants' conduct, and (2) fuel anger at the company defendants. Plaintiff's counsel argued the defense gambled in three ways. First, the corporations gambled by delaying the repair to the hatch. The corporations knew years before Pancho's accident that the hatch was dangerous, and they failed to repair it, taking a gamble on whether someone would get hurt.

Second, defendants gambled by attempting to "cover up" the dangerous condition, claiming they never knew it existed. In numerous interrogatory responses over the course of years of litigation and testimony at trial, the defendants denied knowing about a problem with the hatch. Yet emails going back two years before the accident, indicated a roofing contractor noted the issue for the defendants. In response, the defendants set aside the money to conduct the repairs and paid a roofing company to make the repairs. However, the roofing company never actually made the repairs, and the defendants never saw the project through. These inconsistencies played into plaintiff 's theme and damaged the defendants' credibility in the eyes of the jury.

Third, once plaintiff 's counsel revealed the emails, the corporations deflected, called the hatch a "dangerous condition," and began pointing the finger at everyone else. Plaintiff 's counsel accused the defendants of playing the blame game: they blamed the roofing contractor for failing to fix the hatch; they blamed former employees for failing to note the issue; they blamed Pancho's employer for failing to train him; and ultimately, they blamed Pancho himself for going through the hatch. The corporations' final gamble was failing to take responsibility while trying to thrust it upon anyone and everyone else.

The techniques of (1) focusing the jury on the defendants' conduct, (2) claiming the defense knew about the danger and chose not to fix it, (3) accusing the defendants of intentionally lying under oath, and (4) arguing the defense ultimately shirked responsibility and pointed the finger at everyone else angered the jury. By focusing on the defendants' intentional actions, plaintiff 's counsel successfully framed the negligence case in terms of absolute, intentional corporate cover-ups. This made it easy for the jury to find liability and causation for plaintiff 's injuries.

One of our partners, Ed Leonard, says the party who wins at trial is the one who makes the jury feel good about its decision. The jury in this case (like most juries these days) was already primed to dislike and distrust a corporate defendant. The defense played right into their worst fears, and plaintiff 's counsel made them feel good about their decision: they awarded a Nuclear Verdict.

Plaintiff's Counsel Asked the Jury to Award Almost $15 Million

Plaintiff 's counsel used psychological techniques of priming, recency, and desensitization (all concepts we discuss in Part IV) to anchor jurors to a high damage award, ultimately leading to a Nuclear Verdict. Plaintiff 's counsel walked the jury through the entire verdict form and suggested a verdict for each question, including liability, damages, and apportionment of fault questions.

Plaintiff's counsel introduced the concept of a high damages award early to anchor the jury. Specifically, while plaintiff's counsel did not give a specific number in jury selection, he discussed the concept of awarding "millions of dollars" in pain and suffering with numerous potential jurors. This established a baseline value for the jurors before they had even heard any evidence or made a liability determination.

Counsel ultimately asked the jury to award between $13.9 million and $14.9 million in total damages in closing argument. He framed the numbers in terms of the past and future economic losses and what he called the past and future "human losses." Counsel broke down past and future economic losses in detail and suggested a damages award for each, $872,238 and $1 million to $2 million, respectively.

Plaintiff's Counsel Argued Pain and Suffering

Plaintiff's counsel advanced powerful arguments to persuade the jury to award almost $10 million in noneconomic damages.[2] In addition to painting a detailed picture of Pancho's daily life and human losses, his attorney used other common, effective arguments to support his request for a large noneconomic damages award. Specifically, counsel compared the value of Inanimate Objects and Famous Athlete or Celebrity Salaries; discussed Minutes/Hours/Days of pain and suffering; argued for Inflation Protection; itemized Elements of Damages; and called the jury to consider a scenario where plaintiff Answers an Ad. Plaintiff's compelling arguments regarding the "biggest damages in [the] case . . . the human damages[,]" not only anchored the jury to a high number, but they also made a Nuclear Verdict seem fair and reasonable.

2 *See generally* Appendix A (providing a more in-depth discussion on plaintiff closing tactics).

COUNSEL PAINTED A PICTURE OF PLAINTIFF'S "HUMAN LOSSES"

Counsel vividly and compellingly explained that Pancho's "human losses" were the most significant element in this case: Pancho lost his work due to this accident. Pancho loved his job, loved working with his hands, and wanted to retire from Aurora Systems. Yet this accident rendered him unable to be an electrician again.

Plaintiff's counsel did not make these arguments in support of economic losses in the form of future lost wages; he deployed them as part of a strategy aimed at driving up the noneconomic damages in the case. The jury was confronted with one of the most difficult questions to answer: what is someone's future worth?

Counsel argued the loss extended beyond plaintiff's future professional worth and happiness: this accident took away his social life. Pancho was always the guy going to parties and events. He had to move back home with his parents because he could not afford rent after the accident. He felt like he was going backwards in life. Pancho's attitude also suffered after this accident. Even five years after the accident, he felt like he was a downer and a burden on people.

The accident stole Pancho away from his passions in life. Pancho could no longer ride bikes with his brother like he used to. He could no longer build or work on cars with his dad in the same way. He could no longer walk around a three-day car show with his dad and brother without carrying a chair and taking frequent breaks. With all these passions ripped away from him, Pancho was a shell of the man he used to be. Plaintiff's losses extended beyond activities or hobbies. He lost meaningful connections with the people he loved the most.

INANIMATE OBJECTS

Counsel anchored his almost $15 million ask of the jury by comparing Pancho's loss to expensive, unique things valued in society: $200 million buildings and the *Mona Lisa*, valued at over $1 billion. Although the court never received a $200 million building or the *Mona Lisa* in evidence, and any reference to them was certainly irrelevant, these arguments anchored the jury in a high-verdict tier and made such large sums of money seem reasonable. Plaintiff's attorney explained Pancho is not the "$200 million dollar building that can be replaced." He is an irreplaceable human being.

FAMOUS ATHLETE OR CELEBRITY SALARIES

Plaintiff's counsel briefly mentioned to the jury that LeBron James makes $40 million a year. Again, this technique anchored the jury to an irrelevant and exorbitant sum. When a jury compares plaintiff's damages request of almost $15 million to Lebron James' salary of $40 million a year, $15 million seems fair and reasonable.

MINUTES, HOURS, AND DAYS

Counsel used a variation of the standard Minutes/Hours/Days noneconomic damages argument. Looking ahead to Pancho's future noneconomic losses, counsel explained his 39-year life expectancy was not just a number. Instead, counsel broke those 39 years down into 468 months, 14,000 days, and 336,000 hours. Counsel did not tie a dollar amount per hour to Pancho's future life expectancy, as often seen in plaintiff's closing arguments. Instead, he explained he hoped Pancho will live even longer than 39 years, but the pains and losses previously described in detail will be with Pancho every day of his remaining life. This argument ultimately justified the $15 million request.

FUTURE INFLATION PROTECTION

Counsel then put Pancho's 39-year life expectancy in context of the increasing cost of goods over time, essentially urging the jury to return a verdict that would protect plaintiff against future potential inflation. Plaintiff's attorney reminded the jury that about 39 years prior, in 1982, a gallon of gas cost $1.30. A new house cost $83,000. Counsel emphasized, based on these changes, how Pancho's financial reality could change significantly over the next 39 years, inviting the jury to speculate about what amount of money might be sufficient to make up for the future cost of goods. The jury's single verdict was Pancho's one chance for justice, and the verdict award needed to be substantial enough to support him through future economic changes.

ITEMIZED ELEMENTS OF DAMAGES

Plaintiff's attorney spent a significant amount of time breaking out each available element of noneconomic damages relevant to Pancho under the applicable jury instructions and assigning a dollar amount to each element. By calling out every potential element of past and future noneconomic damages and multiplying each by the applicable factor of time, plaintiff's counsel easily guided the jury toward a Nuclear Verdict. This argument also equipped the jury with a formula to use in calculating noneconomic damages, despite a clear jury instruction that no such formula exists. Below is what plaintiff's counsel blackboarded out for the jury for each category of damages:

Past Noneconomic Damages

- Pain: $200,000 per year x 5 years = $1,000,000
- Mental Suffering: $50,000 per year x 5 years = $250,000
- Loss of Enjoyment of Life: $100,000 per year x 5 years = $500,000
- Physical Impairment: $25,000 per year x 5 years = $125,000
- Inconvenience: $10,000 per year x 5 years = $50,000
- Anxiety: $25,000 per year x 5 years = $125,000
- Humiliation: $20,000 per year x 5 years = $100,000
- Emotional Distress: $40,000 per year x 5 years = $200,000

Total Past Requested Noneconomic Damages = $2.35 Million

Future Noneconomic Damages

After originally arguing Pancho had a 39-year life expectancy, counsel used a 38-year life expectancy for these calculations.

- Pain: $95,000 per year x 38 years = $3,610,000
- Mental Suffering: $35,000 per year x 38 years = $1,330,000
- Loss of Enjoyment of Life: $45,000 per year x 38 years = $1,710,000
- Physical Impairment: $15,000 per year x 38 years = $570,000

- Inconvenience: $15,000 per year x 38 years = $570,000
- Anxiety: $5,000 per year x 38 years = $190,000
- Humiliation: $5,000 per year x 38 years = $190,000
- Emotional Distress: $25,000 per year x 38 years = $950,000

Total Requested Future Noneconomic Damages = $9.12 Million

TOTAL REQUESTED NONECONOMIC DAMAGES = $11.47 MILLION

ANSWER AN AD

Plaintiff's attorney concluded his closing rebuttal argument with a hypothetical story, a version of the traditional Answer an Ad argument. In essence, counsel posed to the jury: suppose a black car pulled up to Pancho as he entered the electrical room that day. A man gets out of the car and says, "[Mr. Medina], stop for a second. I have a proposal for you." The man then proposes two options to Pancho.

Option one: in the trunk of the black car, the man has $15 or $20 million. Pancho can take all the money in exchange for suffering this accident, having a lifelong pain, undergoing surgeries, losing his career, and deteriorating his relationship with his closest loved ones. Option two: Pancho passes on the money. In return, he wakes up the next day feeling good. He works in the same job for the rest of his life. He lives his normal life, going to car shows, building cars, and being happy. He does not have millions, but he continues his wonderful life as he knows it.

Counsel explained to the jury, "100 out of 100 times [Pancho Medina] is going to say, 'Keep your damn money. I am happy with my life. I love the life I have and the friends I have, the family I cherish.'" But, plaintiff's counsel argued, the defendant corporations did not give Pancho that choice. They had two years before the accident to fix the hatch, and they failed. Regardless of the jury's final verdict, no amount of money would ever bring Pancho back to where he was before the accident.

Final Notable Trial Techniques

Plaintiff's counsel employed several final, powerful trial techniques to fuel juror anger and secure a Nuclear Verdict.

DEFENSE ASKING FOR A "DISCOUNT"

Plaintiff's counsel effectively used the theme that the defense not only failed to *Accept Responsibility* but was also asking for a discount on plaintiff's injuries. When discussing the defense medical billing expert's defense number for past medical damages, plaintiff's counsel stated:

> Just think about what they're trying to do here, and what it is[,] is these companies are not accepting responsibility, but they want a discount. To cut his medical bills? The guy went through two major surgeries. And he is going to owe that money, despite what they want to say that, oh, he'll just waive his bill.

Counsel later reiterated the defense was seeking a "corporate discount." Ultimately, plaintiff's attorney discussed the defense seeking a discount *15 times* in closing argument, and in delivering a Nuclear Verdict, the jury awarded almost every dollar plaintiff's counsel requested.

PARTIES' APPEARANCE AT TRIAL

The plaintiff's bar has embraced a trend not to have their client sit at trial for the duration of trial proceedings. Instead, it is common to see plaintiff only appear at trial one day, for his or her direct and cross-examination. In this case, however, it is clear Pancho appeared at trial for more than just his testimony and perhaps attended every day for the two-week trial.

In contrast, the defense chose to present the majority shareholder of the property management defendant to testify on behalf of the defense and to appear at trial every day. The owner of the building, a practicing physician, however, did not appear at trial. Plaintiff took the opportunity to slam the owners of the building for failing to appear at trial: "[W]here have they been this whole trial? I haven't seen them once. If it's just a small family-owned company and someone is lifetime [sic] injured because of something they did, and you don't think you did anything wrong, I would be showing up. I would be here." This argument effectively fueled juror anger at the defense and cultivated a belief that the defense simply did not care.

CONCLUSION

The final verdict in this case—over $12.6 million—and the arguments deployed leading to it, indicates plaintiff's counsel successfully incited juror anger and the defense failed to defuse it. How could the defense have defused this anger? In the face of plaintiff's permanent injuries, was this an uphill battle for the defense? Is there any way the jury could have returned a defense verdict or even a more reasonable damages award considering plaintiff's counsel's effective presentation? Despite plaintiff's powerful arguments and evidence, we believe this verdict may have been avoided.

EPILOGUE: THE APPEAL

After the jury rendered a Nuclear Verdict for the plaintiff in excess of $12.6 million, the defendants filed Motions for Judgment Not Withstanding the Verdict and for a New Trial, which the Trial Court denied. The defendants then appealed the judgment, arguing the jury's verdict was not supported by substantial evidence because Pancho knew or should have known of the dangerous hatch, and they provided a warning about the hazard.

The Appellate Court concluded:

> [Plaintiff] does not contend that defendants exercised any retained control over the work site, and the undisputed evidence established that [plaintiff] and his employer could reasonably have ascertained the hazardous condition of the site—i.e., that the mechanism designed to hold the roof hatch open was broken and the ladder that provided access to the hatch did not reach all the way to the roof.

The Court reversed the jury's verdict and remanded the case with a directed entry of judgment for the defense. As of the date this manuscript was completed, the case continued with the Trial Court.

Regardless of the successful appeal result, this trial demonstrates how juror anger fuels a Nuclear Verdict, a verdict even the Appellate Court agreed was unjust. The Apex equips the defense to win at trial, eliminating the need to appeal a jury's Nuclear Verdict.

CHAPTER 8

THE POWER OF ACCEPTING RESPONSIBILITY

"Most people do not really want freedom, because freedom involves responsibility, and most people are frightened of responsibility."
—Sigmund Freud

DEFUSE JUROR ANGER: *ACCEPT RESPONSIBILITY*

THE NUMBER ONE EMOTION DRIVING Nuclear Verdicts is anger. This is the goal of every good plaintiffs' lawyer: get the jury angry. What is our goal? To defuse that juror anger. Everything we do in trial, in front of that jury, is intended to defuse anger.

The most effective way to defuse juror anger through validation is to *Accept Responsibility* for something in every single case, even when we are seeking a defense verdict. The defense must be a good human being and let the jury know we do care about the plaintiff. Accepting responsibility does this. It positions the defense as the most reasonable party in the courtroom. The Apex requires the defense to *Accept Responsibility* (note we did not say *liability*)—for something—in every trial, without exception, to reach the apex and defuse juror anger.

The Defense Must Validate

Since we published *Nuclear Verdicts*, we dug further into the topic of anger and the psychological methods to defuse this powerful emotion outside the context of trial with Dr. Jennifer Staples as part of the defense trial attorney training program we created, the Nuclear Verdicts Defense Institute. Dr. Staples introduced us to the critical psychological concept at play when it comes to defusing anger that supports our belief in the importance of accepting responsibility: validation.

"Validation is the recognition and acceptance of another person's thoughts, feelings, sensations, and behaviors as understandable"[1] to establish trust and help navigate emotionally charged situations. "Validating someone shows you understand their feelings and point of view, *even when you disagree*."[2] Dr. Marsha Linehan included validation as a core component of Dialectical Behavior Therapy, the gold standard for treating PTSD and suicidal patients through talk therapy. This critical communication technique is "used to demonstrate empathy, understanding, and acceptance of another person's feelings, thoughts, and behaviors."[3] Validation is also a practice commonly recommended for parents, especially parents of toddlers and teenagers.

Recent research[4] and theory indicate that validation works to reduce the intensity of negative emotions.[5] Validation "can help to defuse anger"

---

1 Karyn Hall, *Understanding Validation: A Way to Communicate Acceptance*, Psych. Today (Apr. 26, 2012), https://www.psychologytoday.com/us/blog/pieces-of-mind/201204/understanding-validation-a-way-to-communicate-acceptance (on file with the Apex Defense Consulting library).

2 Maureen Salamon, *Validation: Defusing intense emotions*, Harv. Health Publ'g: Harv. Med. Sch. (Aug. 14, 2023) (emphasis added), https://www.health.harvard.edu/blog/validation-defusing-intense-emotions-202308142961 (on file with the Apex Defense Consulting library).

3 *The Power of Validation in Dialectical Behavior Therapy*, Grouport, https://www.grouporttherapy.com/blog/dbt-validation (on file with the Apex Defense Consulting library) (last visited Jan. 18, 2025).

4 Cinthia Benitez, Kristen P. Howard & Jennifer S. Cheavens, *The effect of validation and invalidation on positive and negative affective experiences*, 17 J. Posit. Psych. 46 (2022), https://doi.org/10.1080/17439760.2020.1832243 (on file with the Apex Defense Consulting library).

5 Janice R. Kuo, Skye Fitzpatrick, Jennifer Ip & Amanda Uliaszek, *The who and what of validation: an experimental examination of validation and invalidation of specific emotions and the moderating effect of emotion dysregulation*, 9 Borderline Personal. Disord. & Emot. Dysregul. Article 15 (2022), https://bpded.biomedcentral.com/articles/10.1186/s40479-022-00185-x (on file with the Apex Defense Consulting library).

(a powerful, negative emotion), resolve conflicts, and build trust.[6] A recent study concluded that validation significantly reduced the heart rate in individuals initially reporting the feeling of anger.[7]

It is difficult to think, to make sound decisions, to be reasonable, and to be yourself when you are angry. In fact, if you are angry enough, you cannot even hear when someone is talking to you.

What if our jury is angry? What if plaintiff's counsel has done his job during opening statement and left us with 12 angry jurors, or 12 people who were at least on the verge of anger? What should we do to address this very powerful emotion? How do we get angry people to be persuaded by us, or to even listen to us? The first thing we must do is validate. We must address the anger in the room so the jury will listen to us and be open to our version of the case.

Importantly, to validate does not imply approval or agreement with another's feelings. Validation does not condone poor behavior. Validation is also not caving to another person or lying. Effective validation is not based in judgment or criticism. It is simply understanding and acknowledging another's perspective. It is seeing the world from the other person's point of view and maybe finding a kernel of truth in another person's perspective or situation.

Wait, there is some truth in the plaintiff's case?! Is that even possible? Yes, of course. Litigation and trial are emotionally charged processes; they beg for validation. With a point of view not clouded by intense negative emotions, we, as humans, are equipped to make better decisions. A jury free from the cloud of anger is equipped to reach a just verdict, a verdict fair to both parties.

---

6 *Using Validation to be Assertive with Difficult People*, Cognitive Behav. Therapy L.A. (June 1, 2014), https://cogbtherapy.com/cbt-blog/2014/6/1/using-validation-to-be-assertive-with-difficult-people (on file with the Apex Defense Consulting library).

7 Kuo et al., *supra* note 5 (describing how researchers explained the heart rate reductions in those feeling angry may simply be attributed to the individuals increasing their attention to their feelings while receiving the validating feedback).

The Typical Defense Approach—Deny, Deny, Deny, and Invalidate

So, what does the typical defense lawyer do in trial? The exact opposite. We do not accept responsibility. We do not validate. On the contrary, we typically deny everything. We make plaintiff prove her case, even if our research shows we have little to no chance of a defense verdict. We also bring in a whole slew of witnesses and experts to deny any liability on behalf of our client. We invalidate.

Emotional *in*validation occurs when someone's feelings or experience are "rejected, ignored, or judged."[8] Invalidation, "which communicates that another is wrong in their description or analyses of their experiences,"[9] can increase the intensity of negative feelings. A study "found that those who received validating responses experienced a decline in frustration and anger, compared to an increase in frustration and anger among those who received invalidating responses."[10]

In our personal lives, very few of us would intentionally invalidate someone's internal experience and feelings. Doing so just feels *wrong*. But within the heightened stakes and contentious nature of litigation, defense attorneys (and claims professionals) invalidate the plaintiff all the time. We may feel invalidating the plaintiff is necessary to zealously defend our client. Or we feel that to validate means we are weakening our case or admitting liability. "Sometimes people invalidate because they believe if they validate they are agreeing."[11]

Under the traditional defense approach to jury trials, we fight everything at all costs and make plaintiff prove her case. Deny, deny, deny. Plaintiff has the burden of proof, so we make her prove it. Defense teams spend all kinds of time and money denying things that we know only have a slim chance of winning. This approach has worked for a long time. A lot of very accomplished

---

8 Hall, *supra* note 1.

9 Kuo et al., *supra* note 5, at 1 (citing MARSHA M. LINEHAN, COGNITIVE-BEHAVIORAL TREATMENT OF BORDERLINE PERSONALITY DISORDER (1993)).

10 Kuo et al., *supra* note 5, at 2 (citing K.L. Vangronsveld & S.J. Linton, *The effect of validating and invalidating communication on satisfaction, pain and affect in nurses suffering from low back pain during a semi-structured interview*, 16 EUR. J. PAIN 239 (2012)).

11 Hall, *supra* note 1.

defense attorneys have achieved many defense verdicts over the last 30 or 40 years using just this approach.

This approach no longer works. Plaintiffs' lawyers have studied psychology. They know jurors get angry at defendants who fail to do the right thing, to accept responsibility for their actions. Jurors feel the need to punish corporations who not only are clueless about what they did wrong, but continue to deny it in the face of overwhelming evidence. This punishment will take the form of higher compensatory awards, especially pain and suffering, not just punitive damages.

Some of the ways we invalidate include: blaming, judging, denying, trivializing, minimizing, ignoring, misunderstanding, misreading, misinterpreting, and disbelieving. These typical defense methods are so bad and so wrong from a psychological perspective. Think about it: the defense is left with 12 angry people who are deciding our client's fate, and what do we do? We stand up in opening statement and tell them the plaintiff is wrong, dead wrong in fact.

Yes, it is absolutely the responsibility of defense counsel to ask the tough questions in the case. But if it feels wrong outside the courtroom, it is probably wrong inside the courtroom too. We can ask tough questions, be a strong advocate for our clients, *and* deliver on the foundation of The Apex: *Be a Good Human*. Again, "[v]alidation is not agreeing."[12]

Does this make sense? Think about in your own life, how frustrating is it when someone you know does not take responsibility for their actions? How awful does it feel to be invalidated? How does that make you feel? Depending upon the gravity of the situation, it can be infuriating.

It is the same in a jury trial. When defendants behave badly and do not appreciate the gravity of their actions, own up to them, and validate the plaintiff, a jury will punish them. It is simple human nature. We would do it in our personal lives, and jurors do it in real life at trial.

12 *Id.*

Validating Shows We Care About the Plaintiff

Can validation work in a jury trial? Of course it can. Is it used? Not by the defense. Why not? Because it has never been done that way. It has not been necessary to do it that way. It is only in the last 20 years that plaintiffs' lawyers have been actively trying to get the jury angry. Before that, there was no need to validate the jurors' feelings since jurors mostly felt sympathy, which is a less powerful emotion. But anger is such a strong, motivational emotion that calls jurors to act. We must address it.

Plaintiffs' counsel expects the defense to come to trial and present our case in the traditional defense method where we blame the plaintiff for her actions or inactions. Indeed, based on our experience and analysis, the traditional defense trial methods involve blaming, denying, minimizing, and judging—all methods that invalidate[13]—as well as making excuses and burying our heads in the sand. By only pointing fingers at other parties, we signal to the jury that we are making excuses and that we do not care about the plaintiff, which plays right into plaintiff's counsel's hand, making the defendant appear cold, greedy, out of touch, and worthy of punishment—all things the plaintiff's attorney wants the jury to believe. In fact, when the defense does not accept responsibility, plaintiff's counsel regularly points it out to jurors and effectively implores them to hold the defense accountable.

Through The Apex, validating the plaintiff is one of the primary ways we are good humans at trial. When we validate, we demonstrate to the plaintiff that we genuinely care about her. Validating from a place of empathy allows us to connect with plaintiff and defuse her anger. For a plaintiff to have reached the point of trial, she must have experienced *some* kind of an ordeal. We may disagree fundamentally with the nature of her claims or the extent of her injuries, but we can show up as good humans and acknowledge the reality of her experience while defending our client. Here lies the key to this concept: validating the plaintiff reduces juror anger because it reduces *plaintiff's* anger.

A jury connects with the parties through storytelling at trial. Plaintiff's attorneys are very skilled at storytelling (look no further than Gerry Spence

13 *Id.*

and the phenomenon of psychodrama in the law!), and they use it to effectively tell the plaintiff's life story as one where she lived out her absolute dream before the accident. They craft narratives around how the accident ruined her life, and how she will never be the same again.

This creates the perfect opportunity for the defense to validate the plaintiff in trial, validate any anger felt by the jury, and tell a more compelling story than the plaintiff—one where plaintiff is a victor in her own life and justice is served. Apex calls the defense to show up at trial every day and explicitly and genuinely show how much we care. From the moment they take their seats in the jury box until long after they sign the verdict form, jurors should know the defendant cares about the plaintiff, has the community's best interest at heart, and is striving to do the right thing. There is little room for anger when a jury sees the defense as the most reasonable party in the room. Validating accomplishes all of these goals.

The Six Levels of Validation

Dr. Linehan identified six levels of validation as part of Dialectical Behavior Therapy. As the levels of validation progress, so, too, does the strength and power of the validation. The six levels and examples of validating behaviors are:

1. Being Present—Pay attention; look and act interested in the other person.
2. Accurate Reflection—Reflect back; say back what you heard the other person say or do without judgmental language or tone of voice.
3. Mindreading—Read a person's behavior and guess what they might be feeling or thinking. Be sensitive to what is not said by the other person. Pay attention to facial expressions, body language, what is happening, and what you know about the person already.
4. Understand from their Point of View—Understand the person's behavior in terms of their history and biology. Look for how the other person is feeling, thinking, or doing makes sense based on

their past experiences, present situation, or current state of mind/ physical condition. Put yourself in their shoes.

5. Acknowledge the Valid—Normalize or recognize emotional reactions that anyone would have. Look for how the person's feelings, thinking, or actions are a logical response to the current facts. Anyone may feel this way.
6. Radical Genuineness—Show equality. Do not patronize, condescend, or treat the person as fragile or incompetent. Treat the other as an equal and use a radically genuine tone.[14]

We encourage defense counsel to engage in all Levels of validation, but especially Levels One, Two, Five, and Six.

Accepting Responsibility is the Highest Level of Validation

It is clear the defense must validate if we would like the jury to listen to and be persuaded by us. So, what is the best way to validate in a trial?

Accept Responsibility. Accept Responsibility for the defendant's actions, even if the defendant was not at fault. Defense counsel employs the highest level of validation when we genuinely *Accept Responsibility* for something at trial. Accepting responsibility shows we care. It will show we are being reasonable. Accepting responsibility for something is radically genuine and dispenses with the ego typically associated with corporate defendants. Accepting responsibility connects with the plaintiff, and thus the jury, on a human-to-human level. It will acknowledge fault, if appropriate, and it will gain the defense credibility—all things critical for reaching the apex and defusing anger.

Accepting responsibility is the easiest and clearest way to validate both the plaintiff and the jury's feelings about the evidence presented and the emotions that evidence produces. As discussed in *Nuclear Verdicts*, accepting responsibility at trial (1) effectively demonstrates to the jury the defense is the most reasonable party in the room. Accepting responsibility also (2) shows you care about the plaintiff, which is a powerful tool to defuse the anger a

14 *Id.*

plaintiff's attorney begins cultivating as early as jury selection. Accepting responsibility also (3) builds the credibility of the defense in the eyes of the jury, building trust between jurors and defense counsel. Finally, accepting responsibility (4) shifts the jury's focus to other possible culpable parties. If you remember nothing else from this chapter, remember this: the defense cannot shift responsibility without first accepting it.

Three Ways to *Accept Responsibility*

If you read *Nuclear Verdicts,* then you know there are three different ways to *Accept Responsibility* at trial depending on the likelihood the jury will assign liability/fault to the defense. Depending on the liability posture in the case, we say a case falls into one of three "baskets" (Cayce affectionately calls them "designer baskets"): (1) Full Liability; (2) Partial Liability; or (3) No Liability, discussed below.

Regardless of the (designer) Liability Basket you determine is best for your case, remember: words matter. When we say we must *Accept Responsibility* at trial, we mean exactly that. Defense counsel must stand in front of the jury as early as possible in the trial, say this exact sentence: "**[We/my client/corporate representative/XYZ Company] accept(s) responsibility in this case,**" and then explain to the jury for what and how the defendant accepts responsibility.

Depending on how we *Accept Responsibility*, a jury will not think it is an admission of guilt. A jury trial is much more than a sentence or paragraph, or opening statement. Trial takes days and weeks and months. The jury will understand for what we are sorry, and for what we are accepting responsibility. By the end of trial, there is no confusion. If we show remorse as appropriate and genuinely *Accept Responsibility*, not necessarily liability, we will defuse jurors' anger and reduce the chances of a Nuclear Verdict.

THE FULL LIABILITY BASKET

Full Liability

The first basket into which your case may fall is where the defense agrees it is completely at fault and, therefore, fully liable for both negligence and causation. In these cases, the defendant accepts responsibility *and* full liability. It was our fault and no one else's. Here, the defendant assumes full legal responsibility for the harm caused to plaintiff, and the only remaining debate is the extent of damages. The defense acknowledges the defendant injured the plaintiff and is willing to be held accountable. Responsibility is accepted, and juror anger is abated when it comes to awarding any damages, avoiding a Nuclear Verdict.

But this is only the case when the defense speaks to jurors in human words rather than legalese. It is insufficient and ineffective to stand before a jury to announce we "stipulate to liability." This is confusing to even the most educated jurors and carries no psychological benefit. Words matter.

If you are headed to trial and have determined that your case falls into the Full Liability Basket but you have not yet formally stipulated to liability: buckle up and prepare for battle. Plaintiffs' attorneys do not want us to accept fault. Why? Because it very often limits plaintiffs' attorney from talking to the jury about the accident and facts surrounding the accident because liability and evidence about liability are no longer relevant. Plaintiffs' lawyers want to talk about liability evidence and fault so they can make a jury angry.

When we accept responsibility in the Full Liability Basket, we argue in pretrial motions the jury does not need to hear about what the defendant did or failed to do. We are at fault. We *Accept Responsibility* and liability. We increase judicial economy and remove an arrow from plaintiff' s coun-sel's quiver.

THE PARTIAL LIABILITY BASKET

In the example of the second basket, the defendant accepts responsibility *and* partial liability. In this scenario, we *Accept Responsibility* for our reasonable share of fault and acknowledge we are partially liable, while arguing others are also at fault. Here, there are other liable tortfeasors. In the Partial Liability Basket, we *Accept Responsibility* and then go a step further to empower the jury to determine who else bears responsibility and fault in the case. As we discuss in Chapter 9, the Partial Liability Basket is often the most difficult kind of case in which to convince defendants and insurance carriers to *Accept Responsibility*.

Sometimes a co-defendant or empty chair is also at fault. Quite often, the comparative fault lies with the plaintiff herself. In the Partial Liability

Basket, the defense's apportionment of fault suddenly becomes much more reasonable in the eyes of the jury, stopping a Nuclear Verdict.

"Stipulating to partial liability" does not validate, as you will see in our discussion of our data below. Humans care about right and wrong. We must tell the jury we "accept responsibility in this case" as early as possible. Words matter. We should say, "You will not have to determine whether we were at fault. We are, and we accept responsibility for our actions. What you will need to determine is who also has responsibility in this case."

THE NO LIABILITY BASKET

In the third basket, the defense accepts responsibility without accepting any liability, and asks the jury to return a defense verdict. This scenario causes discomfort for defendants and claims professionals. Why? Because defense teams—the defendant, defense counsel, and the insurance carrier—often believe that responsibility is the same as fault. This is not true, as discussed below. Especially when the defense is seeking a defense verdict, we must defuse anger by accepting responsibility for our actions because an angry jury will quickly assign liability and award a Nuclear Verdict.

How can we genuinely *Accept Responsibility* and still obtain a defense verdict? As always, our goal is to defuse juror anger and demonstrate we are the most reasonable person in the room. The defense may *Accept Responsibility* for something within our control and for which we are proud. For example, we can genuinely *Accept Responsibility* for meeting the applicable standard of care, for following policies and procedures set by governing bodies, following our company policies, or for making a reasonable decision based on facts available at the time.

Words still matter in the No Liability Basket. We must stand before the jury and say, "We accept responsibility in this case," and explain for what we *Accept Responsibility*. Unfortunately, this approach to trial is missing in so many Nuclear Verdicts. The defense accepted responsibility in only three of the 100 cases we analyzed when the defendant was asking the jury to award a defense verdict (and see later in this chapter for the impact). In most of these cases, instead of accepting responsibility, counsel often did the exact opposite and told jurors their client had "no responsibility" or "were not responsible" in the case. This approach and this word choice invalidates. It plays right into plaintiffs' tactics to anger a jury, and it fuels a Nuclear Verdict.

False Barriers to Accepting Responsibility

Accepting responsibility sounds easier than it is. Accepting responsibility for something is one of the more difficult elements of the Core Four and the entire Apex for defense teams to fully embrace.

TOO MANY REASONS TO COUNT

There are many reasons a defendant does not *Accept Responsibility* in a jury trial. First of all, the defense traditionally never has! The defense fights everything. The common belief is if you poke enough holes in plaintiff's case, you will win. Plaintiff has the burden of proof, after all. The defense has to prove nothing. So, make plaintiff prove it.

Second, defendants often refuse to *Accept Responsibility* for anything, because they believe if they do, they are admitting fault and, thus, unnecessarily accepting liability. This belief is incorrect. Responsibility is not the same thing as fault.

Responsibility ≠ Fault

Mark Manson calls equating responsibility and liability the "responsibility/fault fallacy." Through the lens of self-improvement, he describes the distinction:

> A lot of people hesitate to take responsibility for their problems because they believe that to be responsible for your problems is to also be at fault for your problems. Responsibility and fault often appear together in our culture. But they're not the same thing.
>
> If I hit you with my car, I am both at fault and likely legally responsible to compensate you in some way. Even if hitting you with my car was an accident, I am still responsible. This is the way fault works in our society: if you [mess] up, you're on the hook for making it right. And it should be that way.
>
> But there are also problems that we aren't at fault for, yet we are still responsible for them. For example, if you woke up one day and there was a newborn baby on your doorstep, it would not be your fault that the baby had been put there, but the baby would now be your responsibility.[15]

When we accept *liability* in the courtroom, we admit legal fault. That term carries legal weight and significance. In contrast, when we accept *responsibility* in the courtroom, we validate the plaintiff's experience in the eyes of the jury, we acknowledge our role in the situation, we show empathy, we demonstrate we care about the plaintiff, we become the most reasonable party in the courtroom, and we defuse juror anger.

Third, there are countless, varying "business" reasons for why the defense declines to *Accept Responsibility* in Nuclear Verdict trials. In many scenarios, the case falls into the No Liability Basket and the defense team falls prey to the "responsibility/fault fallacy." In others, the case falls into the Full Liability Basket or the Partial Liability Basket and the defense team is concerned about the implications of stipulation to some portion of liability.

For example, sometimes the defendant client will not allow us to *Accept Responsibility* because they are concerned about the reputational risk of an

15 Mark Manson, The Subtle Art of Not Giving a F*ck: A Counterintuitive Approach to Living a Good Life 97-98 (2016).

adverse judgment. There can be a concern that if we stipulate to liability in this jury trial, it will have a precedential impact on liability in another jury trial, or it will be used against us somehow in a later proceeding. Sometimes the client does not want to *Accept Responsibility* because plaintiff has alleged punitive damages and the client believes if we give up liability, we are one step closer to getting hit for punitive damages, which are often not covered by insurance. A carrier in the tower of insurance may be concerned that by accepting responsibility for something we may be bringing their layer of insurance into play for an adverse verdict. Underwriting or the insured's broker may be pressing the defense to go for a defense verdict or deny any responsibility, because of long-standing relationship reasons. And there are many more reasons members of the defense team push back on accepting responsibility in trial.

FOCUS ON THE JURY, NOTHING ELSE

For all the reasons to not *Accept Responsibility* in any given jury trial, guess what reason is never given? Because of the impact accepting responsibility will have on 12 people deciding the client's fate in trial!

All the reasons given to not *Accept Responsibility* are business reasons that have almost nothing to do with the effect it will have on the 12 people making the decision. There is no psychological or sociological reason to refuse to *Accept Responsibility*. Failing to *Accept Responsibility* does not validate the jurors' feelings or defuse their anger. The rationale given by insurance professionals and corporate decision makers has nothing to do with the impact it will have on the people deciding our fate.

Instead, the reasons are tied to things going on behind the scenes, business things. It has nothing to do with getting in touch with what 12 people may be feeling or wanting to hear from the defense. So, if you are stuck in this debate, look up. What is at the top of The Apex? *Defuse Juror Anger*. Ask yourself: what will *not* accepting responsibility do to defuse juror anger? The answer is a big, expensive NOTHING.

You know who is 100% focused on the feelings and thoughts of these 12 people? Yep, our competition: plaintiffs' attorneys. They show up with one goal and one goal only: to get the jury to award as much money as possible. And what about us, do we show up with just one goal? Do we show up to get the lowest verdict possible? No way!

When the defense shows up for trial, we are balancing all types of competing factors. Sometimes we do not want the lowest possible verdict at all; we only want a defense verdict. Going for a defense verdict can be very different than trying to achieve the lowest verdict possible. Why on earth would a client not want the lowest verdict possible?

For the reasons listed above, sometimes the defendant client does not want the lowest verdict possible because of the perceived impact any adverse jury verdict might have on a company's reputation or their product, or a doctor's reputation or other professional. Sometimes an excess carrier only wants to prevent the verdict from coming into their layer of insurance. There are legal reasons as well, such as a particular state's contribution, indemnity, and comparative fault laws. How about the fact the plaintiff has the burden of proof, so why not fight everything and make them prove everything, and you never know what a jury may do?

Again, these reasons have nothing to do with what is going on in the heads of 12 decision makers. It is all behind the scenes, business issues and decisions. The defense side of trying big jury trials is so much more complicated than the plaintiffs' side. The plaintiff's team all shows up with only one goal: to get as much money as possible. Our side, not so much.

Yet, when the defense team is united in achieving the lowest, most reasonable verdict possible, we can harness the incredible power of The Apex. When the defense team understands the reasons for accepting responsibility, agrees in which Basket the case falls, and defense counsel is brave enough to stand before jurors and authentically declare, "We accept responsibility in this case and we are asking you to hold us accountable," the jury can relax. Jurors know they are hearing from a party who cares about people and justice, not an entity looking for a way out. Jurors can now focus on the evidence we present, and they know they can trust us. This increases the likelihood that the defense will avoid a Nuclear Verdict.

CASE STUDY OVERVIEW: *ACCEPT RESPONSIBILITY*

Bottom line: anger drives Nuclear Verdicts, and accepting responsibility, in conjunction with the other skills and strategies that comprise The Apex, defuses that anger. It is difficult to be angry with people who care, are reasonable, and are interested in justice. Although it can be difficult and uncomfortable to *Accept Responsibility*, it is imperative in every trial. The data we analyzed bears this out.

In the majority of the cases we analyzed, the defense did not *Accept Responsibility*, and in most cases denied any and all responsibility. What happened? A Nuclear Verdict.

Methodology

We standardized our analysis of 100 closing arguments from Nuclear Verdicts to determine the role accepting responsibility or not accepting responsibility played in these outsized awards. Specifically, if defense counsel used the exact phrase "accept responsibility," or any tense of this term, we considered this an application of The Apex. If there was no reference in defense counsel's closing argument to "accepting responsibility," we considered this an omission of The Apex.

Hypothesis

Our trial experience shows that accepting responsibility at trial defuses juror anger and helps prevent a Nuclear Verdict. Thus, our hypothesis was: In the majority of Nuclear Verdicts, defense counsel does not *Accept Responsibility* in front of the jury.

Results

Our case study analysis supported our hypothesis. In the majority of Nuclear Verdicts, the defense did not *Accept Responsibility* in front of the jury. Our data analysis revealed much more about the impact of failing to *Accept Responsibility*, and how plaintiffs' counsel capitalizes.

THE DEFENSE DOES NOT *ACCEPT RESPONSIBILITY* IN MOST NUCLEAR VERDICTS

Out of the 100 Nuclear Verdicts we analyzed, the defense failed to *Accept Responsibility* for *anything* in 85 of them. Put another way: **the defense accepted responsibility only 15% of the time**.

Frequency of the Defense Accepting Responsibility

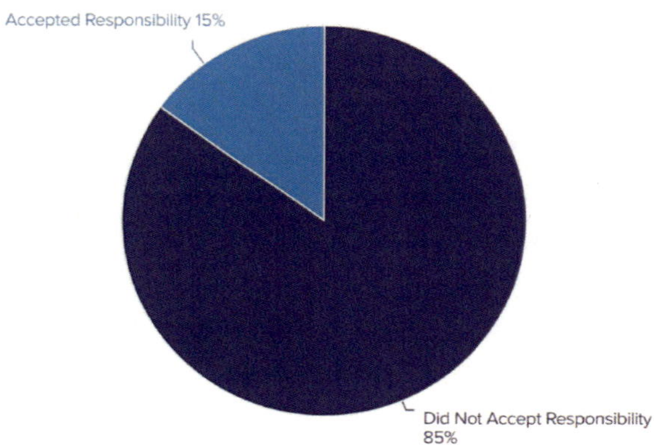

This is not surprising, given the false barriers to accepting responsibility we have already discussed and the pushback we receive when we tell a room full of defense counsel they must *Accept Responsibility* for something in every single case. The defense does not use the number one tool available to us to defuse juror anger: we fail to validate. The problem is even more striking when we peer inside the three liability baskets to take a closer look at what is happening.

Three Liability Baskets

THE FULL LIABILITY BASKET

The most common concern we hear when we talk about accepting responsibility sounds something like this: "But if I accept responsibility for something, I am confessing liability!" So, what happens when liability has already been confessed? The easiest case to *Accept Responsibility* should be the Full Liability Basket, the one in which the defense has stipulated to liability, right? That would align with the most common reason for refusing to *Accept Responsibility*. However, our analysis does not support this conclusion.

Of 100 Nuclear Verdicts analyzed, the defense stipulated to liability in ten trials. We categorize these cases as falling into the Full Liability Basket. Of these stipulated cases, the defense used the phrase "we accept responsibility" (or some iteration thereof) in only four cases. Thus, the defense "accepted responsibility" in only 40% of Nuclear Verdicts where the defense also stipulated to liability.

In those stipulated liability cases where the defense accepted responsibility, the verdicts averaged 58% of plaintiff's ask compared to stipulated liability cases where the defense did *not Accept Responsibility*, where the verdicts averaged 71.3% of plaintiff's ask. Put another way: accepting responsibility in stipulated liability cases resulted in lower overall verdicts.

Impact of Accepting Responsibility in Stipulated Liability Cases

Verdict Amount as Percentage of Plaintiff's Ask

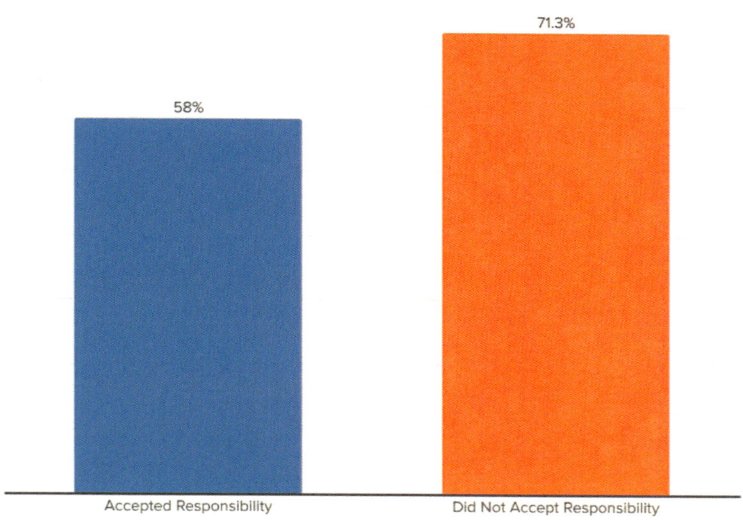

The defense has nothing to lose by accepting responsibility when liability is not a question the jury will have to answer, and yet, the defense still does not do it. The reason may be as innocent as believing a jury will understand the defense has accepted responsibility by stipulating to liability, but that reasoning is rooted in the fundamental misconception that jurors think like lawyers. They do not.

Remember: responsibility is not the same as liability, both in the law and in the eyes of our jurors. Words matter. Even in the Full Liability Basket, defense counsel must stand before the jury and say, "We accept responsibility in this case," instead of, "My client stipulates to liability." Doing so carries a measurable benefit for the defense.

THE PARTIAL LIABILITY BASKET

Our data also shows the defense similarly does not *Accept Responsibility* in Nuclear Verdicts when the case falls within the Partial Liability Basket. Of 100 Nuclear Verdicts analyzed, the defense stipulated to partial liability in six trials. Of the six cases in the Partial Liability Basket, the defense accepted responsibility in only two cases. Thus, the defense "accepted responsibility" in only 33% of Nuclear Verdicts where the defense also stipulated to partial liability.

Our analysis reveals that accepting partial liability resulted in no measurable impact to the ultimate award compared to plaintiff's trial ask. Where the defense accepted partial liability, awards averaged 128.3% of plaintiff's ask. Where the defense did not accept partial liability, awards averaged 122.2% of plaintiff's ask. This is a negligible difference in a small universe of data.

Essentially, admitting to partial liability did not result in a statistically significant change in the ultimate verdict awarded. There is good news to be found here: in cases where the defense has learned through mock trial or focus groups that there is a substantial likelihood of at least some liability being assigned to them, there is no measurable impact on the verdict by admitting to partial liability. The bad news? The defense gains no benefit in these partial liability basket cases if they do not use the human (and effective!) words: "We accept responsibility."

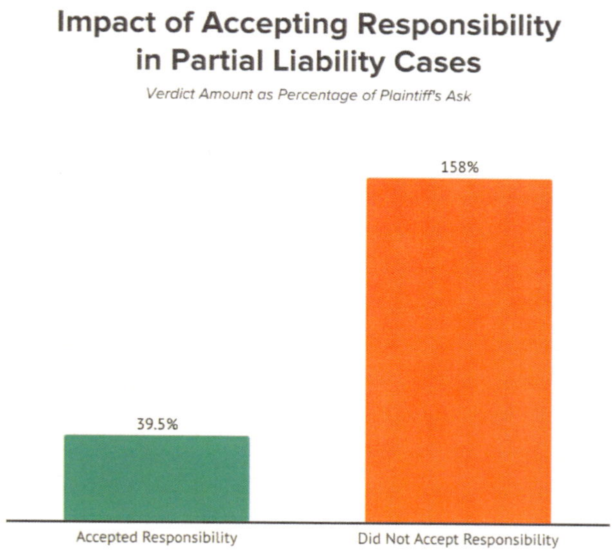

Of the six cases where defense stipulated to partial liability, they accepted responsibility in only two. But, in those cases, verdicts averaged 39.5% of plaintiff's ask, compared to 158% of plaintiff's ask in stipulated partial liability cases where the defense did *not Accept Responsibility*. This represents a reduction of 118.5%!

The defense may still be stuck in an "admit nothing, deny everything" mindset (even where the defense has already "admitted" liability). In either case, we are missing the mark. Jurors respond to human words, and if we fail to genuinely *Accept Responsibility*, we are missing a powerful opportunity to stand and deliver as good, reasonable humans.

THE NO LIABILITY BASKET

Of the 100 Nuclear Verdicts analyzed, the defense sought a defense verdict in 54 trials. Of the 54 cases in the No Liability Basket, the defense accepted responsibility in only three cases. Thus, the defense "accepted responsibility" in 5.5% of Nuclear Verdicts where the defense simultaneously contested liability.

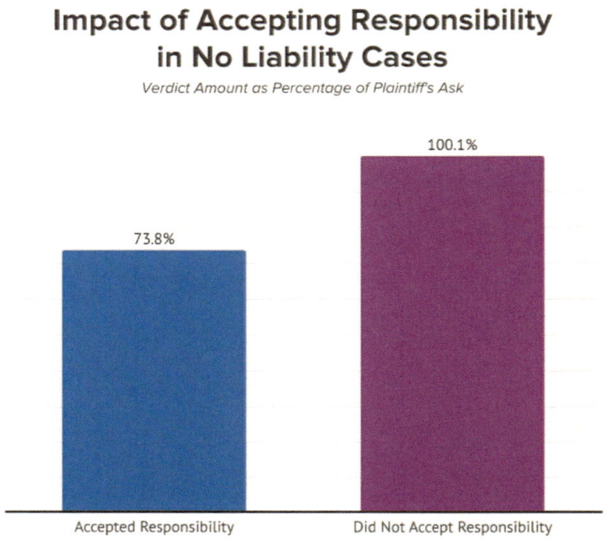

And, where the defense sought a defense verdict and accepted responsibility, the verdicts averaged 73.8% of plaintiff's ask. On the flip side, where the defense sought a defense verdict and did *not Accept Responsibility*, the verdicts averaged 100.1% of plaintiff's ask, representing a 26.3% difference.

Again, accepting responsibility is beneficial for the defense *even while seeking a defense verdict*.

Plaintiffs' Counsel Slams the Defense for Not Accepting Responsibility

When we decline to *Accept Responsibility*, we give plaintiffs' counsel another arrow in their quiver. We tracked what we termed "reverse accepting responsibility," where plaintiffs' counsel attacked the defense for not accepting responsibility. Plaintiffs' counsel used this method in 64% of the Nuclear Verdicts we analyzed, more than any other "reverse" method. Why might this be? Because *they* know the power of accepting responsibility, and they know to capitalize on it when the defense falls short to drive juror anger and increase the Nuclear Verdict.

Where plaintiffs' counsel attacked the defense for failing to *Accept Responsibility*, verdicts averaged 138% of plaintiff's ask, compared to 90.1% where they did not use this attack. And where the defense accepted responsibility and plaintiff did not use the reverse method (likely because the defense was insulated from the attack because of their acceptance of responsibility), the verdict was the lowest in this analysis, averaging 68.6% of plaintiff's ask. In cases where the defense refused to *Accept Responsibility* but plaintiffs' counsel did *not* attack them for it, verdicts averaged 92.6% of plaintiff's ask. The most dangerous combination occurred (unsurprisingly) when the defense failed to *Accept Responsibility* and plaintiff's counsel attacked them for it. In this scenario, verdicts averaged 154.7% of plaintiff's ask.

Defense Does NOT Accept Responsibility
+ Plaintiff Attacks Defense for Not Accepting Responsibility
= Verdict 1.5x Plaintiff's Ask.

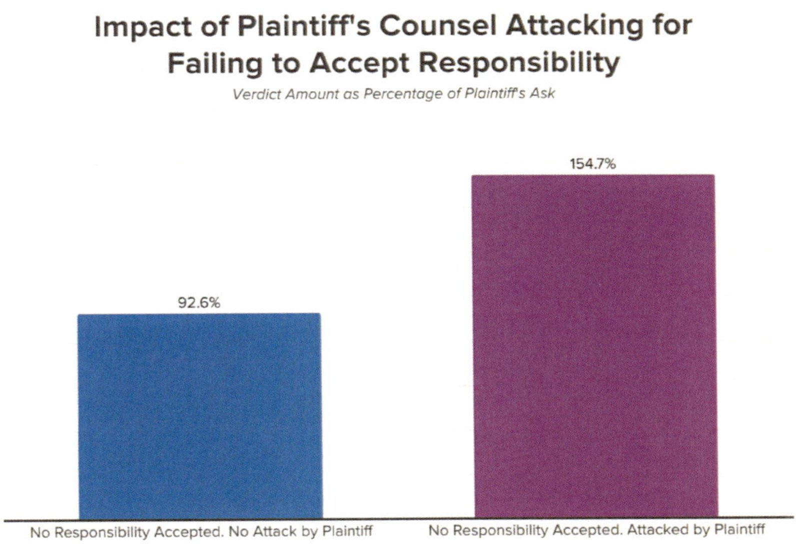

This speaks both to the power of accepting responsibility and to the anger-generating power of plaintiffs' counsel pointing out a failure to *Accept Responsibility* to the jury.

In case all this number crunching makes your brain hurt as much as ours, let us put it this way: declining to *Accept Responsibility* is bad for the defense, but the worst possible scenario for the defense is one where they refuse to *Accept Responsibility and* plaintiffs' counsel takes them to task for it in front of the jury. Do you remember our discussion surrounding anger? This data confirms anger is in the driver's seat when a jury awards a Nuclear Verdict, and the defense is paving the road for plaintiffs' counsel to direct the jury straight over a cliff by refusing to *Accept Responsibility.*

Even in Nuclear Verdicts, Accepting Responsibility is Impactful for the Defense

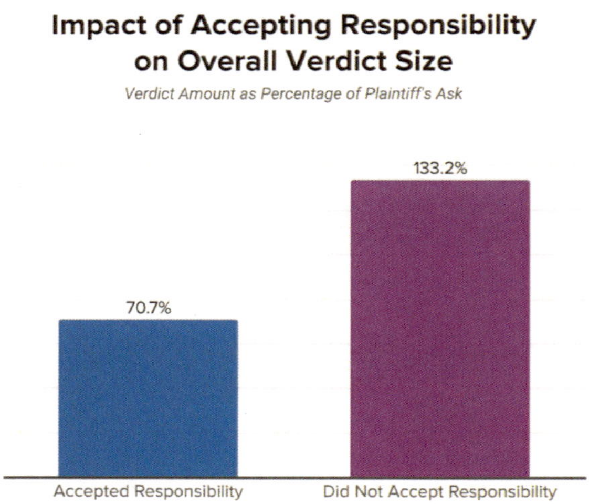

We started off with some bad news, but we also want to highlight some good. Our analysis reveals that even where a Nuclear Verdict is ultimately awarded, accepting responsibility is impactful for the defense. In cases where the defense did not *Accept Responsibility*, verdicts averaged 133.2% of plaintiff's ask. However, where the defense did *Accept Responsibility*, verdicts averaged 70.7% of plaintiff's ask, representing a 62% difference in Nuclear Verdict awards.

We talk about why plaintiffs' counsel gives a number in Chapter 11, and the power of giving a number in general, but for this discussion, consider how angry a jury must be to *exceed* plaintiff's already astronomical ask. The 33% increase from plaintiff's ask where the defense refused to *Accept Responsibility* did not even require the plaintiff to attack the defense. Jurors got there on their own because a failure to *Accept Responsibility* infuriates *humans.*

The *Reptile* Loves a Defense Failure to *Accept Responsibility*

We will give credit where credit is due: the *Reptile* truly did announce a plaintiff's revolution, as billed. And its impact has not dissipated despite its rebranding; it is wildly effective at driving up damages. The *Reptile* thrives in a courtroom where the defense refuses to *Accept Responsibility*, perhaps unsurprisingly because of its penchant for punishment.

Where the defense did not *Accept Responsibility* and plaintiff's counsel deployed *Reptile* buzzwords, verdicts averaged **161.7% of plaintiffs' counsel's ask.** The combination of a failure to *Accept Responsibility* and *Reptile* is deadly for the defense. Accepting responsibility does make a dent on the impact of *Reptile*, however. Where the defense accepted responsibility and plaintiff's counsel used *Reptile* buzzwords, the average verdict was 94.6% of plaintiff's ask, compared to only 46.8% of plaintiff's ask in cases where the defense accepted responsibility, but plaintiff did not use the *Reptile.* So, yes: the *Reptile* is still alive and well, and it is still wildly effective at fueling juror anger to deliver Nuclear Verdicts.

Not Accepting Responsibility
+ Reptile
= 61.7% Increase in Verdict Over Plaintiff's Ask

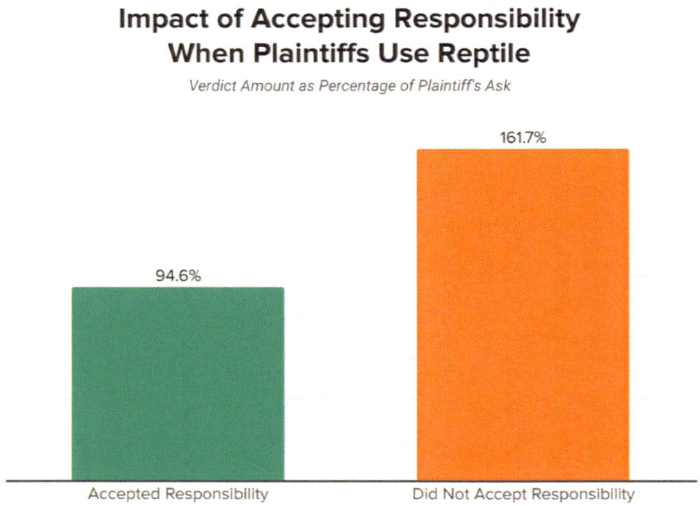

This makes sense: the *Reptile*'s obsession with so-called "tentacles of danger" is productive only when a perceived danger actually exists. A corporate defendant's failure to *Accept Responsibility* strikes at the heart of the *Reptile*'s call to action: the incalcitrant corporate defendant who refuses to *Accept Responsibility* for anything represents a danger to the community at large, greater than the harm suffered by this specific plaintiff, and ripe for the punishment and control the *Reptile* bestows upon jurors.

As we have said before and will say ad nauseum, The Apex represents a singular method and blueprint containing a set of skills and strategies that work together and build on one another toward the goal of defusing juror anger and delivering justice. The *Reptile* is only effective if anger is not defused. Anger is most effectively defused through the application of every single building block contained within The Apex.

THE DATA-BACKED CONCLUSION: ACCEPTING RESPONSIBILITY REDUCES JURY AWARDS

Plaintiffs' lawyers are more finely attuned to the power of accepting responsibility than defense attorneys. Skilled plaintiffs' lawyers lay the groundwork with jurors early to prime them for a defense's refusal to *Accept Responsibility* and will marry that with *Reptile* buzzwords designed to incite fear and fuel anger. The defense insulates our clients from the effectiveness of these tactics by accepting responsibility early, clearly, and genuinely.

Identifying into which Liability Basket a case falls as early as possible (but certainly well before trial) will equip the defense with the tools we need to connect with the jury in human terms rather than legalese. As always, the defense is wise to heed the information it receives from mock trials and other sources of pretrial intelligence. The first step to accepting responsibility in trial may very well be accepting what the science we paid for tells us rather than fighting it or holding out hope it is wrong.

The defense has at our disposal the most impactful way to validate juror anger, regardless of into which Liability Basket the case falls. We are empowered to speak as humans—good humans, who believe in reasonableness, common sense, and responsibility. Jurors are receptive when we do. Our clients deserve it, and justice demands it.

CHAPTER 9

HOLD MY CLIENTS ACCOUNTABLE

BOB'S ALTERNATIVE, APEX CLOSING ARGUMENT

OUR DEFENSE THEMES

RESPONSIBILITY, REASONABLENESS, COMMON SENSE. THAT is what I told you this case was about three weeks ago. I believe that is what the evidence has shown this case to be about today.

Let's talk about responsibility.

PERSONALIZE THE DEFENDANT

Only one person has unconditionally accepted any responsibility in this case. That person, that corporate citizen, is my client, Arendelle Center. Mr. Gonzalez has sat here on behalf of these corporate citizens every single day. He sat here and has been doing the right thing, every day, really every day since this accident occurred five years ago. He is here accepting responsibility. He has shown how much he cares about Mr. Medina. He is here for you to hold him and this company accountable. How do you hold my client accountable? You award plaintiff what is fair and reasonable, nothing more, nothing less.

It is easy to throw around accusations. It is very easy to file a lawsuit in America, but it is very difficult to defend one. I do not mean financially, because you cannot consider the costs of all of this, or attorneys' fees over the last several years—you will receive a jury instruction on that.

It is difficult to put your and your company's reputations in the hands of 12 strangers and say, "Hold me accountable." But that is what my clients are doing. They accept responsibility for their actions and say, "Hold me accountable; here I am."

ACCEPT RESPONSIBILITY

We accept responsibility. We were negligent. We made a mistake. We had a plan to fix our mistake, the broken hatch, but we didn't fix it. We also didn't hide it; we didn't conceal it. Rather, we warned people about the broken hatch.

APOLOGIZE

We could have fixed our hatch sooner than we did; we should have fixed it; we wish we had fixed it. As you heard, we are sorry. We are sorry this ever happened to Mr. Medina. It should never have happened.

We accept responsibility for our actions. The hatch was broken. We knew it. We knew it for two years. That was our fault. We put up a sign letting folks know it was broken. But we could have done more; we should have done more. We were at fault. You are not going to have to decide that. Our responsibility is not even a question for you on the jury verdict form. We are sorry, and we accept responsibility for our actions in this case.

SHIFT RESPONSIBILITY

So who else has fault? Who else has responsibility for this accident? Well, we know no one else has accepted any responsibility for this accident—only my clients. But what about the plaintiff? You have heard a lot of accusations by plaintiff 's counsel. You have heard a lot of blaming by counsel. A lot of criticism of the way we have accepted responsibility in this case. But not once, after weeks of evidence, have you heard plaintiff or his lawyer accept any responsibility in this case. Not once.

You heard that Mr. Medina has been doing this kind of work for a long time. He has gone through over 600 hatches in his career. We don't know how many of those hatches had a sign on them telling folks not to use the hatch. We don't know how many of those 600+ hatches had a sign telling him it was broken, stay away. We don't know how many times in his career, as an expert in this field, he ignored warning signs and went right through a dangerous hatch. We don't know how many times in his career he ignored any kind of warning sign when he was working.

What we do know is that in this case, Mr. Medina did not follow directions. He did not stay away from the broken hatch. He did not follow the warnings. He did not stop when he felt the hatch was heavier than normal. He did not stop when he realized the hatch was broken. Mr. Medina failed to follow instructions not to use our hatch. All these failures, this was negligence. And for this, he is responsible. Mr. Medina and his counsel have accepted none of it.

ASSIGN PERCENTAGE OF FAULT

It is time to hold plaintiff and his attorney responsible for his actions in this case. He messed up, too. He is negligent. On the jury verdict form, you should find and write that plaintiff was 80% negligent.

MY RESPONSIBILITY STORY

When you look at the concept of responsibility, it is actually two things: acceptance and accountability. I learned that concept from a very young age. I've shared with you that I'm from Staten Island, New York. Growing up there, the summer was hot and muggy, but my sister and I lived for summertime. We used to ride our bikes to our grandparents' house. We would head down our tree-lined street to the buzz of cicada bugs humming loudly in all the towering green oak trees. The louder the cicadas, the hotter the day was going to be.

We loved to go to my grandparents' for two main reasons. First, they had candy. Second, they had air-conditioning. We had a window AC unit in our 1,100 square foot ranch home, and my parents only allowed us to run it at night when they were home. Being at my grandparents', basking in their air-conditioning during the hottest heat of the day, was a treat.

So off we would go to my grandparents' in the late morning. It was a short bike ride, mostly downhill. But inevitably, my sister and I would start to race to see who could get there first and "win." So we often showed up panting and sweaty, dropping our bikes in the back yard. Up the steps we would race, into their old two-story brick home. We would swing the back door open and there it was, the rush of cool air. *Aahhh*. It felt like an ice chest. With big smiles on our sweaty faces, we would hug Grandma while Grandpa yelled, "Shut the door!"

We got the air conditioning. Now bring on the candy! While the air conditioner blew full blast, we held candy in our hands and put our sodas on the side table. My grandfather's chair was fully reclined. We found which of the five TV channels was showing Abbott and Costello reruns. It was too good to be true! Well, unfortunately, it was.

After about an hour of doing absolutely nothing but eating candy and watching TV in the cold air, my grandfather would insist we go outside. He would say, "Get out of the house. You can't just sit around and watch TV all day!" So, off we would go.

One day, as we went out into the sun and unbearable heat, we decided it was time for a game of catch. I played Little League, and my sister Denise played softball. We both had our gloves and started throwing a rubber ball back and forth. That was my grandfather's rule: no throwing a hard ball or a baseball.

My grandparents' home had a small grassy backyard that abutted the cinderblock wall of a dry cleaner on one side. The dry cleaner had a couple of windows along the wall that let the wonderful dry cleaner smell escape.

My sister and I started throwing a rubber ball, but after a while that became no fun. So, I got my baseball and began throwing some pretty impressive pitches. I remember throwing a perfect strike that my sister did not catch. (She, of course, says it was a wild pitch!) You guessed it, I broke the dry cleaner's window.

I was scared to death. I knew my grandfather would be angry and disappointed in me for disobeying. But I walked into that air-conditioned house, which didn't feel as good as it did earlier that morning, and told my grandfather the truth. As I expected, he was livid!

My grandfather took me by the hand and said, "We are going to the dry cleaner's, and you are going to take responsibility for this, young man!" We walked around to the front of the building and into the dry cleaner. My grandfather asked for the owner. When he came to the front, my grandfather said, "Tell him what you did." I was terrified, but I somehow managed to squeak out, "I broke your window, Sir, with my baseball."

The owner was surprised. He told us to wait a minute, and he went to the back of the store. It felt like an eternity, but he returned with my baseball in his hand. I held my breath to see what would happen next.

The owner approached and handed me back my ball. He said, "Son, I want to thank you for taking responsibility for your actions. Here is your baseball back."

"YES!" I thought to myself. I had my ball back! The owner seemed pleased with me. I had done the right thing; I had taken responsibility. I guess it was time to go back to the air-conditioning and candy!

As I turned and started to walk out of the store with a big feeling of relief, I felt a pull on my collar jerking me backwards. It was my grandfather. His hand was firmly on my shirt and neck, and he seemed even angrier than before. "Hold on," my grandfather said. "You are not done yet. You are going to pay this gentleman back for the window you broke."

My heart sank. I knew what that meant, and it wasn't good. I knew I would be mowing lawns for the rest of the summer to pay back the dry cleaner for his window. Instead of being in the air-conditioning watching TV, I was going to be cutting lawns in the sweltering heat.

And, ladies and gentlemen of the jury, I learned the meaning of the word "responsibility" that day. I learned responsibility is really two words: acceptance and accountability. I had accepted responsibility for the broken window, but I also had to be held accountable.

HOLD PLAINTIFF ACCOUNTABLE

It is time for you to teach plaintiff and his counsel what responsibility really is. Sure, it would have been nice if plaintiff's counsel had stood up here before you three weeks ago and accepted responsibility for his client's negligence. But he didn't do it and will probably never do it. He gets the final word, so listen to see if he finally accepts responsibility for his own negligence, after five years of denying it.

How do you hold plaintiff and his attorney accountable for his negligence? You find that plaintiff was 80% negligent. You find that plaintiff failed to act as a reasonable person, a person who had been through over 600 hatches before, and failed to observe or follow the warning signs about the broken hatch. And you award damages that are fair and reasonable, nothing more, nothing less.

Now let's talk about damages.

PATTERN OF RESPONSIBILITY

Our research shows the overwhelming majority of Nuclear Verdicts happen when the defense has failed to truly *Accept Responsibility*. The above is an example of how the defense could have accepted responsibility in the *Medina* case. It is not a criticism of a particular defense lawyer. In fact, our research shows who the defense lawyers are in any particular case really does not matter. What matters is recognizing the pattern of Nuclear Verdicts, and most importantly, taking steps to stop it.

Data shows the defense must *Accept Responsibility* for something to avoid a Nuclear Verdict. Failure to *Accept Responsibility* by the defense was present in **85%** of all Nuclear Verdicts we researched. Lack of responsibility is an overwhelming theme used by plaintiff's counsel to get jurors angry.

The good news is that breaking the pattern of failing to *Accept Responsibility* in a jury trial is pretty easy. All you have to do is—*Accept Responsibility*! The research shows declining to *Accept Responsibility* is no longer working and, in fact, plays right into plaintiffs' lawyers' hands. In every single jury trial, even when going for a defense verdict, we must *Accept Responsibility* for something.

Plaintiffs' lawyers are baiting the defense to deny responsibility. They are setting the jury up to get angry when the defense fails to accept what it did wrong. Just like in this *Medina* case, plaintiffs' attorneys often challenge the defense to accept any responsibility. Why? Because they know the defense will not do it, and then plaintiff's counsel will be the most reasonable person in the room. Every time the defense tries to poke a hole in plaintiff's liability arguments and fails, we fuel juror anger. When we refuse to accept any responsibility, the defense is wrong in the eyes of the jury and, therefore, less credible and less reasonable.

Partial Liability Basket

Under The Apex responsibility analysis, we believe the *Medina* case falls into the Partial Liability Basket of responsibility.[1] Given the facts about the hatch, when it broke, when the defendant was notified that it broke, the steps (or lack thereof) the defendant took to repair it, and the notice the defendant posted about the hatch, we believe it would have been highly unlikely a jury would have found the defense 0% liable.

Yes, we have the benefit of 20/20 hindsight to help us with this case assessment, but we also come to the same conclusion by tapping into the core value of The Apex: reasonableness. We believe a reasonable jury would find the defendant at least some percentage at fault. In this case, the defense should position itself as the most reasonable party in the room and accept both responsibility *and* liability.

At the same time, others are also at fault here! Plaintiff failed to exercise reasonable care in his use of the hatch and awareness of his surroundings, including his awareness of the sign indicating the hatch was broken. Third parties the defendant hired to fix the hatch may also be liable for not

1 For more behind-the-scenes insight into Bob's thought process and the development of this Apex closing, join our Apex Defense Community at www.apexdefenseconsulting.com.

remedying the danger, but our sample Apex closing above focuses only on plaintiff's comparative negligence.

Do The Opposite: Own It!

So, what should the defense do when we only have partial liability, but little to no chance of a defense verdict? Our research shows the defense should do the opposite. Do the opposite of what the defense industry has been doing for the last 50 years. The plaintiffs' bar has completely changed the way they try lawsuits, and they are hoping we do not change a thing.

So, change it up! Own what we did wrong, and then focus the jury on the conduct of everyone else. A trial is about what you make it about. Most defense lawyers make trials about their client. And so does the plaintiff! So, most trials are about the defendant, and it is just a matter of how angry plaintiff's counsel can get the jury. Stop it, please! We must stop fighting points we know we will lose.

Stipulate to negligence. Yes, if we are not going to get a defense verdict, do not make the plaintiff prove his case. Own it. Stipulate our client made a mistake; we were negligent. The jury will not have to decide this. Defuse anger. We can stand before the jury and say, "We are sorry. We accept responsibility for our actions, and we are here to be held accountable. How do you do that, ladies and gentlemen of the jury? How do you hold my client accountable? You award what is fair and reasonable, nothing more, nothing less. Now, let's look at who else has fault in this case."

Instead of focusing the next several weeks on our client's actions and waging a losing battle at that, we spend time talking about the actions of others. We make the trial be about what we want it to be about—the real wrongdoers. The jury does not have to evaluate the defendant's actions at all. The jury does not have to punish us either, like the plaintiff wants them to do. There is no need. We owned what we did wrong, we learned from our mistake, and we are in court to do the right thing: to fully and reasonably compensate the plaintiff.

We have conceded nothing. This is not rolling over or playing from a position of weakness. This is a power move, made from a position of strength. We are taking control of the narrative and making the trial be about what we want it to be about—the wrongful conduct of others. We have defused juror anger, and we have refocused their attention for the entire trial on the plaintiff and others. Powerful!

CONCLUSION

There is a pattern to Nuclear Verdicts. As evidenced by this particular case, as well as most others, the defense's failure to *Accept Responsibility* is a critical reason for this outrageous result. Responsibility is not a weakness in the courtroom—it is a strategic advantage. When the defense accepts responsibility early and genuinely, we build credibility, earn the jury's trust, and defuse the anger that fuels Nuclear Verdicts. As we demonstrated in the *Medina* case, even when the facts put us in the Partial Liability Basket, there is immense power in owning what we did wrong. This allows us to reframe the trial around the conduct of others and empower the jury to focus on fairness rather than punishment.

The Apex approach flips the traditional defense strategy on its head, urging us to lead with empathy, honesty, and strength. *Accept Responsibility.* Tell a true story about acceptance and accountability. Apologize and mean it. And then shift the spotlight. Plaintiff and his counsel do not get a free pass. They must be held accountable, too.

The good news is that the fix is pretty simple. *Accept Responsibility* in every jury trial and break the pattern of Nuclear Verdicts, reclaim the narrative of the case, and achieve justice for all.

PART IV:
GIVE A NUMBER

CHAPTER 10

THE CASE OF A NEW, 24/7 JOB

COMING BACK TO LIFE

In the Hospital (One Month After Accident)

DAVID BLACKWELL SHOULD BE DEAD right now. The combination of fractures, lack of consciousness, and gray skin did not give anyone much hope. When he arrived at the emergency room, Dr. LeRoy Peterson confirmed he had no carotid pulse and was, in fact, dead.

This did not prevent Dr. Peterson from attempting the impossible—reviving David through an emergency thoracotomy. Nurses rushed David to the operating room, making quick use of the limited time available to prep him for a potentially life-restoring procedure. Dr. Peterson sliced open the left side of David's chest and pried open his ribs to expose his heart. Dr. Peterson then compressed David's heart with his hands to stimulate blood flow and try to restart his heart's electrical activity.

With any other patient, death would have been practically inevitable, but David proved to be one of the most resilient patients Dr. Peterson had ever seen. While the surgery was successful, doctors immediately placed

David in an induced coma, where he remained for a month. He was alive, but just barely.

He Was Alive, But Just Barely

When he came into consciousness, David could tell he was breathing, but where was he? He tried to peel his eyes open, but his eyelids felt like boulders, heavy and immovable. A tube filled his throat and open mouth. "Just breathe," he thought to himself. "Don't panic. Open your eyes slowly on the count of three. 1…2…3."

The dim light of the room around him seared into his skull. He silently questioned, "How long have I been out of it?" With eyes half open, he scanned the space around him and realized he was in a hospital room. Next, he saw his wife, Ann, sleeping on the recliner next to his bed. Then, the realization struck him: he could not move his torso, arms, or legs.

Sleepless Nights: The New Normal (Two Years After Accident)

After a sleepless night with periodic spasms, David finally decided to ask Ann for help getting up at seven a.m. Waking up at this time may be early for his teenage daughters, but David had been awake since being put into bed the night before. This is David's new normal.

During the night, he wrestled with whether he should speak up about his pain. He did not want to wake his wife every two hours when he needed to be moved, but doctors said he is highly susceptible to bed sores and infections. So, wake her he did, and every single waking broke his heart just a little more.

Today, even two years after the accident, David still dreads nightfall. When the house is quiet and everyone is asleep, his fears take over. David has anxiety attacks as bedtime approaches each night. He grieves the loss of his independence and mobility. He grieves the experiences he looked forward to that he will never have, like walking his daughter down the aisle and dancing with her at her wedding. He grieves the vacations his family will never take. He grieves never feeling his wife's touch again. He grieves losing his life's passion of being a truck driver. He grieves playing sports with his high school-aged daughters. He grieves the years of life expectancy lost because of this accident.

FREEDOM FROM FLASHBACKS

Worst of all, David re-lives the accident at night. In the blink of an eye, his mind takes him back to the moment his cement truck flipped over, trapping him inside the truck's cab. He did not know whether he would survive. While almost everything from that day is a blur, he clearly remembers two things: First, he remembers the pain, worse than anything he ever imagined. While he prayed to make it out alive, all he really wanted in that moment was for the pain to stop. Second, he remembers telling a stranger, "Please call my wife, but don't let her hear my pain." He could not keep himself from screaming as first responders pried his body free from the truck cab, shearing through metal with the Jaws of Life. Even despite the trauma and chaos, in that moment, he had enough clarity to know he did not want his wife to hear him scream.

In the weeks after the accident, he learned the right front tire of his cement truck exploded as he drove on the highway that morning. The explosion caused his 32,000-pound truck to veer sharply to the right, hit an embankment, and flip over. First responders freed his crushed body from the truck cab. Most shocking of all, David learned he had no heartbeat when he arrived at the ER.

IF ONLY HE COULD GO BACK

For now, David is ready for Ann to lift him out of bed and into his motorized chair. He uses a special control for his chair that he can manipulate with just his fingers since he is unable to move his arms. Ann uses the lift straps to move David from the bed to his wheelchair. David follows her in his chair, gliding it toward the bathroom using his finger controls. Ann prepares his toothbrush with some toothpaste. As she approaches him with the toothbrush, they exchange smiles, and she begins brushing his teeth.

David flashes back to brushing his teeth alongside Ann as they served in Iraq, the place where he found his purpose and got a glimpse of his dream to drive trucks. It was also the time he and Ann fell in love. Serving together got him through the stress of their overseas military service tour. He looks back at those memories fondly and knows that he will always have that time, even though he will never drive a truck again.

As Ann helps David rinse his mouth one final time, his nurse arrives. A nurse must now help David every day with basic bodily functions. Thankfully, a hired professional assists David with these most private needs, not Ann. After 17 years of marriage, David and Ann know everything about one another, but helping him in the bathroom is simply too embarrassing an ask for David to make. He thinks to himself that "in sickness and in health" might be the hardest vow there is to keep.

He would give anything to go back to the day of his accident and do it all differently. What started as a regular day on the job, driving the cement truck, has turned into a 24/7 job for Ann and others taking care of him. He wishes he would not have driven the concrete mixer that day. He wishes with everything left in his body that he could go back to being the "guy who fixed people's problems." For the rest of his life, he is now the problem, and there is no "fix."

A NUMBER TO PROTECT SAFETY

David Blackwell filed a products liability lawsuit against Dynatrax Tire Co. in Federal Court stemming from his accident. David asserted he was driving a cement mixer truck for Sussex Concrete when the right front tire, a Dynatrax tire, experienced a tread separation and suddenly deflated. David was unable to maintain control of the cement truck; the truck veered to the right, struck an embankment, and rolled over completely before coming to a stop.

The accident rendered David a wheelchair-bound quadriplegic who depends on assistance from others for all of his activities of daily living. When he woke up from an induced coma, he learned he suffered paralysis from the nipple down as a result of the rollover accident. David suffered several fractures, including a broken neck, three thoracic fractures in his back, and twelve fractured ribs. Additionally, David sustained a ruptured spleen, a pulmonary embolism, and neurological trauma to the brain. His spinal injury also caused autonomic dysreflexia, which causes severe headaches, hypertension, visual disturbance, and vasoconstriction.

After a four-day trial, the panel of eight jurors awarded every penny of the verdict requested by plaintiff's counsel: $37,835,259.23:

- $2,049,675.23 for past medical expenses
- $6,109,381 for future medical expenses
- $115,545 for past lost wages
- $560,656 for future lost wages
- $14,000,000 for past noneconomic damages
- $15,000,000 for future noneconomic damages

If you added up those numbers and arrived at a different total, we did too. Plaintiffs' counsel's math did not add up in the numbers he provided, but the jury delivered exactly what he requested, right down to the last, incorrectly totaled dollar. Plaintiff's attorneys secured this Nuclear Verdict by effectively giving the jury a number and delivering other powerful arguments.

Importantly, the defense in this case requested a defense verdict but did not give the jury a number at all. This strategy likely failed, at least in part, due to the stipulation to past economic damages. Plaintiff effectively used compelling arguments to support his large request, and the defense sat silent. Ultimately, the importance of giving a number is clear by comparing the final verdict award to plaintiff's ask: they match, dollar for dollar.

Plaintiff's Counsel Gave a Number Early and Often

The jury awarded David the full dollar amount requested by plaintiff's counsel—$37.8 million. The case reveals how powerful giving a number and backing it up with a powerful narrative can be in guiding a jury toward a specific outcome.

PSYCHOLOGICAL PRIMING

Plaintiff's counsel leveraged the psychological method of priming[1] to effectively instill their requested number in the jurors' minds early, and ultimately, to fuel a Nuclear Verdict. Plaintiff's attorney deployed his number as early as was permissible in order to prime jurors to accept his valuation for the case and return a large damages award.

Jury Selection

In this federal case, the jury was not primed with a number in jury selection. The court conducted jury selection on behalf of both the plaintiff and the defense, and unsurprisingly, the judge did not discuss damages numbers in his selection of the jury.

Opening Statement

Plaintiff's counsel first primed the jury with his damages request in opening statement. Interestingly, counsel chose only to discuss economic damages numbers with the jury in opening. He revealed plaintiff's medical bills for the preceding three-and-a-half years were "over $2 million . . . $2,049,675.23." He also stated, "[W]e have an economist who'll explain that if you give him $6,109,381 today, that will pay for his $7 million plus of care that he needs for the next 15 years." Counsel offered context for the large number, explaining, "It's actually a minimal plan to try to keep him alive for those 15 years."

Counsel previewed that the evidence would show his past lost wages were "$115,000 . . . for the past 3.5 years." Also, "his future lost wages . . . [are] over $600,000, but when it's reduced to dollars you give him today, an award of $560,000 will take care of his not being able to work" until age 67. In total, plaintiff's counsel asserted David's economic damages were "$8.8 million in this case."

Notably, counsel did not propose a number to the jury for noneconomic damages in opening statement. Instead, counsel emphasized, "What you also need to understand is that this amount of money that we're looking at here,

---

1 We discuss priming in detail in Chapter 11.

this $8.8 million, doesn't allow for one penny for the human harms and losses in this case." Counsel previewed the elements of noneconomic damages the jury was charged to consider under the applicable jury instructions: "[P]ain and suffering for the past three and a half years and for the next 15 years[,]" "mental anguish in the past and in the future[,]" "disfigurement and humiliation[,]" and "inconvenience." Counsel drove home the significant impact the accident had on David's life by showing photos of him and his family before and after the accident.

Counsel ended his opening statement by previewing a massive number that encompassed both the disclosed economic numbers and the undisclosed "human losses": "So at the end of the case, we're going to be asking for a large sum of money which will fully and fairly compensate [David Blackwell] for each and every one of his real harms and losses. The real harms and losses, the evidence and the facts that are in the box about what he lives with every day of his life."

PSYCHOLOGICAL RECENCY

Plaintiff's counsel used psychological recency[2] to drive home plaintiff's request for economic damages by highlighting the number during witness testimony. Counsel discussed plaintiff's economic damages in his case-in-chief through direct examination of plaintiff's retained physical medicine and rehabilitation physician as well as his retained economist.

Plaintiff's retained physical medicine and rehabilitation expert testified the full value of plaintiff's future medical care was $7.1 million. Plaintiff's expert economist confirmed the present value of plaintiff's future medical care and lost wages. Both of plaintiff's experts testified on day three of trial. Plaintiff's counsel did not discuss numbers with the jury for three days—between opening statement and direct expert examination.

2 We discuss recency in detail in Chapter 11.

Plaintiff's Counsel Discussed Numbers in Closing Argument

Plaintiff's counsel finalized and formalized his full damages request to the jury in closing argument. He drove home the economic damages numbers previewed for the jury earlier in trial and placed a number on plaintiff's noneconomic damages, delivering on his promise to request a large sum of money.

PAST MEDICAL EXPENSES

The parties stipulated David's past medical bills were $2,049,675.23 for the preceding three-and-a-half years of medical treatment he received. Accordingly, the jury did not need to make a determination as to the award for past medical expenses. Nevertheless, plaintiff 's counsel stated this num-ber to the jury again in closing argument. The jury awarded this stipulated damages figure for past medical care.

FUTURE MEDICAL EXPENSES

Counsel argued this accident reduced David's life expectancy by 12 years. Counsel then presented future life care expenses for his expected 15 remaining years of life were $6,109,381. Counsel persuasively argued that while plaintiff might live longer, his ask of just over $6.1 million was appropriate. This argument likely built credibility behind the number, and it clearly resonated. The jury agreed and awarded this exact amount of damages for David's future medical care.

PAST LOST WAGES

David was unable to work a day after the accident. His lost wages for the three-and-a-half years since the accident were $115,545. Based on this requested amount for damages, plaintiff earned approximately $33,000 per year as a truck driver, his dream job and his passion. It also appears the defense did not contest this amount. And once again, the jury awarded exactly plaintiff 's requested damages for past lost earnings.

FUTURE LOST WAGES

Plaintiff 's counsel argued the present value of David's requested damages for future lost wages was $560,656, an amount that would replace his lost wages until age 67. The defense did not contest this requested damages amount, and the jury awarded exactly this amount for future lost wages.

PAST NONECONOMIC DAMAGES

Plaintiff 's counsel asked the jury to award a total of $14,000,000 for past noneconomic damages. As discussed in more detail below, counsel broke down the elements of past noneconomic damages into elements provided under the applicable jury instructions: past bodily injuries, past physical pain, past mental anguish, and past inconvenience. Counsel asked the jury to award $3,500,000 for each of these elements of past noneconomic damages. The jury agreed.

FUTURE NONECONOMIC DAMAGES

Plaintiff 's counsel requested the jury award a total of $15,000,000 in future noneconomic damages. Again, counsel broke down the damages request into the only three elements of future pain and suffering specified in the applicable jury instructions: future physical pain, future mental anguish, and future inconvenience. Plaintiff 's attorney asked the jury to award $5 million for each of these elements, and (you guessed it) the jury agreed.

Summary of Giving a Number

In plaintiff's first closing, counsel totaled the requested damages amount for the jury before the defense presented its closing argument. Plaintiff's counsel suggested the total damages "for the harms and losses of [David Blackwell] is $37,835,259.23." Counsel said this total damage number only once, and he did not repeat his damages request in rebuttal. This simple method of giving a number, in addition to the creative and effective noneconomic damages arguments used by plaintiff 's counsel, shows the power of simply giving a number to the jury.

PLAINTIFF'S OTHER EFFECTIVE TRIAL TACTICS

In addition to giving a number, plaintiff's counsel deployed several other tactics often seen in Nuclear Verdicts to support plaintiff's request for a verdict over $37 million, including arguing Elements of Damages, attacking defense counsel, and arguing this trial is plaintiff's only shot at justice.[3]

Plaintiff's Counsel Argued Elements of Noneconomic Damages

Plaintiff's attorney used a common method to argue noneconomic damages in closing argument by itemizing every element of noneconomic damages available under the applicable jury instructions and assigning an arbitrary, large dollar value to each element of available damages. Once the jury awarded plaintiff's counsel's requested dollar figures for each element, plaintiff's counsel successfully obtained a Nuclear Verdict.

The applicable jury instructions provide the following categories of damages for the jury to consider if it found in favor of the plaintiff: bodily injuries, physical pain, mental anguish, disfigurement or deformity, any associated humiliation or embarrassment, or any inconvenience. Plaintiff's counsel insulated the jury's deliberations from potential jury nullification by arguing they must follow the law on each of these elements of damages, regardless of their personal beliefs. Plaintiff's counsel then delivered detailed arguments to the jury on each of these elements of damages to support his request for noneconomic damages, both past and future.

BODILY INJURY

Counsel called out the first element of damages for pain and suffering for the jury allowed under the applicable jury instructions in a PowerPoint presentation: bodily injury. Counsel argued, "[L]et's go to bodily injuries. This is for the past bodily injuries, for the past three and a half years for the injuries we discussed with you, the fractures, the brain injury, the fact that he can't walk again from his cervical fracture, can't dance, can't swim." Plaintiff's

3 *See generally* Appendix A (providing a more in-depth discussion on plaintiff closing tactics).

attorney suggested the value of plaintiff's bodily injury for the past three and a half years was $3,500,000.

PAST PHYSICAL PAIN

While the jury's award for past physical pain would compensate David for three-and-a-half years of pain, plaintiff's counsel challenged the jury to consider the value of the physical pain David suffered on the day of the accident. Using another proven tactic in graphically describing injuries, counsel recounted graphic details of David being trapped in the cab of the cement truck: "What is it worth to [David Blackwell] just for the day . . ., to be crushed inside that cab[?]" Counsel showed a photo of first responders rescuing David from the accident and stated, "I smelled the smoke, I saw the blood." Counsel then requested the jury award $3,500,000 for past physical pain for the entirety of the preceding three-and-a-half years.

PAST MENTAL ANGUISH

Counsel urged the jury to weigh the value of David's mental anguish over the three-and-a-half years from the day of the accident up until the time of trial. "What is it worth for [David Blackwell] to understand that he will never walk again, [David Blackwell] recognizing that he will never dance with his daughter if she gets married or stand there to receive her as she comes down the aisle." Counsel argued David is learning to cope with the mental anguish of knowing he is going to live a significantly shorter life because of this accident. Counsel told the jury David's past mental anguish was worth $3,500,000.

PAST INCONVENIENCE

Counsel compellingly argued David suffered significant past inconvenience:

> [I]t's inconvenient when [David Blackwell] needs to be turned over in the middle of the night and he can't do it by himself. It's inconvenient when he wants to get out of bed in the morning and he can't do it by himself. He can't bathe himself[;] he can't feed himself[;] he can't brush his teeth.

Plaintiff's attorney urged jurors that this inconvenience was connected to David's mental anguish because of the constant need to make a choice when he needs help. For example, the jury heard of the internal debate when David needs to move in the middle of the night, whether to disturb his wife's sleep again to ask for help or continue to lie in the same position and risk sores and infections. For the preceding three-and-a-half years of inconvenience, counsel requested the jury award another $3,500,000.

FUTURE PHYSICAL PAIN

Looking at the fifteen years of life expectancy remaining, counsel argued the jury needed to award significant future noneconomic damages. David continued to suffer from headaches, and the accident caused him to suffer from a condition called autonomic dysreflexia. With this condition, any amount of physical discomfort, such as clothes being too tight, raises his blood pressure even though he is on blood pressure medication. "He has to be wary of ulcers, pulmonary embolism, [and] infections." All of these things contribute to his future physical pain, counsel argued, ultimately urging the jury to award $5,000,000 for this element of damages.

FUTURE MENTAL ANGUISH

The evidence the jury received supported counsel's argument that the accident took away the essence of who plaintiff is. Counsel masterfully personalized his client and explained that David "dreamed of being a truck driver" when he was young. When that dream came true, he loved his job. He met the love of his life in the military, and they served together in Iraq. During his military service, David worked as a truck driver, and upon returning home, found joy in fishing, bowling, camping, barbequing, being outdoors, and working around the house.

Counsel painted a dismal picture for the jury, arguing the person he was before the accident—the angler, trucker, outdoorsman—was gone, and would never return for the final 15 years of his shortened life. Counsel suggested to the jury that the value of the future mental anguish for coming to terms with being the problem, being unable to be left alone, and for being a 24/7 burden to his wife was $5,000,000.

FUTURE INCONVENIENCE

Counsel recounted plaintiff's testimony as an example of the ongoing and future inconvenience awaiting his client. When questioned on the stand about the accident, David smiled, but tears came to his eyes. He was then unable to hold a tissue with his hand in order to wipe his eyes. Counsel teased out the importance of this singular moment of testimony: unable to even wipe his own tears.

Plaintiff's counsel capitalized on his personalization of David in reminding the jury that he was the man who used to take care of everyone. He cooked. He cleaned. He mended. He fixed: "I was the guy who fixed people's problems, and now I am the problem." Plaintiff's counsel eloquently summed up his $5,000,000 request for future inconvenience by stating, "I dare say that every aspect of his waking life is an inconvenience."

ELEMENTS OF DAMAGES CONCLUSION

Counsel concluded his pain and suffering argument on the Elements of Damages allowed under the jury instructions by stating his total requested damages number—the only time plaintiff's counsel stated his total number to the jury. Counsel stated, "The total of these damages, we suggest, for the harms and losses of [David Blackwell] is $37,835,259.23." The jury agreed and awarded this exact amount as its final verdict.

Plaintiff's Counsel Blamed Dynatrax Tire for Failing to *Accept Responsibility*

Plaintiff's counsel also advanced several pointed attacks at the defense and defense counsel in order to drive juror anger and fuel a Nuclear Verdict. After delivering his request for over $37 million, counsel posed a rhetorical question: "What will the defendant say about these damages? They won't say anything. They've taken a cavalier approach to this case with the position that they never make a defective tire."

Counsel leveraged the defense's refusal to accept responsibility for anything and argued the defense essentially buried its head in the sand when it claimed the company never made a defective tire. This, no doubt, fueled juror anger and positioned the plaintiff's number as the only reasonable conclusion to the case. Counsel questioned Dynatrax's defense as simply "smoke and mirrors."

Plaintiff's attorney recalled Dynatrax sells 100 million tires a year, perhaps one billion tires every ten years, and Dynatrax's corporate representative testified that the company has never sold a defective tire. Counsel called this testimony an "absurd proposition," especially when measured against other evidence that Dynatrax acknowledged it manufactured almost 8,000 defective tires.

The testimony and overall approach by the defense to deny responsibility telegraphed to the jury an unwillingness to acknowledge wrongdoing. Plaintiff's counsel's effective and unmitigated arguments laid the defense bare for what the jury perceived to be just punishment in an outsized jury award, even though no punitive damages were on the table.

Plaintiff Would Never Get a Mulligan When it Comes to Justice

Tapping into jurors' desire for justice and instilling a sense of urgency, counsel argued to the jury essentially that David would never get a "mulligan" in this case. "We can't come back[,]" argued counsel. "This is our only day in court." While jurors would move on with their lives after the conclusion of the case, David would still suffer all these problems because of the accident for the rest of his life, and he would get no do-overs. Counsel empowered the jury: "Today is the day we make an award for the damages to [David Blackwell] for the rest of his life."

CONCLUSION

Plaintiff's attorney successfully incited and fueled juror anger toward the defendant, Dynatrax Tire, and equipped the jury with the specific number to award. The jury agreed Dynatrax was liable for manufacturing a defective tire driven on David's cement truck on the day of the accident, and plaintiff's counsel guided the jury toward a nuclear result by giving a number and repeating it.

Interestingly, in this case, plaintiff's counsel stated the total damage request only once, and he did not repeat it in rebuttal. However, plaintiff's counsel primed the jury at the earliest possible opportunity and rooted its expectations for a large total sum in the economic damages number. This strategy worked well in conjunction with the powerful argument detailing each element of requested damages, particularly each element of noneconomic damages.

How might the defense have avoided a nuclear result in this catastrophic case? Could the defense have sponsored an alternative damages number to the jury and still obtained a defense verdict? If so, how could the defense have given a number while seeking a defense verdict and maintaining integrity with the jury? We believe the defense could have given a number to the jury in this case while still credibly seeking a defense verdict.

EPILOGUE: THE APPEAL

After the jury awarded this Nuclear Verdict, the defense appealed on several grounds, including the claim that the pain and suffering award of $29,000,000 was excessive, and requested the Appellate Court overturn the verdict or lower the verdict. Only about four months after the jury awarded the verdict, the Appellate Court agreed with the jury when it came to their finding of negligence and the need for damages. The Court found the jury's verdict only slightly excessive, determining that the jury's award for future lost wages was issued based on the full amount of plaintiff 's alleged lost wages before the required reduction to present value.

The Court lowered the jury's verdict by $65,515 to a total verdict of $37,767,742. The defense was allowed to accept the reduced verdict or to retry the case. It appears the case later settled and further appeals were dismissed about ten months after the original trial. This appeal reinforces the need for the defense to utilize The Apex at trial to fully equip ourselves with the tools and skills to prevent a Nuclear Verdict, thus eliminating the need to appeal an excessive verdict.

CHAPTER 11

GIVE A NUMBER, DELIVER JUSTICE

"The phenomenon we were studying is so common and so important in the everyday world that you should know its name: it is an anchoring effect."

—Daniel Kahneman

DAMAGE CONTROL: *GIVE A NUMBER*

ONE OF THE MOST EFFECTIVE ways to influence the jury's verdict at trial is to sponsor a defense number in every single case, even when seeking a defense verdict. Giving a defense number counters plaintiff's psychological tactics about money at trial and, again, positions the defense as the most reasonable party in the room. The Apex calls the defense to *Give a Number* in every trial, without exception, to reach the apex and avoid a Nuclear Verdict.

We see this strategy work time and again in every single one of our trials. And yet, the defense routinely neglects this tool and gets hit with Nuclear Verdicts. Are we saying you *will not* get hit with a Nuclear Verdict if you *Give a Number?* No. But we are saying the chances are substantially decreased, and studies confirm its effectiveness for the defense.

How Do Plaintiffs' Attorneys Get a Nuclear Verdict? They Ask for It!

The plaintiffs' bar knows the most effective way to get a Nuclear Verdict is to simply ask the jury to award one. This was not always the case; plaintiffs' lawyers used to be shy about discussing money. We have partners at our firm who were once plaintiffs' lawyers, and they remember the days of debating whether asking for a big number would offend the jury.

Those days are long gone, because the plaintiffs' bar realized something pretty basic: most community members who show up for jury service have no idea how to value a loss like pain and suffering, loss of a limb, or loss of a life. This means they are desperate for guidance, and the plaintiffs' bar is more than happy to give it. Here is an example of common responses from jury surveys after the jury awarded a Nuclear Verdict:

> Question: How did the jury arrive at the decision to award the plaintiff $20 million in damages?
>
> Actual Juror #1: We came up with a percentage approach, and that's what we all discussed. We started with what she was asking for—$80 million, which seemed like a very high amount—and we went down and down from there.
>
> Actual Juror #2: None of us had been on a jury before, so we had no idea where to start. What's a life worth? It would have been nice to have some precedent to go by, but we didn't. So, we started with what they gave us and then we took a percentage.[1]

Because most jurors do not have life experience or specialized education to value this kind of loss, they look to attorneys for guidance.[2]

In response to this truth, plaintiffs' attorneys ask juries to award large dollar amounts at trial. Let us remember that is their singular goal in trial:

---

1 Christina Marinakis, *How to Counteract the Anchoring Effects of a Plaintiff's Damages Request*, The Nat'l L. Rev. (May 5, 2022), https://natlawreview.com/article/how-to-counteract-anchoring-effects-plaintiff-s-damages-request (on file with the Apex Defense Consulting library).

2 Brian H. Bornstein & Edie Greene, *Jury Decision Making: Implications For and From Psychology*, 20 Curr. Dir. Psych. Sci. 63 (2011), https://www.law.nyu.edu/sites/default/files/upload_documents/Jury-Decision-Making.pdf (on file with the Apex Defense Consulting library).

they are laser-focused on a big number, and they want jurors laser-focused, too. The reality is that jurors do not arrive at a Nuclear Verdict on their own.

What juror wakes up the morning they report for jury duty and tells their spouse, "Honey, today I think I will award a plaintiff hundreds of millions of dollars."? No one. And the first time they hear an ask for hundreds of millions of dollars, it feels like a big number—because it is. But over the course of trial, that number starts to feel reasonable. And, eventually, on the last day of trial, that same juror may very well wake up and say that exact sentence to their spouse.

Put simply: the bigger the ask, the bigger the verdict. The plaintiffs' bar knows that everyday Americans will not award $20 million, $50 million, or $100+ million verdicts on their own. Juries only arrive at these astronomical awards because plaintiffs' counsel lead them there.

The Psychology of Anchoring

Anchoring is a form of cognitive bias. A 1974 study examined and explained the concept of "anchoring" as a tool individuals use to predict the value of something: "In many situations, people make estimates by starting from an initial value that is adjusted to yield the final answer[.] [D]ifferent start points yield different estimates, which are biased toward the initial values. We call this phenomenon anchoring."[3] This makes sense. Just as the juror surveyed above articulated, humans want precedent, especially about difficult or unfamiliar concepts.

This is one of the craziest things about anchoring: even when the anchor number is completely random, the anchoring phenomenon still works. In one famous experiment, college students were asked to write down the last two digits of their social security number and then place a bid on a bottle of wine. Obviously, the students' social security numbers were completely unconnected to the wine's value. Nevertheless, the study found that students who wrote down higher social security numbers bid higher on the wine than

---

3 Amos Tversky & Daniel Kahneman, *Judgment under Uncertainty: Heuristics and Biases*, 185 SCIENCE (n.s.) 1124, 1128 (1974), https://sites.socsci.uci.edu/~bskyrms/bio/readings/tversky_k_heuristics_biases.pdf (on file with the Apex Defense Consulting library).

those with lower numbers. "The recent memory of a large number caused students to think of large numbers when valuing the bottle of wine."[4] Nobel Prize winner and one of the founders of Behavioral Economics, Richard Thaler, described this study: "People are anchored on some number they were given, even when they constructed it at random, like the last two digits of their social security number. It's an almost irresistible force."[5]

ANCHORING INFLUENCES EVEN JUDGES' DECISION-MAKING

Studies on anchoring have revealed even judges are susceptible to anchoring. Just a few of these studies show:[6]

- Rolling dice before issuing a criminal sentence increased prison sentences by 60% depending on the number rolled;[7]
- A defendant filed an "absurd" motion to dismiss a case, arguing that the plaintiff could not meet the minimum jurisdictional requirements of $75,000 (the anchor), resulting in a 29.38% reduction in plaintiff's award from the judge;[8]
- The mention of a compensation award from a court TV show resulted in a 700% increase in compensation awarded by the judge;[9] and,

4 Josh Yazman, *Attempting to Replicate Ariely's Anchoring Bias*, MEDIUM (Nov. 30, 2017) (emphasis omitted), https://medium.com/@joshyazman/attempting-to-replicate-arielys-anchoring-bias-dba6a6c03b1b (on file with the Apex Defense Consulting library).

5 NOVA: *Mind Over Money* (PBS television broadcast, aired Apr. 27, 2010).

6 Rod Hollier, *Anchoring Bias in the Courtroom*, THE L. PROJECT (May 2017), https://static1.squarespace.com/static/5817bb2746c3c4a605334446/t/5921b1b0f5e23119eaf8bda6/1495380412134/Anchoring+Bias+in+the+Courtroom+by+Rod+Hollier.pdf (on file with the Apex Defense Consulting library).

7 Birte Englich, Thomas Mussweiler & Fritz Strack, *Playing Dice With Criminal Sentences: The Influence of Irrelevant Anchors on Experts' Judicial Decision Making*, 32 PERS. & SOC. PSYCH. BULL.188 (2006), https://homepages.se.edu/cvonbergen/files/2013/01/Playing-Dice-With-Criminal-Sentences_The-Influence-of-Irrelevant-Anchors-on-Experts-Judicial-Decision-Making.pdf (on file with the Apex Defense Consulting library).

8 Chris Guthrie, Jeffrey J. Rachlinski & Andrew J. Wistrich, *Inside the Judicial Mind*, 86 CORN. L. REV. 777 (2001), https://scholarship.law.cornell.edu/cgi/viewcontent.cgi?article=2844&context=clr (on file with the Apex Defense Consulting library).

9 Chris Guthrie, Jeffrey J. Rachlinski & Andrew J. Wistrich, *The "Hidden Judiciary": An Empirical Examination of Executive Branch Justice,* 58 DUKE L.J. 1477, 1504 (2009), https://scholarship.law.duke.edu/cgi/viewcontent.cgi?article=1406&context=dlj (on file with the Apex Defense Consulting library).

- In a personal injury case stemming from an auto accident, when judges were told the amount of a damages cap on the case, knowing of the damages cap resulted in a 47.83% increase and 150% increase in the judge's damages award.[10]

Ideally, judges would be able to deliver blind justice because they would be wholly unbiased. In reality, judges are humans who carry bias based on their life experience and beliefs. Even judges, who are trained in the law and whose responsibility it is to serve as the "neutral" in a case, are influenced by anchoring. If judges are susceptible to anchoring, what hope does our neighbor serving as a juror have of withstanding the powerful psychological impact of anchoring? None.

ANCHORING IMPACTS JURY DECISION-MAKING

Studies are also replete with the data-driven conclusion that anchoring also influences juror decision-making. "Extensive research and numerous case studies have shown that when plaintiffs present exorbitant damages claims, juries tend to use these figures as anchor points for their own award decisions, leading to higher damage awards."[11] The higher plaintiff's attorney's request, the higher the jury's award, "even at comically high requests, such as $1 billion."[12] Notably, "the more money the plaintiff requested, the more the jurors thought the defendant was liable."[13] Let us say that again for the people in the back: the plaintiff asking for a higher damages amount resulted in higher *liability* findings. Talk about putting the (very expensive) cart before the horse.

Humans' judgment gets skewed during trial. "Research indicates that even jurors who initially find the plaintiff's request excessive eventually

---

10 Jeffrey J. Rachlinski, Andrew J. Wistrich & Chris Guthrie, *Can Judges Make Reliable Numeric Judgments? Distorted Damages and Skewed Sentences*, 90 IND. L.J. 695 (2015), https://ilj.law.indiana.edu/articles/13-Rachlinski-Wistrich-Guthrie.pdf (on file with the Apex Defense Consulting library).

11 *Mastering the Counter-Anchor as part of a Defense Strategy*, COURTROOM SCIS., INC.®, https://www.courtroomsciences.com/blog/litigation-consulting-1/mastering-the-counter-anchor-as-part-of-a-defense-strategy-690 (on file with the Apex Defense Consulting library) (last visited June 18, 2025).

12 Hollier, *supra* note 6.

13 *Id.*

accept it as reasonable."[14] When presented with an exceptionally high damages ask from plaintiffs' counsel, jurors believe plaintiff and their attorney are "more selfish and less generous," but the initial distaste jurors feel fades over the course of trial.[15] Jurors in this study ultimately awarded the plaintiff higher compensation than those exposed to a lower, less offensive, request.[16]

Plaintiffs have nothing to lose and a lot to gain by asking for astronomically high numbers. The defense can no longer rely on jurors being offended by a ridiculous plaintiff's ask. A jury's initial feelings about plaintiff's exorbitant number are not enough to overcome the powerful effect of plaintiff's attorney's anchoring tactics.

The Defense Must Always *Give a Number*

We have seen firsthand that when the defense gives a number, the risk of a Nuclear Verdict *decreases*. Why? Giving a counter anchor is the most powerful way to ground the jury in reason and offset the exorbitant ask made by plaintiffs' counsel. Sponsoring a reasonable defense damages number shows that the defense is the most reasonable party in the room and cares about plaintiff. This builds credibility and trust with the jury.

"By openly addressing damages and providing a well-reasoned argument, the defense demonstrates their commitment to transparency and fairness. This can enhance the defense's overall credibility and increase the likelihood that the jury will consider their perspective when deliberating on the case."[17] We must use every opportunity to demonstrate our reasonableness to the jury. Giving a number is one of those opportunities.

Recent articles support our position that the defense should provide a counter-anchor, but qualify that the defense should not *Give a Number* in

---

14 *Mastering the Counter-Anchor as part of a Defense Strategy*, *supra* note 11.

15 Gretchen B. Chapman & Brian H. Bornstein, *The More You Ask for, the More You Get: Anchoring in Personal Injury Verdicts*, 10 Appl. Cogn. Psych. 519, 537 (1996), http://www.communicationcache.com/uploads/1/0/8/8/10887248/the_more_you_ask_for_the_more_you_get-_anchoring_in_personal_injury_verdicts.pdf (on file with the Apex Defense Consulting library).

16 *Id.*

17 Bill Bower, *Drop the Anchor*, CLM Mag. (Oct. 3, 2024), https://www.theclm.org/Magazine/articles/drop-the-anchor-nuclear-verdicts-anchoring/3105 (on file with the Apex Defense Consulting library).

every case and should instead only sponsor a number when it is "appropriate." We disagree. Our experience, our research, and others' psychological studies show that giving a number is *not* a sign of weakness. It is *always* appropriate, because human psychology is always at play in the courtroom! We must not allow plaintiffs' lawyers to dictate the story the jury believes in the deliberation room. We must equip jurors to deliberate with their reason and common sense intact. The Apex calls the defense to *Give a Number*. In. Every. Single. Case.

False Barriers to Giving a Number

"A nickel ain't worth a dime anymore."
—Yogi Berra

Perhaps unsurprisingly, as you will see later in this chapter, the defense rarely sponsors a number in cases that result in a Nuclear Verdict. The primary reason we have heard from carriers and counsel alike is a belief that giving a counter-anchor is a sign of weakness or a confession of liability. This belief is misguided.

The defense also refuses to *Give a Number* because of various business considerations: we worry about excess towers, policy limits, future claims, and carrier relationships. This barrier ignores the humans in the jury box and unfairly hamstrings the defense. Our clients (insurer and insured) deserve a complete defense, not one hampered by irrelevant business considerations. When we are in the arena, we must give it everything we have got. Giving a number is one of the most effective arrows in our quiver; why overlook it?

GIVING A NUMBER IS NOT A SIGN OF WEAKNESS

The Apex calls defense counsel to *Give a Number* in every single case, regardless of the (designer) Liability Basket in which the case resides. Jurors do not interpret our proposal of a defense damages number as a sign of weakness nor an admission of liability.[18] Rather, "focus groups and juror

18 *Counter-anchor or play it safe?*, Courtroom Scis., Inc.®, https://www.courtroomsciences.com/blog/litigation-consulting-1/counter-anchor-or-play-it-safe-82 (on file with the Apex Defense Consulting library) (last visited June 18, 2025).

interviews have shown that jurors *want* to hear the defense's perspective on damages[.]"[19] Of course they do.

It is the plaintiff's demand for money that brings jurors to the courthouse, asking them to sacrifice days or even weeks away from their real lives. We owe it to *jurors* to address the elephant in the room. The defense must *Give a Number* in every single case, even when seeking a defense verdict.

In fact, studies have shown the defense is *more likely* to get a defense verdict if they *Give a Number*. A study conducted by the Iowa Law Review in 2016 analyzed the impact of anchoring for both the plaintiff and the defense. Unsurprisingly and consistent with earlier studies, the Iowa Law Review study found jury awards jumped significantly when the only changed variable was a higher ask from the plaintiff.[20] Put another way: when nothing in the simulation changed except plaintiff giving a higher number, the verdicts awarded were higher. But the most impactful strategy the defense employed in this study was giving a counter-anchor.

The study found that the chances of obtaining a defense verdict were the *highest* when the defense sponsored their own number, increasing to almost an 82% likelihood. The study also found that attacking the plaintiff's number had the biggest negative impact on the defense's chances at a defense verdict. Similarly, ignoring the plaintiff's number was not as impactful as countering it. **Most simply: giving a defense number has been shown to *increase* the chances of a defense verdict.**

GIVING A NUMBER PREVENTS NUCLEAR VERDICTS, WHICH IS GOOD FOR BUSINESS

We can present dozens of stories with additional reasons why insurance carriers or insured clients do not want to give the jury a number. All of these reasons are business or financial reasons, reasons the jury will never learn about—policy limits, towers of insurance, excess coverage, reinsurance, the

19 Bower, *supra* note 17 (emphasis added).

20 John Campbell, Bernard Chao, Christopher Robertson & David V. Yokum, *Countering the Plaintiff's Anchor: Jury Simulations to Evaluate Damages Arguments*, 101 Iowa L. Rev. 543 (2016), https://ilr.law.uiowa.edu/sites/ilr.law.uiowa.edu/files/2023-02/ILR-101-2-Campbell.pdf (on file with the Apex Defense Consulting library).

duty of primary insurance to reasonably settle the matter within its layer, loss ratios, similar pending cases, business appetite for risk, etc. These reasons for not giving a number have nothing to do with human psychology. None of these reasons defuse anger nor ground the jury.

The plaintiffs' bar is *hoping* we will let business reasons dictate our trial strategy. They hope we will be too scared to give the jury a number. They hope we will ignore the humans in the jury box and focus instead on complicated business considerations. They hope we will cower and shrink and stay silent on the ultimate reason we are all in court, and they hope we will let them run away with the game.

The Apex demands instead that we show up boldly for our clients, and it demands we *Give a Number* in pursuit of justice. When we avoid a Nuclear Verdict, we deliver justice for the plaintiff while simultaneously avoiding the nuclear fallout for businesses that comes from outsized jury awards. We protect our client, we make right what was wronged, we serve the jury, and we ensure American consumers do not unwittingly fund the plaintiffs' bar's lavish lifestyle.

Follow Four Rules When Giving a Number

Did we pump you up? Are you convinced we must *Give a Number*? Good. Now, let us show you how to do it.

The Apex lays out four rules the defense must follow to effectively *Give a Number*. As with every element of The Apex, all four rules are rooted in *Be a Good Human:* (1) give the number early; (2) repeat the number often; (3) never increase the number; and (4) the number must be reasonable.

GIVE THE NUMBER EARLY—PRIMACY EFFECT

When remembering items presented in a series, humans tend to remember the first and last items in the series better than those presented in the middle. This is a form of cognitive bias called "serial position effect," caused by the ways the brain processes and stores information in our memory.[21] The tendency to remember information presented earlier in a series is called the "primacy effect."

"Priming is a technique used to influence (i.e., control) attention and memory, and it can have significant impacts on decision-making. Specifically, priming is an implicit memory effect in which exposure to stimulus influences a response to later stimulus. This means that later experiences of the stimulus are processed more quickly by the brain."[22] Put another way: once we have seen or heard something, we recognize and process it more easily the next time we see or hear it.

In light of this psychological truth, the defense should sponsor a defense number to the jury as early as permitted in trial in order to tap into the primacy effect. "By prioritizing damages early on, defense counsel can mitigate the risk of time-related limitations compromising the damages argument."[23] Specifically, the defense should *Give a Number* in jury selection where permissible to identify any potential jurors who would not be able to award such an amount or less at the end of trial. Just as plaintiffs give their number early to remove jurors who cannot award their number (in other words, "prequalify" the jury to award a Nuclear Verdict), the defense must ensure the sworn jury is capable of issuing a reasonable award.

If a court does not allow the defense to discuss numbers in jury selection, then the defense must prime the jury with its valuation in opening statement. But remember: if it's good for the goose, it's good for the gander. If plaintiff's counsel is permitted to *Give a Number* in jury selection, the defense is permitted, too. Go to bat on this one if need be. If plaintiff's counsel opens the door in opposition to a court order precluding either party from giving a number, follow suit. That bell cannot be unrung.

---

21 Saul McLeod, *Serial Position Effect (Glanzer & Cunitz, 1966)*, Simply Psych. (Apr. 19, 2025), https://www.simplypsychology.org/primacy-recency.html (on file with the Apex Defense Consulting library).

22 Bill Kanasky, *Debunking and Redefining the Plaintiff Reptile Theory*, Courtroom Scis., Inc.® 7, https://www.iadclaw.org/assets/1/19/6.1-_Kanasky-_Debunking_Reptile_Theory.pdf?3034 (on file with the Apex Defense Consulting library) (last visited June 18, 2025).

23 *Mastering the Counter-Anchor as part of a Defense Strategy, supra* note 11.

REPEAT THE NUMBER OFTEN—RECENCY AND DESENSITIZATION

In addition to giving the defense number as early as possible in the case, the defense must work to repeat the number throughout the course of trial, including during plaintiff's case-in-chief. Doing so keeps our number at the forefront of jurors' minds as they are receiving and processing evidence. We cannot wait one, two, or four or more weeks to talk about our defense valuation after originally presenting it to the jury in jury selection and opening statement. Defense counsel must strategically plan when and with which witnesses to discuss the defense number on cross-examination during plaintiff's case. And, of course, we must use our case to repeat the number again.

The defense must finally repeat our number in closing argument. The "recency effect" is the tendency for humans to remember the information they heard last or most recently.[24] Closing argument is the final opportunity to share our number. When supported by primacy and repetition, closing argument is the chance for the defense to fully educate the jury about *why* the defense's number will make plaintiff whole, as discussed in Part V, and send jurors to the deliberation room to deliver a defense verdict or the defense number.

Repetition is also key for the defense to counter plaintiff's anchoring tactic of desensitization. "Desensitization" occurs when repeated exposure to something decreases one's negative response to the item over time.[25] For example, plaintiff's counsel may ask the jury in jury selection if they could ever come to award $50 million in damages in their final verdict. To most everyday Americans who report to jury duty, $50 million initially sounds outrageous. But after hearing plaintiff's counsel repeat "$50 million" over the course of many days or weeks, that outrage diminishes if not altogether vanishes.

---

24 McLeod, *supra* note 21.

25 Andreas Miles-Novelo & Craig A. Anderson, *Desensitization*, *in* The International Encyclopedia of Media Psychology 315 (Jan Van den Bulck, David R. Ewoldsen, Marie-Louise Mares & Erica Scharrer eds., 2020), https://www.craiganderson.org/wp-content/uploads/caa/abstracts/2020-2024/20-2M-NA.pdf (on file with the Apex Defense Consulting library).

Similarly, the defense must repeat our defense number to the jury throughout the course of trial. We must keep our number in front of them so they remember it and are not manipulated into accepting plaintiff's valuation as reasonable when it comes time to deliberate. Instead, they will be "prehabilitated" and inoculated against plaintiff's anchoring tactics.

NEVER INCREASE THE DEFENSE NUMBER

The defense should have confidence in the number we choose to share with the jury at the beginning of trial. It must be supported by the evidence, and it must never go up. A defense attorney who tells the jury in jury selection that at the end of the trial, he is going to ask for a verdict of $2 million or less needs to conclude trial asking for a verdict of $2 million or less. To increase the defense's requested verdict during trial tells the jury that the defense was persuaded by plaintiff's case or that the defense did not have a good basis for the initial number they sponsored. A defense attorney who increases his defense number during trial will lose credibility with the jury, and credibility is currency in trial.

THE DEFENSE NUMBER MUST BE REASONABLE

Finally, the number the defense sponsors to a jury must be *reasonable*. It must be a real number, meaning not "zero," not "less than plaintiff's number," and not "a reasonable number." It must be an actual number, and it must deliver on the foundation of The Apex: it must be a number a good human would convey. It must pass the straight-face test.

To give the defense wiggle room, it is appropriate to give a range for the defense number such as "$500,000 or less." This allows the defense to adjust to what happens in trial without losing credibility, but in every case, the defense must give an actual number.

The evidence in the case must also reasonably support the defense number. "By presenting reasonable alternatives to extreme awards and engaging jurors with a pragmatic mindset, defense attorneys aim to guide them toward realistic assessments of damages. The key is to present a counter-anchor that aligns with the case's facts and provides a logical rationale for the proposed figure."[26]

This particular rule is sometimes difficult for insurance carriers to adopt, especially in excess exposure cases. The number the defense sponsors must be reasonably supported by evidence to gain credibility and avoid a Nuclear Verdict, even if that number is higher than insurance policy limits.

For example, consider a case where Joe rear-ends another car at a high speed, totaling his car and significantly damaging the car he hit. Both the plaintiff and defense medical experts agree the driver of the other car sustained significant neck and back injuries from the whiplash, which required one surgery and to a reasonable degree of medical probability will require a second surgery in the future. Unfortunately, Joe carries a nonstandard auto policy limit of $15,000. Joe's insurance carrier allegedly botched tendering the full policy limits in response to plaintiff's policy limits demand, and plaintiff is now claiming the policy limits are now open. Plaintiff never makes a demand less than $5 million, and the case proceeds to trial. The jury hears past medical specials alone are $600,000, and plaintiff's counsel asks the jury to award $10 million.

It would be *unreasonable* for the defense to argue the jury should award $15,000! The defense's own expert agrees the injuries were substantial. Yet we have seen insurance carriers instruct the defense team to never *Give a Number* to the jury above policy limits because they believe doing so is arguably admitting the carrier is in bad faith. While the jury verdict could be evidence of bad faith in a subsequent first-party lawsuit against the carrier, which would you rather argue about, a $1 million verdict or a $10 million verdict?

Obviously, this a tough example for any carrier, having your defense counsel ask a jury to award more than the insurance policy limits. But remember your goal. If it is to get a defense verdict, then give a reasonable number. If it is to get the lowest award possible, then give a reasonable number. The

26 *Mastering the Counter-Anchor as part of a Defense Strategy*, *supra* note 11.

jury has no idea what the insurance policy limits are, but they do know what reasonable is. And being reasonable will avoid a Nuclear Verdict.

Blaze Your Own Trail

The Apex goes further than simply mimicking plaintiff's counsel when it comes to giving a number. Apex empowers the defense to *Give a Number* to the maximum extent permitted by the court, *even when the plaintiff does not give a number.* The defense receives the psychological benefits of giving a number to a jury even when plaintiff does not sponsor a number. Just as only hearing an astronomical number for damages from plaintiff anchors the jury toward awarding a Nuclear Verdict, only hearing a reasonable number for damages from the defense anchors the jury toward awarding a reasonable verdict, even when that reasonable verdict is a defense verdict.

The defense benefits from the psychological benefits of anchoring, priming, recency, and desensitization when we give a number, even when plaintiff does not. We should not allow our strategy to be dictated by plaintiffs' counsel! When have they ever waited for us before deciding to think creatively? This is our trial, too—our client's day in court! Anchor for them. Anchor for justice.

CASE STUDY OVERVIEW: *GIVE A NUMBER*

The data we analyzed shows the defense must sponsor a number with the jury at trial. Our preference and practice is to give a single total number and then show our work by explaining components of our economic and noneconomic numbers. However, the data we analyzed shows that giving *any kind of number* helps the defense, even a stipulated number. And yet, as predicted, the defense falls abysmally short, even in "damages only," admitted liability cases.

Methodology

We standardized our analysis of 100 closing arguments from Nuclear Verdicts to determine the result choosing to *Give a Number* had in these outsized awards. Specifically, if defense counsel sponsored an exact defense number for any element of damages, we considered this an application of The Apex. If there was no reference in defense counsel's closing to a defense number, we considered this an omission of The Apex.

We also tracked whether the defense gave an economic number, a non-economic number, both, or a single total number. This ensured uniformity, but it was also overly inclusive. We wanted to truly gauge how much guidance the defense offers the jury as to damages in cases where the jury returns a Nuclear Verdict.

Hypothesis

Our trial experience shows that giving a defense number helps prevent a Nuclear Verdict. Thus, our hypothesis was that in the majority of Nuclear Verdicts, defense counsel does not *Give a Number* in closing argument.

Results

Our case study analysis supported our hypothesis. In the majority of Nuclear Verdicts, the defense did not give any version of a defense number in closing argument, even when plaintiff did. We also saw a benefit we had hoped the data would bear out: even in our universe of only Nuclear Verdicts, giving a defense number was impactful in reducing damages.

CASE STUDY DISCUSSION: THE DEFENSE ROUTINELY FAILS TO GIVE ANY NUMBER AT ALL

Out of the 100 closing arguments in Nuclear Verdicts reviewed, defense counsel gave some version of a number (either a noneconomic number, an economic number, or both) in 46 cases. **This means that in 54% of the Nuclear Verdicts analyzed, the defense gave no number whatsoever.** By contrast, plaintiffs' counsel gave a number 87% of the time.

Plaintiff vs Defense Giving a Number

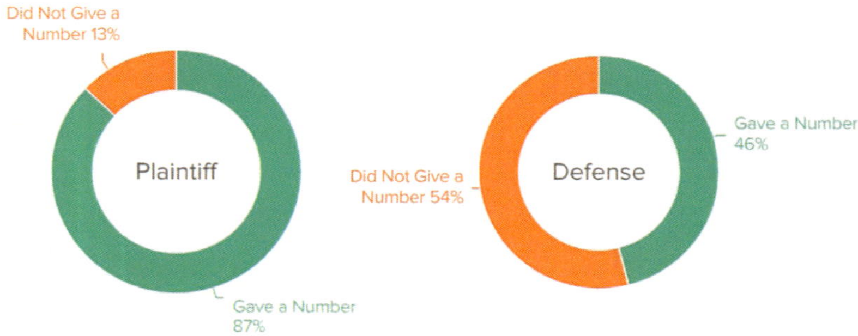

Giving a number is wildly effective for plaintiffs, and we suspected that giving a number would prove to be effective for the defense, even in Nuclear Verdicts. We were surprised to see that even merely saying a stipulated number had an impact on the overall verdict.

The average verdict in cases where the defense gave a number was 75.3% of plaintiff's ask, while the average verdict in cases where the defense did not give a number was 150.7% of plaintiff's ask, representing a 50% decrease.

Impact of Giving a Number on Overall Verdict Size

Verdict Amount as Percentage of Plaintiff's Ask

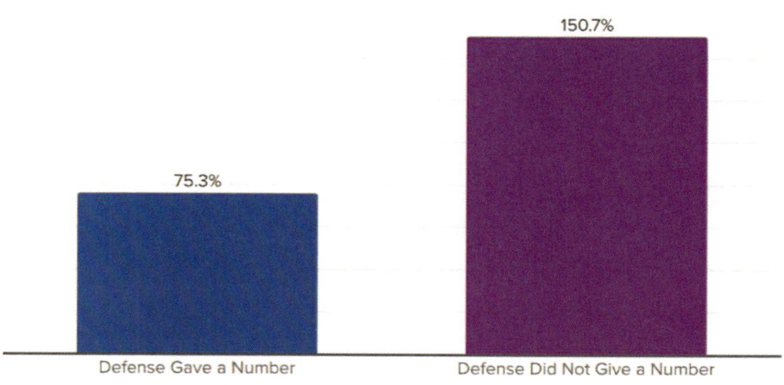

Put another way: the average verdict *exceeded* plaintiff's ask by more than 50% when the defense failed to give a number. Giving literally any number at all has a measurable impact on the ultimate verdict, even in the face of plaintiff's anchoring and other tactics.

Giving Economic and Noneconomic Numbers

Drilling down further, we examined the impact of giving an economic number, a noneconomic number, and giving both. There were 24 cases where the defense gave an economic number and 26 cases where the defense gave a noneconomic number. However, there were only 11 cases where the defense gave both.

Of the cases where the defense gave an economic number, the average verdict was 80.4% of plaintiff's ask, compared to 139.6% where the defense did not give an economic number. Similarly, in cases where the defense gave a noneconomic number, the average verdict was 69.8% of plaintiff's ask, compared to 145.7% where the defense did not give a noneconomic number. **So, again: giving any kind of a number results in lower damages awarded, and failing to give a number results in an average verdict that *exceeds* plaintiff's ask.**

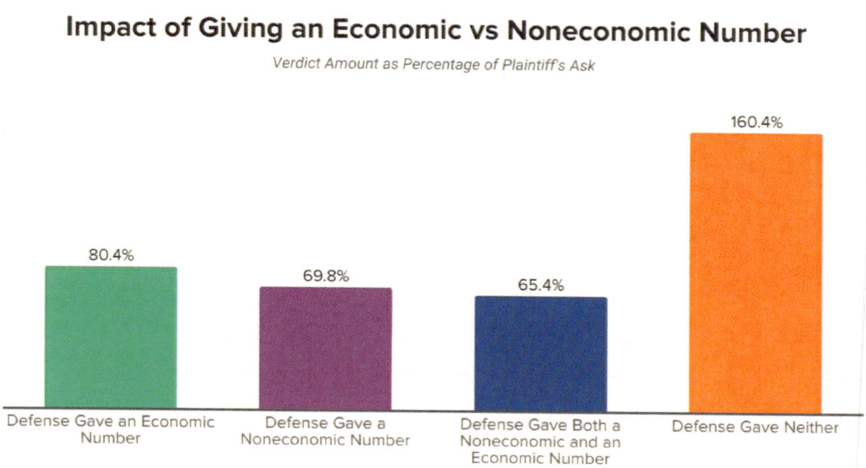

What happened in cases where the defense gave both an economic and a noneconomic number? Though the data set was small, it returned the *lowest*

average verdict compared to plaintiff's ask, at 65.4%, compared to 160.4% where the defense gave neither.

Because our practice and preference is to give a single total number and then explain how the noneconomic and economic numbers fit into it, we also analyzed how frequently the defense gave a single total number. The defense did so in only 15% of cases, but in only *three* cases did the defense give a single total number along with both an economic number and a noneconomic number. We believe, our experience supports, and the data shows that offering a clear number to the jury and explaining it is critical for the defense.

The defense's number was convoluted, or worse, inconsistent in several Nuclear Verdicts we studied. We observed several instances where the defense said different numbers for the same category of damages. *We* were confused, and we are experts! Any psychological benefit the defense gains in giving a number is severely undermined if we do not give a number clearly. But saying literally *any number* helps.

Do Not Say Plaintiff's Number

Our analysis shows the defense is more willing to repeat plaintiff's number than give its own. The defense repeated plaintiff's number (in whole or in part) in 54 Nuclear Verdicts analyzed but only gave a number (any number at all) in 46 cases.

What happened in the cases where the defense repeated plaintiff's number? The average verdict was 104% of plaintiff's ask. Interestingly, the damage of repeating plaintiff's number was mitigated in those cases where the defense also gave their own number (any number at all), with the average verdict coming in at 61% of plaintiff's ask.

To avoid doing plaintiff's counsel's job for them by delivering on recency and desensitization of plaintiff's number, we also avoid repeating plaintiff's number. If the defense reiterates to jurors *plaintiff's v*aluation of the case, we are further desensitizing them to that astronomical ask, even if we are repeating it in order to highlight its absurdity. This is why, we believe, in the Iowa Law Review study, "attacking" plaintiff's number resulted in the lowest defense verdict rates.[27] In order to attack plaintiff's number, the defense must *say* plaintiff's number, and doing so adds credence to it in the minds of our jurors.

A textbook application of The Apex would, therefore, be to give a single total defense number, explain it by offering both an economic and a non-economic number, and not repeat plaintiff's number. This did not happen in a *single* Nuclear Verdict.

The Defense Does Not *Give a Number* in Stipulated Liability Cases

The number one reason we have heard from carriers and their counsel alike for not giving a number is: "We are going for a defense verdict. Giving a number would mean we are confessing liability!" Setting aside the falseness of this presumption (remember the Iowa Law Review study that concluded the chances of getting a defense verdict actually increase when we give a number?), we examined how often the defense gives a number when liability is not at issue. What happens when the roadblock of contesting liability is removed? Does the defense put their money where their mouth is (literally)? Our data says: No.

Of the ten admitted liability cases contained within our data set, the defense gave a number in five. So, even when liability is not at issue at all (the biggest roadblock to giving a number), the defense still does not give a number half the time.

Giving A Number + Asking for a Defense Verdict is Good for the Defense

Next, we were curious about the impact of asking for a defense verdict while giving a number, understanding that in this universe of cases, no defense verdicts were awarded. The defense asked for a defense verdict in 54 of the Nuclear Verdicts we analyzed, and the defense gave a number in 12 of

27 Campbell et al., *supra* note 20.

these cases. In other words, the defense gave a number 22% of the time when seeking a defense verdict.

On the other hand, asking for a defense verdict without giving a defense number is lethal for the defense. In cases where the defense requested a defense verdict but did not give any number, the average verdict was 200.2% of plaintiff's ask. In these cases the jury gave double what plaintiffs asked for in the final verdict.

Request a Defense Verdict
+ DO NOT Give a Number
= Verdict 200+% of Plaintiff's Ask

The winning combination? Asking for a defense verdict while giving a number! When the defense both requested a defense verdict and gave a number, the average verdict was 66% of plaintiff's ask.

Impact of Giving a Number While Seeking a Defense Verdict on Overall Verdict Size

Verdict Amount as Percentage of Plaintiff's Ask

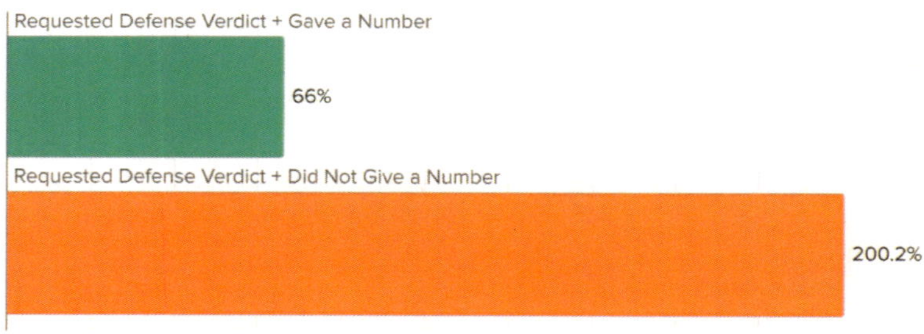

Request a Defense Verdict
+ Give a Number
= Verdict 34% Less Than Plaintiff's Ask

Our takeaway? Arguing the plaintiff has not met their burden without offering the jury guidance will result in the jury dishing out punishment in the form of a verdict double what plaintiff's counsel requested. On the flip side, asking for a defense verdict and giving a number helps drive down damages, contrary to popular belief. **Takeaway: if you are going to ask for a defense verdict, you had better also *Give a Number*.**

When Punitive Damages are Available, The Defense is Even Less Likely to *Give a Number*

Of the 100 Nuclear Verdicts we analyzed, punitive damages were available in 41 cases. This category of cases arguably represents the greatest risk to defendants because in these cases the law allows plaintiffs to argue that the defense should be punished. In other words: anger is at the core of plaintiff's counsel's arguments, and the jury is offered a blank line on which to assign a dollar value specifically to punish and deter. Of these 41 cases, the defense gave a number (any number at all) in only 16. And, where they did give a number, verdicts averaged 71% of plaintiff's ask, compared to 212% where they did not.

Plaintiffs' Counsel Likes Attacking the Defense's Number, but Doing So is Not Effective

Over the past several years, we and our partners have seen an uptick in arguments by the plaintiff attacking our number. We have also seen in our anecdotal study of Nuclear Verdicts a similar trend toward attacking the defense for giving a number. In this study, we often saw plaintiffs' counsel going after the defense for *failing* to give a number! Darned if you do, darned if you don't.

One of the most common tactics we have seen is the plaintiff's counsel telling the jury the defense either *should* be embarrassed by or ashamed of the number they gave, or the reason they *haven't* given a number is that they are embarrassed or ashamed.

The average verdict where the plaintiff did not attack the defense in this way was 130% of plaintiff's ask, even in cases where they attacked the defense in other ways. However, when the plaintiff did attack the defense in this way, the average verdict dropped to 59.9% of plaintiff's ask.

We have also observed a recurring argument advanced by plaintiff's counsel that the defense "wants a discount." Plaintiff's counsel advanced this argument in 17% of Nuclear Verdicts. So, we analyzed whether these types of arguments resulted in verdicts as a higher percentage of the plaintiff's ask. Some more good, empowering news, here: This argument is only effective for plaintiffs when the defense fails to give a number!

In cases where the defense gave a number and plaintiff's counsel argued the defense "wants a discount," the average verdict was 59.2% of plaintiff's ask. However, where the defense failed to give a number and plaintiff's counsel argued the defense "wants a discount," the average was 111.7% of plaintiff's ask (meaning that it exceeded plaintiff's ask by almost 12%).

Our takeaway? Juries like it when the defense gives a number, and do not appreciate the plaintiff shaming or attacking us for doing so.

THE DATA-BACKED CONCLUSION: GIVING A NUMBER (ANY NUMBER) IS GOOD FOR THE DEFENSE AND IS WILDLY UNDERUTILIZED

Where the defense did not use any component of the Core Four, the verdict averaged 148.6% of plaintiff's ask.

Failure to Use Any of the Core Four = Verdict
Almost 50% Higher than Plaintiff's Ask

However, this measure dropped to 75.3% when the defense gave any number at all.

Giving Any Number = Verdict 24.7% Less than Plaintiff's Ask

Either because jurors consciously appreciate guidance, or because counter-anchoring subverts the effectiveness of plaintiff's lawyers' psychological tactics, giving a number has a measurable impact in trial, even in cases where Nuclear Verdicts are awarded. And, because it is the area where we get the most pushback, we will say it again:

Giving a number while seeking a defense verdict
= Verdict 34% Less than Plaintiff's Ask.

Ultimately, The Apex calls the defense to be bold, consistent, and grounded in reason. It demands that we reject outdated fears and inapplicable business-driven justifications for silence in the face of plaintiff's anchoring tactics. When we *Give a Number*, we empower the jury to reach a just result, we serve our clients with integrity, and we fulfill our duty to the court. Whether the number is large or small, what matters most is that a number comes from us clearly and credibly. The time has come for the defense to own the narrative around money at trial. *Give a Number.* In every single case.

CHAPTER 12

I MUST ADDRESS ALL THE EVIDENCE

BOB'S ALTERNATIVE, APEX APPROACH[28]

JURY SELECTION

THE LAW SAYS THERE IS no place for bias, sympathy, or prejudice in this courtroom. As you have heard, plaintiff's attorney is asking you to award a large sum of money.

- How many of you think that because counsel asks for a certain amount, it means the case must be worth that?

We will ask you for a defense verdict, meaning that Dynatrax Tire is not at fault for this tragic accident, or, if you disagree and find we were at fault for this accident, to award Mr. Blackwell a substantial amount of money, $13 million or less.

You must set aside bias, sympathy, and prejudice to make some hard decisions.

- Juror Ms. Abell, if the evidence shows in your opinion that Dynatrax Tire was not at fault for this accident, would you be able to give no money and return a defense verdict?

28 Special thanks to our San Diego Partners Kristi Blackwell and Chris Schon for their trial work that served as inspiration and a point of reference for this Apex example.

- Mr. Houston, it is clear that Mr. Blackwell suffered significant, life-changing injuries in this accident. How do you feel about listening to the evidence for the next few weeks and ultimately awarding a defense verdict in this case, which would mean that Mr. Blackwell leaves with $0?
- Ms. Barnard, what trouble would you have if plaintiff's attorney is asking for tens of millions of dollars in damages, but you believe evidence supports a significant award, but one much less than plaintiff is asking? Would you be able to put aside sympathy for plaintiff and award $13 million or less?

OPENING STATEMENT

[*Concluding Opening Statement*]

...

At the conclusion of this trial, we will request a defense verdict.

We will also discuss in closing, because you will be instructed on the law on damages, how to reach a fair and reasonable number for pain and suffering. Even though we do not believe you ever get to this part of the special verdict form our Judge will ask you to fill out, we will discuss a number that is not based upon emotion, or anger, or pleas of prejudice. A number that does not involve lawyers.

We will discuss a number much, much lower than plaintiff's lawyer wants. You just heard a number from plaintiff's counsel for only economic damages. The final number you hear from plaintiff's attorney is going to be significantly higher than what he just requested.

I'm going to share my client's total and final number in this case with you now because even though we are asking for a defense verdict, I want you to keep it in mind. Our number is life-changing. Our number is going to make a meaningful difference in the Blackwell family's life. As I told you in jury selection, if there is any liability for the tire failure, the evidence will show a fair and reasonable award for all of plaintiff's damages in this case is $13 million or less.

Thank you.

CROSS-EXAMINATION

[*Cross-examining plaintiff's retained life-care planner*]

Q: Ms. Stotts, are you aware doctors have put together another plan to address plaintiff's future care needs?

A: Yes.

Q: Have you seen that plan?

A: Yes.

Q: And that plan costs between about $3.3 million and $4.6 million, correct?

A: Yes, I believe so.

[*Cross-examining plaintiff's accident reconstructionist*]

Q: Are you aware that doctors in this case have put together a $3-4 million plan to give Mr. Blackwell the future medical care he needs?

Plaintiff's counsel: Objection. Relevance. Outside the scope.

Judge: I will allow it.

[*Cross-examining plaintiff's wife*]

Q: Mrs. Blackwell, is it safe to say your family life has been completely changed since this accident?

A: Yes, completely.

Q: Your husband has many worries about the future now, correct?

A: Yes.

Q: And a lot of those worries have to do with money, correct?

A: Absolutely.

Q: You know he worries about how your family will afford the cost of your teenagers' college tuition, for example?

A: Yes, that's true.

Q: Would $5,000,000 have a meaningful impact on your family's life?

A: …

DIRECT EXAMINATION

> [*Examination of our Corporate Representative*]
>
> Q: You've heard me talk to the jury in this case as early as jury selection about how we are seeking a defense verdict. Do you agree with that?
>
> A: Yes, we accept responsibility for manufacturing safe tires.
>
> Q: But if the jury disagrees with us and believes we are at fault for this tire failure, we believe there is a fair, full, and reasonable value of this case. What is that value?
>
> Q: I think that number is $13 million or less.

CLOSING ARGUMENT

> [*Conclude Closing Argument by Giving a Number and Arguing Pain and Suffering.*]
>
> ...

The evidence you heard over the many weeks of this case shows that the tire was not defective. As we have discussed, Dynatrax Tire accepts responsibility for properly manufacturing and distributing a safe tire. As I just detailed, the evidence shows the tire failure in this case was caused by an impact that happened before Mr. Blackwell's accident. That impact broke the steel cords in the tire and allowed compressed air into the structure of the tire. This impact happened nine years into the tire being used on a concrete mixer. It was improper usage and maintenance that caused the tire to fail, and we urge you to issue a defense verdict in this case.

[*Display the jury verdict form.*]

On question one of the verdict form, "We, the jury, on the issues joined, unanimously find in favor of the Plaintiff," you are going to answer "No."

[*Display "no" on the jury verdict form for the jury.*]

On question two, "We, the jury, on the issues joined, unanimously find in favor of the Defendants," you are going to Answer "Yes."

[*Display "yes" on the jury verdict form for the jury.*]

Then, your work will be done in this case. You will not have to answer any other questions. You will date the form and alert the bailiff you have reached a verdict.

Now, I need to talk to you about what happens if you do not find in favor of my client. We defense lawyers struggle with this. How can I tell you I believe the evidence supports a defense verdict, but also tell you in jury selection, in opening, and throughout the case that the case is worth $13 million or less?

Well, I have a duty to my client and to this court to address all the evidence and the law you are considering. This is an ethical duty to my client. You've heard evidence about money damages for weeks and it is my responsibility to address that evidence with you now. This is a responsibility I take seriously.

If you answer "Yes" to question one, then you are also going to have to answer question three: "We unanimously award damages in the amount of ________________ in favor of David Blackwell and against the Defendants, jointly and severally."

If you get this far, if you find liability, then you are going to write a number between $10,951,559 and $12,244,576 into question three. How did I get to this number?

Well, as you have heard from our experts, if you get to this part of the jury verdict form, we agree with plaintiff's counsel that Mr. Blackwell's past medical expenses were $2,049,675, his past lost wages were $115,545, and the present value of his future lost earnings are $493,141.

[*Display these three categories of economic damages and amounts for the jury.*]

Past medical expenses: $2,049,675

Past lost wages: $115,545

Future lost earnings: $493,141

You *would* need to decide the fair and reasonable value of three remaining categories of damages: future medical expenses, past pain and suffering, and future pain and suffering.

For future medical expenses, as you heard from our doctors, the reasonable value of Mr. Blackwell's medical treatment for the rest of his life is between $3,293,198 and $4,586,215. [*Argue why the jury may choose either value or something in between.*]

[*Display our defense number for future medical expenses for the jury.*]

Future medical expenses: $3,293,198 to $4,586,215

If you get this far, we accept responsibility for Mr. Blackwell's noneconomic damages as well—his pain and suffering. A pain and suffering award of $2,000,000 for past pain and suffering and $3,000,000 for future pain and suffering will fully and reasonably compensate Mr. Blackwell for what he went through in this awful accident. $5,000,000 in pain and suffering is not only reasonable, but it will be life-changing for Mr. Blackwell and his family.

[*Display each category of noneconomic damages for the jury.*]

Past noneconomic damages: $2,000,000
Future noneconomic damages: $3,000,000

Now, again, I don't think you're ever going to get to this part of the jury verdict form. I think you are going to award a defense verdict in this case. But, if you find my client was at fault for this tire failure nine years after the tire was made, in response to question three on the verdict form you will write a total verdict of between $10,951,559 and $12,244,576.

[*Display the total defense number for the jury on the jury verdict form.*]

"We unanimously award damages in the amount of **$12,244,576** in favor of David Blackwell and against the Defendants, jointly and severally."

When it comes to every aspect of plaintiff's damages, including damages for pain and suffering, the law requires you to award fair compensation.

[*Display Jury Instruction for the jury.*]

> "Your verdict shall be for such sum as will **fully and fairly compensate** the plaintiff for the damages sustained as a result of the defendant's negligence."

How should you determine what is fair? There are two main things to consider when addressing pain and suffering...

WHY GIVE A DEFENSE NUMBER?

Jurors Need Guidance

We know in this Nuclear Verdict the defense did not sponsor a defense number for damages in closing argument. The outcome? The jury awarded plaintiff every penny of damages his attorney requested. After the jury found the defendant liable, the only framework the jury had to determine what would "fully and fairly compensate" plaintiff was the number and argument provided by plaintiff's counsel.

The same psychological truths that work for plaintiffs in trial work for the defense, too! Again, there is no study of "plaintiff psychology" and "defendant psychology." It is just "human psychology." The same techniques that plaintiffs' attorneys use work for us, too, when we are brave enough to use them.

Anchoring is perhaps the most powerful psychological phenomenon we studied and discussed in this book. The power of numbers to frame someone's reasoning on an issue is truly mind blowing.[29]

Even Appellate Judges Think You Should *Give a Number!*

In this particular case study, the defense appealed the verdict on several grounds, claiming the noneconomic damages award of $29,000,000 was excessive, and requested the appellate court lower the verdict. The defense informed the appellate judge the jury's verdict was the largest tort verdict in the jurisdiction not involving punitive damages in the last 10 years. They also argued most of plaintiff's attorney's presentation at trial was meant to

29 For more behind-the-scenes insight into Bob's thought process and the development of this Apex closing, join our Apex Defense Community at www.apexdefenseconsulting.com.

elicit the "passions" of the jury. From a defense perspective, it is easy to agree with this, right?

The appellate court's opinion on the noneconomic damages award is essentially "Exhibit A" of why the defense cannot rely on an appeal to correct an outsized jury verdict. The Court explained its ruling:

> "[I]n closing argument, counsel for [Blackwell] laid out a reasonable calculation of each element of non-economic damages. He asked for $3.5 million each for the elements of past bodily injuries, physical pain, mental anguish, and inconvenience (over 3.5 years). He then asked for $5 million each for the elements of future mental anguish, inconvenience, and physical pain. Each of these harms, in the Court's view, was well-supported by the thoroughly presented damages evidence."

Now, hold onto your seat for what the court said next: "**Additionally, Defendants offered no conflicting evidence of damages and did not cross-examine any of the damages witnesses at trial. Thus, they gave the jury no basis on which to question the requested damages amount. It is unsurprising, then, that the jury awarded [Blackwell] exactly what he sought.**" Mic drop. Even the appellate court judge practically begged the defendants to give a number![30] If this does not convince defense attorneys and our clients to give a number, we do not know what will.

CONCLUSION

The plaintiffs' bar uses the most powerful psychological tools to connect with jurors and drive Nuclear Verdicts. The pattern of Nuclear Verdicts reveals most defense attorneys are not giving the jury a number in these outsized awards. When it comes time for the jury to deliberate and jurors

30 The court concluded, "A reasonable and fully-informed juror, unmotivated by passion, corruption or prejudice, could certainly conclude that $29,000,000 was necessary to compensate [Blackwell], *i.e.*, to make him 'whole,' for the extraordinary suffering that he has endured and will continue to endure and for the alteration of his entire life." Ultimately, the court determined the jury erroneously awarded a "slightly excessive" verdict for not awarding future lost wages before reducing it to present value and provided a means to correct the error. The case apparently settled, and the further pending appeal was dismissed.

decide the defense is at fault, the jury has no other guide to help them value the case other than the anchor given early and often by plaintiff's attorney.

It is time for the defense to come out of the Stone Age and use these psychological tools, too. We must anchor the jury in every single case, even when we are seeking a defense verdict. When the defense chooses to *Give a Number*, it helps the defense, even in nuclear results.

It is time to break the pattern of Nuclear Verdicts. Apply The Apex and always *Give a Number*, even when seeking a defense verdict. *Give a Number* even if plaintiff's counsel does not give one. *Give a Number* even though it feels "risky," "counterintuitive," or "scary." *Give a Number* to deliver justice for all.

PART V:

ARGUE PAIN AND SUFFERING

CHAPTER 13

THE CASE OF A LOST IDENTITY

A PASSION MAKES LIFE SWEET

Easy Like Saturday Morning (1999)

SPENCER'S EYES SPRANG OPEN AS the sun gleamed through the blinds in his room. Children's artwork lined the walls around him: fingerpaint, crayons, marker, and colored pencil kaleidoscopes of fire-breathing dragons, heavy haulers, and jungle tigers. He remembered it was Saturday morning—cartoon morning!

Spencer slipped out of his Spiderman sheets and tiptoed quietly past his parents' bedroom. Spencer's mom made him a deal a few years back: if Spencer would agree to let his parents sleep, she would buy him a boatload of art supplies, and he would be allowed to draw while watching Saturday morning cartoons until his parents woke up. As he rounded the corner to the living room, Spencer spotted another week's worth of fresh colored pencils and a stack of crisp construction paper waiting for him on the coffee table in front of the TV.

The seven-year-old expertly turned on the TV with the big remote control and changed the channel until he found his Saturday morning cartoons on the Kids' WB. His favorite show, *Pokémon*, was about to start. Spencer returned the remote to the coffee table and carefully opened his new supplies.

When his mother stepped into the living room a couple of hours later, she found the small room filled with pieces of decorated construction paper. Spencer lined the couch, the chairs, the floor, and even the top of the television with his work for her to see. The corners of her mouth turned up into a sleepy smile as she sighed to herself. *"He has such a gift,"* she thought as she embraced him. She wished she could afford art lessons, but Spencer was refining his work on his own initiative.

Spencer's mother's eyes scanned the drawings around the room, impressed by his attempts to copy what he saw in each cartoon. She observed his work with a bittersweet heaviness in her chest. She missed the fingerpaint smears and scrambled crayon lines he used to show her. Now, it was undeniable his skill improved each week, and she was immensely proud of his self-driven progress, though it was further evidence her little boy was growing up.

"Just Do It" (2012)

Spencer tried to calm the butterflies in his stomach as he stepped toward the larger-than-life glass doors. The Nike campus was buzzing with creativity and innovation. Among the lush greenery, sleek walls, and expansive art installations, Spencer heard confident voices and even some laughter.

For 20-year-old Spencer, the atmosphere was both invigorating and intimidating. Two thousand students from across the country had applied for this internship. Spencer was one of only two people accepted to an art position. Most important to him, Spencer was accepted on his own merit. He did not know Phil Knight. He did not have a parent who called in a favor. Nike accepted him based on his own skill, promise, grit, and determination. And now he was ready to dive in and make good on his childhood dreams.

After only a moment, Melissa, his mentor, welcomed Spencer with a beaming smile and firm handshake. She guided him through bustling corridors and busy elevators to the graphic design department. As they approached an open-concept meeting space, Spencer took in the iconic quote on the wall.

> *"...I've failed over and over and over again*
> *in my life. And that is why I succeed."*
> —Michael Jordan

The weight of the words hung in the air. The quote resonated deeply with the budding designer. Spencer knew the only way to achieve something great is to step outside his comfort zone and risk failure.

Spencer was ready. He was ready to embrace risks. He was ready to explore new possibilities. He was ready to *Just Do It*.

Graduation Day (2014)

As he sat on the floor of the Marsee Auditorium among a sea of 125 blue robes, Spencer was hyper-aware of his heartbeat. The building itself swelled with pride from graduates, faculty, and loved ones. He looked to his right, squinted, and panned the audience slowly until he found her again. His mom's delight radiated through her smile as the commencement address began.

Spencer was not a 4.0 student, but he dove in and committed himself to the Nance College of Art + Design on day one. Today, he was so close to receiving his bachelor's degree. He was four credits short, but the school recognized everything he poured into his education and allowed him to walk at graduation in anticipation of his completion.

As graduation day approached, Spencer received the Outstanding Contribution Award from Student Affairs. This award, given to a student who significantly impacted campus life, was an acknowledgment of all the late nights and tireless efforts he poured into making the Nance a better place.

This moment was a long time coming. Truthfully, Spencer never liked school and hardly applied himself to his studies. During his junior year of high school, he tagged along with a buddy to a college fair. There, he found Nance. Suddenly, a light turned on for him in ways it never had before. He was excited at the prospect of learning something he really cared about—art.

He applied right away, but the school denied him admission. His grades from high school were just too low.

Spencer was undeterred. He applied for, was accepted, and attended junior college. It was hard to go to a school where he knew no one while all his friends went off to four-year universities, but he was determined to get grades good enough to attend Nance. He did just that. He always knew he was a fighter, that he could battle through anything. Today, this graduation proved it to everyone else, too.

After what seemed like an endless crowd of people parading across the stage, the Dean finally neared the end of the list of students with a "Q" last name. Spencer and his fellow "R" classmates stood and shuffled out of their rows to form a single-file line along the edge of the arena floor.

His chest swelled as he heard the announcer call "Raabe," then "Raaj." He took a deep breath and remembered what his best friend told him this morning: "Enjoy the moment, Dude!"

"Rabinowitz."

"Rabito."

Then, at last,

"Spencer Raines."

The 22-year-old put one foot in front of the other and walked across the long stage toward the podium to receive his diploma for a bachelor's degree with a handshake from the Nance College President.

As he descended the stage to return to his seat, he locked eyes again with his mother. She had supported him through countless challenges and celebrated every little victory since the day he was born. His degree was as much her achievement as Spencer's. He knew this day would stay with both him and his mother forever.

Preparing for the Hike of a Lifetime (2018)

13…14…15, Spencer counted in his head as he exhaled deliberately. He replaced the heavy dumbbells on the rack and looked at himself in the gym mirror. At 26 years old, Spencer was finally happy with his physical fitness and physique. He was confident in who he was, how his body looked, and what his body was capable of. His workouts were paying off.

In just two short months, he and his two best friends would check off a bucket-list item by hiking part of the John Muir Trail. Spencer's friend had won the trail lottery and secured a coveted permit for the trip. The 211-mile hike through some of the most rugged and stunning California wilderness was sure to put his body to the test. The trip would be unsupported—the young men would trek almost three weeks with only the supplies they had on their backs. On the final day of the journey, the trail would take the group over the tallest summit in the continental United States—Mt. Whitney, at 14,505 feet of elevation.

This would be the longest hike Spencer had ever trekked, and he knew it was going to be life-changing. His body and his mind were ready. He had only to stay healthy and finalize his supplies before the group began their road trip to Mammoth. But for now, on to deadlifts.

Days Later

Spencer awoke to the sterile scent of antiseptic and the soft beep of machines echoing in the background. His body felt foreign, bound by a weight of pain, as if it no longer belonged to him. His right wrist throbbed with an unrelenting ache, and his leg was immobilized in a heavy cast. The doctors were thorough and their diagnoses grim: a shattered wrist, a fractured femur, and significant spinal injuries. Each word landed like a blow, underscoring the gravity of his new reality.

Spencer lay on the highway in unbearable, unrelenting pain just hours ago. As he rode his motorcycle, a truck struck him from the side. Spencer's recollection of the accident was still foggy, but he remembered being thrown from the motorcycle, skidding across a nearby trailer moving over 60 miles an hour, and then coming to a stop on the unforgiving asphalt. As chaos unfolded around him on the freeway, he lay there screaming and immobilized, and in shock at the searing pain.

Over the many hours he lay awake in the hospital waiting for his surgeries to begin, Spencer thanked God he "geared up" every ride with equipment designed by the company he worked for: Greiner North America. As the brand's marketing associate for over five years, Spencer most recently helped the company through a rebrand of their website and printed content. Greiner even flew him to their factory in Magdeburg, Germany, a few times. Spencer fully believed in the products he helped market. He wondered if he would be alive if he had not worn Greiner's full protective gear and helmet the day of the accident.

The surgeries began four days later, each one a battle against his own broken body. The first surgery focused on repairing his shattered wrist and snapped femur on the same day. Surgeons performed their own form of art by painstakingly inserting pins and plates to stabilize the damage in his dominant hand like an intricate dance of metal and bone. The doctors stabilized the largest bone in his body—his femur—and weaved tendons back around it.

As he lay in the fog of the recovery room in extreme pain after his surgeries, he looked down at his right side to see the pins sticking out of the bandages around his wrist and his leg in traction in the air. The weight of the pain in his body was so heavy that he could hardly breathe. As he waited for the doctors to give him an epidural to numb all the pain, all he could think about was his shattered future.

Goodbye art, illustration, and graphic design. Goodbye hiking, gym, and motorcycle riding. Goodbye to his career and everything he worked so hard for. Goodbye to the essence of who he was mere days ago.

SPENCER'S NEVER-ENDING PAIN AND SUFFERING

One month after his motorcycle accident, Spencer Raines sued Premier Kia Automotive and its driver of the blue 2015 Kia Optima that crashed into him. He claimed the driver of the vehicle, while in the course and scope of his employment at Premier Kia Automotive, veered out of the HOV lane and collided with Spencer and his motorcycle. The initial impact launched Spencer across three lanes of highway traffic into a passing flatbed trailer, which then propelled him to the pavement below. The entire collision was captured on video by a GoPro camera affixed to another motorcycle rider's helmet.

At trial, the jury heard Spencer sustained extensive orthopedic injuries in the accident. He was admitted to the hospital for 15 days, where he underwent open reduction and internal fixation and screw fixation surgeries to his shattered right wrist and snapped femur. He also suffered an L-1 compression fracture. Five months later, Spencer underwent a third surgery to his right wrist to remove hardware and place K-wires for stabilization. Spencer's doctors attested to his ongoing pain and need for future medical treatment, including potential surgeries.

Spencer was unable to find a job after the accident. He claimed this accident stole his ability to be a competitive candidate and find a job in the open job market. Spencer, therefore, claimed substantial damages for future loss of earnings.

Plaintiff's counsel successfully obtained liability admissions in deposition through effective use of the *Reptile* tactics. The defense stipulated to liability, and trial proceeded before a jury as to damages only. The jury awarded $21,496,420, as follows:

- $279,375 for past medical expenses (stipulated);
- $611,940 for future medical expenses;
- $95,729 for past loss of earnings (stipulated);
- $2,509,376 for future loss of earnings;
- $8,000,000 for past noneconomic damages; and
- $10,000,000 for future noneconomic damages.

Plaintiff's counsel effectively fueled juror anger and used numerous techniques to drive the jury toward a Nuclear Verdict, including a large award for noneconomic damages. Notably, counsel used innovative tactics to argue pain and suffering.

The Defense Stole Spencer's Passions

Plaintiff's counsel effectively framed for the jury that the human losses, the noneconomic damages, are "the real part" of the case. As humans, we live for our passions. In this case, counsel argued, Spencer's passions were stripped away from him. Counsel explained that Spencer "didn't want to be the C.E.O. of Microsoft. He didn't want to be the president. [sic] He just wanted to do his art, do his hiking, hang out, live a nice life, be with his family. And they took it all away from him, through no fault of his own."

Tapping into the compelling human story at the heart of his client, plaintiff's counsel effectively showed that Spencer *loved* his job as a graphic designer; being an artist was his identity. "He loved his job. It was his life, his passion. And all of that—all of that was taken from him through no fault of his own." Counsel generated anger through the argument that the defense unjustly stole from his client the whole of who he was.

Counsel told the jury that some may comment "only" plaintiff's hand and right leg were hurt but argued to the jury that it is impossible to "only" hurt a part of a person. Rather, when someone is injured, the "whole of the man" is injured, and he cannot just be put back together; "this isn't Humpty Dumpty." Plaintiff's counsel told a compelling story of heartbreak and irreparable harm, and the jury was left empowered to deliver vengeance.

Elements of Damages

In order to help the jury evaluate the "human losses" and drive a Nuclear Verdict, plaintiff's counsel used a common tactic called the Elements of Damages argument, in which he walked the jury through each possible element of noneconomic damages available under the jury instruction.[31] For each and every element, counsel provided a detailed argument of what plaintiff suffered and sponsored a number to account for it.

In this case, applicable jury instructions permitted plaintiff to recover past and future noneconomic damages for the following elements: (1) physical pain, (2) mental suffering, (3) loss of enjoyment of life, (4) disfigurement,

31 *See generally* Appendix A (providing a more in-depth discussion on plaintiffs' counsel's closing tactics).

(5) physical impairment, (6) inconvenience, (7) grief, (8) anxiety, (9) humiliation, and (10) emotional distress. Plaintiff's counsel argued to the jury, "[A]ny harm that we've proved, we're entitled to compensation." He examined Spencer's mother and Spencer himself on each of these elements to introduce specific evidence supporting each element of pain and suffering.

Counsel claimed the jury "must assess" each of these elements and together render "[o]ne award for the past" and "one award for the 50.5 years in the future." He further explained, "[s]ome of these overlap...[b]ut you're just going to give one award, and you're going to consider all of these because you must under the law." This argument is particularly effective, as we will discuss in Chapter 14, because it offers context and guidance to some of the most nebulous questions a jury is asked.

It appears plaintiff's attorney displayed a PowerPoint slide in closing argument that suggested a dollar award for each element of the jury instruction on damages. Plaintiff's damages chart displayed to the jury totaled $39.5 million. While defense counsel objected to the slide, the Court merely clarified that the jury was "not to write up an award for each individual element." Instead, jurors were instructed to "consider each individual element" and "come to one total amount for [the] award."

Minutes/Hours/Days

Plaintiff's counsel used another common argument to drive the jury toward a large noneconomic damages award: one we call the "Minutes/Hours/Days" approach. Using this tactic, counsel broke down the minutes, hours, and days that plaintiff will suffer in the future to contextualize the amount of time that will pass, and to legitimize the massive number they request. In this case, counsel said, "You've seen four days of testimony on what this man has been through and the 13,000 days in the future and the 400,000 hours it's going to be." Later, counsel continued, "And if you think in your head, it's 14,400-some days, almost 500,000 hours, over almost 1.5 million minutes left for him." This tactic is effective because it distills down a large concept like "pain and suffering" into easily understood time increments.

However, in this case, plaintiff's attorney did not close out the Minutes/Hours/Days argument in typical fashion. Plaintiff's counsel most commonly ties the minutes, hours, and days in the future to a small dollar amount that, once multiplied over plaintiff's future life expectancy, adds up to tens and tens of millions of dollars. For example, plaintiffs' attorneys typically argue that plaintiff is entitled to earn minimum wage every hour, sometimes even every minute, for the rest of his life as compensation for the pain and suffering he will experience in the future. By the time jurors multiply the current applicable minimum wage ($16.00/hour) by the hours in plaintiff's future life expectancy (about 450,000 hours), they land on an extremely large damages award.

In this case, however, this argument would only lead to a future pain and suffering award of $7,200,000. Therefore, plaintiff's counsel strategically laid out the future minutes, hours, and days of plaintiff's future life expectancy without tying these figures to a specific dollar amount to ask the jury for an even larger future damages award than this method would produce.

Then, plaintiff's counsel effectively used a "reverse" Minutes/Hours/Days argument in rebuttal to discredit the number the defense suggested for pain and suffering. Specifically, plaintiff's counsel disparaged the defense's damages number, $1 million for future pain and suffering, by breaking it down into minute and hourly pay. Counsel argued, "$1 million from today to the future. 50.5 years is... 530 hours. Check me out. 26,542,800 minutes. That's four cents a minute... That's what they say is full compensation. [$]2.40 an hour." This played right into counsel's theme that the defense wanted a discount, and fueled juror anger.

Future Inflation Protection

When speaking to the jury about Spencer's life expectancy, plaintiff's counsel deployed another common tactic: one we have termed "Future Inflation Protection." This argument is as effective as it is speculative. Counsel challenged the jury to look 50 or more years into the future and imagine how much money jurors would need to award now to secure plaintiff's future.

Counsel initially asked the jury to recall who the President was 50 years ago. In rebuttal, he reminded the jury that Lyndon Johnson was the president 50 years ago. At that time, Starbucks did not exist, Bill Gates was a teenager, minimum wage was $1.30 per hour, and Michael Jordan was six years old. Counsel reminded the jury that 50 years is a long time for plaintiff to live and that common sense and the evidence tell the jurors that plaintiff's condition is not going to improve over the next 50 years.

Piggybacking the "reverse" Minutes/Hours/Days argument to dispute defense counsel's noneconomic damages number, counsel stated, "When I was in school, [$]2.40 was, like, the minimum wage. It's much more now, but this is what [the defendant] thinks is fair."

Inanimate Objects

Counsel used the powerful argument technique of comparing plaintiff's pain and suffering, his human losses, to the loss of valuable inanimate objects. Plaintiff's counsel said, "Lovely to look at, great to touch, but if you break it, consider it sold."

FEDEX PLANE CRASH

Plaintiff's counsel compared the value of Spencer's injuries to a plane crashing into the defendant's car dealership to empower the jury to award a Nuclear Verdict:

> Let's say that some FedEx plane crashed into the dealership and it destroyed all of the inventory and the buildings and the structures, and they lost money, and they get some accountants to do the math, and they would say, here's the tab, [$]35 million.... Now, would you hesitate if that was supported by the evidence for a corporation to receive that money? You shouldn't because the law says you can't.
>
> Well, why should it be any different if [Mr. Raines] is entitled to 30 or 40 million? Why should it be any different for him than a corporation? And the law says it isn't. It's the same.

THE DEFENSE MUST SETTLE THE DEBT

Counsel also implored the jury to force the defendant to pay its debt to Spencer for the injuries they caused. Plaintiff's attorney argued, "There is a debt owed by this side of the table to this side of the table. People have debts. They buy things. They have credit cards. They pay. But they settle the debt. And we're here to square that debt because it's owed. And it's been owing for almost two years now. And it's time to square the debt. And that's what you're going to do." Counsel continued, "But there's a debt owed. We're here to collect it. They owe it. Straight up."

PLAINTIFF'S OTHER EFFECTIVE TRIAL TACTICS

In addition to delivering powerful arguments to support a nuclear award for pain and suffering, plaintiff's counsel used several common methods in closing argument to drive juror anger and secure a large jury verdict.

Plaintiff's Counsel Gave a Number

Counsel asked the jury to award over $42 million in closing argument. Plaintiff's counsel empowered the jury to award "full compensation" to Spencer. Counsel equated the verdict to being a cup half full of water and suggested that the perception of whether the cup is half full or half empty depends on one's thirst. Counsel told the jury, "anything less than a full cup of justice is injustice."

Counsel explained to the jury that the court did not allow him to give a specific number in jury selection or opening statement.[32] He gave a specific number in closing, the only time he was allowed to discuss it. "I told you, I want to do it, but I'm not allowed to do it. I followed the rules." Counsel then defended the legitimacy of his $42 million request of the jury: "I was allowed to say tens and tens and tens, which is over 30 million, which is exactly where I have been on [sic] day 1. I never changed for one second in this case, ever."

---

32 Notably, plaintiff's legal team gave an economic damages number in opening statement of $2 to $3.6 million.

Plaintiff's attorney also attempted to separate and distinguish the jury's incoming verdict for pain and suffering from any possible punitive damages, which were not available in this case. Counsel stated, "And as the judge told you, no one's getting punished here. We don't want any punishment. That's not right. We're not looking for punishment. We're looking for full, complete compensation." This approach cultivated trust and credibility for the plaintiff's counsel, even as he advanced arguments clearly aimed at generating anger.

Plaintiff's Counsel Called Out the Defense for Not Accepting Responsibility

While the defense stipulated to liability and conceded they were at fault, plaintiff's counsel argued the defense did not really concede anything meaningful in the case.

BALL THROUGH A WINDOW STORY

Counsel told the story of a boy throwing a ball through a window and having to pay to repair what he broke.[33] When a window is broken, the child who broke it does not get to say, "but that window is 10 years old, so I'm going to get you a 10-year-old window." This is not how the civil justice system works in America. Again, counsel accused the defense of not wanting to pay the full value of Spencer's loss. Instead, counsel told the jury, the defense was looking for a lower jury award because they did not think the jury would award a large verdict.

In rebuttal, plaintiff's counsel again discussed a boy throwing a ball through a window. Counsel reminded the jury, however, that the boy would need to be fully accountable and fully compensate for the damage he caused.

---

33 *See also* Chapter 9 (providing an example of how defense counsel can implement The Apex and effectively deliver a story about responsibility in closing argument). *Cf.* ROBERT F. TYSON, JR., NUCLEAR VERDICTS: DEFENDING JUSTICE FOR ALL 14-32 (2020) (providing the effective use of a narrative story to demonstrate to the jury how the defense accepts responsibility in a case to defuse juror anger and show how the defense is reasonable. Bob shares a story of throwing a ball through a window as a boy as an example of how he learned that responsibility has two components: acceptance and accountability. Plaintiff's counsel regularly use and twist this example story in their damages arguments in closing, as discussed here).

He argued the defense should not get a discount, just as there should be no discount for the boy who broke a window.

IN REALITY, THE DEFENSE CONCEDED NOTHING

Instead of calling their own witness to "prove" their case, plaintiff's attorney argued the defense merely cross-examined all of plaintiff's witnesses. The defense did not call any witnesses and rested immediately after plaintiff's counsel rested his case. Plaintiff's counsel challenged the defense by asking, "Where are their witnesses? They got none."[34]

> But they don't really admit anything. They only concede what they have to. Their job is to defend the financial interests of the defendant. And that's what they're supposed to do. There's nothing wrong with that. But you have to do it with evidence. They don't have any evidence.

Plaintiff's counsel referenced the Bible when arguing again that the jury must require the defense to accept full and complete responsibility for their actions by requiring them to fully compensate Spencer for his loss.

> And it's not going to be an eye for an eye and a tooth for a tooth and an arm for an arm and a limb for a limb. It's going to be, like the next verse says (as read and/or reflected:) "If a man has an ox and it gores another, that oxen shall be killed and the meat not eaten unless he can pay a sum in ransom and that oxen will be spared." And that's what it is here, compensation, to compensate. We're never going to make him whole, but to compensate for what's been lost.

Counsel Referenced Historical Figures and Works

Plaintiff's counsel in this case is one of the very best at weaving references to historical icons, documents, or works of art to craft a compelling closing argument. Counsel's powerful historical references included (1) the United States Constitution, (2) the Magna Carta, (3) four references to the Bible, (4) Latin root words, (5) Julius Caesar, (6) the Founding Fathers, (7) Thomas

34 The defense objected to this argument and was overruled.

Jefferson, (8) Abraham Lincoln, (9) Martin Luthur King, and (10) Blind Lady Justice. These creative, historical arguments are persuasive to jurors.

Counsel Empowered the Jury

Spencer's counsel empowered the jury to render a large award for his client in two powerful ways. First, counsel gave jurors more power in their verdict than they have in the United States electoral system. Counsel stated, "We see so much today on T.V. about political elections. But in that election, and the election that's coming up, you're going to be one of millions of people that are casting their votes. But here, you're one of 12." Counsel added, "Most people come from different backgrounds, from different education, from different training, from different religions, different races, but you're all together as one and you speak as one. And when your verdict is read, you will speak the truth of what will happen to [Spencer Raines]."

Second, plaintiff's attorney made clear to the jurors that they alone held plaintiff's future in their hands—not the judge, not the defense, and not him. He argued, "So they don't get to determine what's reasonable and what's full and complete, the dealership. We don't get to determine it. I don't get to tell you what it should be. I reason with you, make a suggestion, but you all decide. You decide what's fair and just."

Plaintiff's Attorney Explained there are "No Mulligans"

As seen in many Nuclear Verdicts, counsel used the common argument that this trial was Spencer's one and only opportunity to be compensated for his injuries and pain and suffering. The law does not allow Spencer to come back in five years and explain that his future surgeries did not work. Spencer could not come back in 10 years and explain he is experiencing more pain than the jury predicted. "He can't come back. This is it. One shot. No do-overs, no mulligans, no replays. This is it.... That's why it's so important."

Plaintiff's Counsel Attacked the Defense and Defense Counsel

One of plaintiff 's counsel's most effective strategies to fuel juror anger was to attack the defense and defense counsel. Counsel challenged the defense numerous times in closing argument: The defense did not believe that jurors were "going to give the money that [Mr. Raines is] entitled to. And that's why we're here." Plaintiff 's counsel argued that the defense did not bring in expert witnesses to dispute the extent of plaintiff 's injuries "because they don't think you're going to give the money. That's why we're here."

PREDICTED THE DEFENSE'S NUMBER

Plaintiff's attorney attempted to discredit any number the defense would give in closing argument by predicting how much money the defense was going to suggest for pain and suffering. Plaintiff's counsel hearkened back to the defense attorney's opening statement in which the defense said, "His injuries are serious, and the evidence will show it's going to require a substan-tial—substantial amount of money to fully compensate him." Then counsel remarked, "Substantial, I guess, is in the eye of the beholder, but I guarantee you, his substantial is not substantial."

Counsel specifically predicted at two different points in his closing argument that the defense would suggest the jury award $2 million. Counsel also challenged jurors to hear what defense counsel would suggest they award for each element of damages discussed above: pain, suffering, humiliation, anxiety, embarrassment, etc. Plaintiff's attorney then guaranteed jurors that defense counsel would not tell them what each element is worth because defense counsel was "embarrassed."[35]

Defense counsel then suggested the jury award $2 million for noneconomic damages in closing argument: $1 million for past and $1 million for

35 Defense objected. The court sustained and instructed plaintiff's counsel not to "impune [sic] counsel." Plaintiff's counsel responded in front of the jury, "I'm not. They're great lawyers. They can get the best lawyers they want—the big car dealership and they got the best. They have no evidence."

future.[36] In rebuttal argument, plaintiff's attorney discredited the defense's suggested number and claimed it was not substantial: "Is [$]2 million substantial? What is that T.V. show, you answer nine questions, you get a million dollars? . . . Is that substantial? I don't think so."

"NICKEL AND DIME" AND WANTING A DISCOUNT

The defense admitted Spencer "suffered serious injuries[,]" and plaintiff's counsel argued that the defense wanted to "nickel and dime" and cautioned the jury that they would "see him nickel and dime us on the future noneconomic and the past." Counsel also stated, "You heard that phrase, [']going to nickel and dime you to death.['] That's what we're getting here." Plaintiff's attorney drove home the allegation: "That's what car dealers do."

The jury heard from plaintiff's attorney that the defense did not think the jury would award $25 million. Counsel accused the defense of wanting a "discount" and empowered the jury to award a large verdict.

> You're going to see it, I guarantee it. They want a discount. They don't want to pay full and complete. They're looking for a discount.[37]
>
> They've taken it away from him, and they want to come in here and minimize and low-ball, and they don't care. Their job is to defend the financial interest of the company. That's their job to do that. And the lower the amount they get you to award, the better it is for the defendant. And that's their job.

Plaintiff's counsel also used a "reverse" investment and interest argument.[38] Counsel used this argument as an analogy of the defense's argument

36 Defense counsel provided the jury the stipulated economic damages numbers for past medical treatment and past lost wages in opening statement. In opening, defense counsel asked the jury "to award [Mr. Raines] a substantial, but reasonable, amount of money" and that he would "leave it to [the jury] to tell us how to compensate [Mr. Raines]."

37 The defense objected, and the court overruled the objection.

38 *Cf.* ROBERT F. TYSON, JR., NUCLEAR VERDICTS: DEFENDING JUSTICE FOR ALL 50-63 (2020) (providing a discussion on the effective use of an argument discussing the power of interest earned on any potential damages award when arguing pain and suffering, particularly when discussing the impact of money on plaintiff's life).

to demonstrate the defense was asking for a discount in this case.[39] "So let's say that, you know, you borrowed [$]500,000 from the bank. You go back to the bank and say, okay, here's [$]440,000. Just put it in [the bank] and get the interest and you'll get your whole [$]500,000. That's what they're trying to do here." Through each of these arguments, plaintiff's counsel advanced the narrative that the defense was attempting to get out of paying the full amount owed to Spencer for the harm they caused.

VILLAINIZED THE DEFENSE AND DEFENSE COUNSEL

Plaintiff's counsel further fueled juror anger by insinuating that the defense and defense counsel were up to no good. Counsel mocked defense experts in the replay of their video deposition. Specifically, a defense medical expert refused to agree with plaintiff's counsel in deposition that Spencer experiences chronic pain and would have some degree of continuing pain in his leg and hip for the rest of his life. In closing, plaintiff's counsel insinuated it was ridiculous that a doctor would not agree that Spencer experienced pain given the severity of his injuries.

> This is the tactic. This is what's been going on in this case. We've exposed it, and they don't like it, but that's what this case is about. Discount, minimize, reduce, not full and complete. Come on. You hire someone like this because you know what he's going to say. We had to bring it to you. But this is what their defense is.

Plaintiff's counsel also reminded the jury in his closing argument and in rebuttal that defense counsel asked Spencer's mother how Spencer passed the time while he was not working. Specifically, the defense asked her if Spencer sat at home all day watching lawyer commercials. Counsel then asked the jury the rhetorical question of why defense counsel would ask that question, "Do you think it was to determine whether he has future pain and suffering, or was it for another purpose?" Counsel posed the question to the jury, "Why would a lawyer ask questions—well, what is [Mr. Raines] doing at home watching

39 In this case, plaintiff's counsel used this argument in "reverse" to demonstrate how the defense was asking the jury to give them a discount on the damages award.

lawyer commercials? Why would they throw that out there?" This argument effectively insinuated the defense did not care about Spencer and, instead, thought Spencer was abusing the legal system for financial gain.

EMBRACED THE BATTLE OF TRIAL

Plaintiff's attorney fully embraced the adversarial nature of closing argument. He clearly understood that for his client, trial was a fight for justice. In response, defense counsel objected to plaintiff's counsel's closing argument numerous times. Almost every time the defense objected, whether the court sustained or overruled the objection, plaintiff's counsel argued with even more passion and accused the defense of trying to prevent plaintiff's counsel from sharing evidence: "They don't want me to get it out. I'm going to get it out."

CONCLUSION

Plaintiff's counsel's arguments not only fueled juror anger but also provided graphic narratives for the jury to reference in deliberations in support of an astronomical jury award. Counsel used common techniques to argue pain and suffering, including arguing each Element of Damages under the jury instruction; breaking down future Minutes/Hours/Days; and driving the fear of Future Inflation.

How could the defense have defused juror anger in this admitted liability case? How could the defense have secured a more reasonable jury verdict? Was the jury always going to "split the baby" between each party's suggested damages number? In this admitted liability case, was there any way to educate and empower the jury to fully compensate the plaintiff with a number that was also fair for the defendant? While plaintiff's counsel, one of the best in the country, delivered compelling arguments to drive this Nuclear Verdict, we believe defense strategies exist that could have helped mitigate the award while ensuring justice was served—for all.

EPILOGUE: NO APPEAL

Our research did not reveal any appeals on this case after the verdict. It is possible the parties entered into a High/Low Agreement, a type of settlement agreement that guarantees a minimum amount damages a plaintiff will recover and sets a damages cap to protect the defense, prior to trial. High/Low Agreements often waive any right to an appeal by either party.

CHAPTER 14

EMBRACE THE DISCOMFORT: *ARGUE PAIN AND SUFFERING*

"To enjoy bodily warmth, some small part of you must be cold, for there is no quality in this world that is not what it is merely by contrast. Nothing exists in itself."
—Herman Melville, *Moby Dick*

THE GREAT UNKNOWABLE: PAIN AND SUFFERING

OUR PARTNER, ED LEONARD, SAYS this of pain and suffering: "No one on earth is guaranteed a pain-free life." Ed is right, and so is Mr. Melville. A full life brings both the ecstatic highs of love, newness, connection, and beauty, and the crushing lows of loss, grief, disappointment, regret, pain, and loneliness. No one is promised a life free of these things, for these things *are* life. The human experience is layered, complex, and emotionally exhaustive. The richness of joy exists *because* of the contrast of suffering.

But what happens when pain, suffering, loss, and grief are thrust upon you? What light can be found at the end of a tunnel you never signed up to enter? Where does "fair" even begin to enter the equation when discussing the loss of a life? The erasure of a future? And how deeply *unfair* is it to jurors to expose them to the most upsetting stories of human pain, ask them to live in and with those stories, and then mandate that they deliver closure in the form of a verdict, all free of emotion and without any meaningful guidance?

The Role of Pain and Suffering Damages in Nuclear Verdicts

Our civil justice system does its best to determine and award what is fair. It is the best attempt at addressing, in a measurable way, the woes of the human condition. We make our way to the courthouse steps to seek recompense for harms we have suffered—harms that run afoul of what is acceptable. We air our grievances through a set of norms, rules, and standards. Through trial, we empanel a jury that is representative of our community to find the truth, weigh the facts, follow the law, and administer justice.

Our jurors are offered limited guidance through the convoluted jury instructions they receive. Their decisions are guided as much, if not more, by their own moral compass and life experience than by the law. And they are tasked with answering the unknowable: what is another human's pain and suffering worth?

Pain and suffering, otherwise known as "general" or "noneconomic" damages, or as plaintiffs' lawyers call them, "human" losses, comprise the biggest category of damages in Nuclear Verdicts. Plaintiffs' attorneys know this is where they make their money. This is the part of the case where a jury cannot get guidance from an invoice or a receipt. This is the part of trial we cannot see or touch—physical pain, mental suffering, and emotional distress.

Jurors calculate the incalculable through this category of damages as they assess pain, suffering, loss of companionship, humiliation, mental anguish, emotional distress, loss of enjoyment of life, inconvenience, disfigurement, and anxiety. It is right they do this; humans are more than the sum of their economic parts, after all. A person's life is more than their medical bills, their income, their property, or the cost of their funeral. But how do we expect jurors to arrive at a "reasonable" evaluation of these abstract concepts, especially if we cannot do it ourselves?

The jury instructions offer little help. For example, the California Civil Jury Instructions provide, "No fixed standard exists for deciding the amount of these noneconomic damages. You must use your judgment to decide a reasonable amount based on the evidence and your common sense."[40] States across the country vary in how much guidance they offer, but jury instructions uniformly do *not* offer a formula for assessing this kind of harm. And this is where the plaintiffs' bar's creativity comes to life.

After (1) angering a jury as early as jury selection, (2) asking the jury to award a large verdict as early as jury selection, (3) and fueling juror anger the entire trial, the angry jury arrives at closing arguments. Through creative and compelling storytelling, the plaintiffs' bar creates a narrative to support why their outrageous request is fair, reasonable, and warranted by the end of trial. As they deliberate, angry jurors use this amorphous category of noneconomic damages to "send a message" through an astronomical jury award. Even though punitive damages are often unavailable in these cases, plaintiffs' counsel fashion their arguments for pain and suffering damages as a way to punish the defendant. Angry jurors agree with them.

As discussed in Chapter 1, *Reptile* and other plaintiffs' tactics lead the jury to believe that a large dollar award, especially for noneconomic damages, will decrease the likelihood that this kind of accident or incident will happen again. Juries believe a large dollar award will force a defendant, especially a corporate defendant, to change policies, procedures, and behaviors.

In response to the incredibly creative arguments presented by plaintiffs' counsel, most defense attorneys do not argue pain and suffering on behalf of the defense in closing argument. You read that right. **In the majority of Nuclear Verdicts, the defense is silent on the largest damages component of the final jury verdict.** How can we possibly feign surprise at an unreasonable result when plaintiffs' lawyers are so adept at marinating jurors in an emotionally manipulative stew for weeks and months, and the defense *says absolutely nothing about it*? *Of course* noneconomic damages are disproportionate!

40 Judicial Council of California Advisory Committee on Civil Jury Instructions, *Judicial Council of California Civil Jury Instructions: CACI*, Cal. Cts.: Jud. Branch of Cal. 873 (2024), https://courts.ca.gov/system/files/file/judicial_council_of_california_civil_jury_instructions_2025.pdf (on file with the Apex Defense Consulting library).

Five Truths of Noneconomic Damages

1. Noneconomic damages represent the most emotional losses present in the case.
2. Noneconomic damages are the most nebulous and abstract questions a jury will face.
3. The law specifically instructs jurors there is no fixed standard or formula for calculating noneconomic damages.
4. Noneconomic damages offer the jury a chance to restore control.
5. Humans have difficulty exercising reasoned judgment in the face of overwhelming emotion.

The plaintiffs' bar figured out these five truths and adapted their approach accordingly. The defense, however, is an ostrich. Ostriches do not actually bury their heads in the sand, contrary to the popular myth. Far worse for our analogy (and somehow more accurate): ostriches flop to the ground, attempt to camouflage into their surroundings, stay perfectly still, and try to wait out the danger. The problem? The typical defense approach to merely flop and hide does not protect our clients from a Nuclear Verdict.

Taking our safari analogy a little further, The Apex specifically calls the defense to address the elephant in the room. It calls the defense to genuinely, proactively, methodically, and *empathetically Argue Pain and Suffering*. Pain and suffering damages are the biggest damages component of Nuclear Verdicts and the one requiring the least connection to fact, law, or common sense. We must have a game plan. The Apex provides a winning one.

The Human Avoidance of Pain and Empathy

Thorndike's Law of Effect posits that behaviors followed by pleasurable or positive experiences are more likely to be repeated than behaviors followed by unpleasant or negative experiences.[41] This makes sense but may be rooted more in neuroscience than we might expect. Recent studies have

41 Kendra Cherry, *The Law of Effect in Psychology*, VERYWELL MIND (Nov. 6, 2023), https://www.verywellmind.com/what-is-the-law-of-effect-2795331 (on file with the Apex Defense Consulting library).

revealed that neurons at work in the brain (in the ventral pallidum region, to be exact) control behavior intended both to seek rewards/pleasure and avoid punishment/pain.[42] Put more simply: we do not like pain, and we are wired to actively try to avoid it.

The same is true of another's pain. While empathy is considered to be a virtue, it has also recently been revealed as a choice—one that most would rather avoid.[43] Dr. Brené Brown wrote, "Empathy is a choice. And it's a vulnerable choice, because if I were to connect with you through empathy, I would have to connect with something in myself that knows that feeling."[44]

As we have discussed, humans usually do not seek out vulnerability. Empathy may, therefore, be the penultimate feeling to avoid: it is the marriage of pain and vulnerability. And while studies have examined whether, and to what extent, humans will avoid pain or empathy, no study we could find directly addresses how *jurors*, who cannot escape from emotionally painful stimuli, process it.

The Human Desire for Closure

Taylor Swift writes in her aptly-titled song, "How Did It End?," "We must know / How did it end?" It is not just a good song; it is a psychological truth. Psychologists have identified the "need for cognitive closure," noting "…closure affords predictability and a base for action" and "closure may serve as a means of escaping an unpleasant…activity."[45] There exists a spectrum of

42 Marcus Stephenson-Jones, Christian Bravo-Rivera, Sandra Ahrens, Alessandro Furlan, Xiong Xiao, Carolina Fernandes-Henriques & Bo Li, *Opposing contributions of GABAergic and glutamatergic ventral pallidal neurons to motivational behaviors*, 105 Neuron 921 (2020), https://pmc.ncbi.nlm.nih.gov/articles/PMC8573387/pdf/nihms-1546280.pdf (on file with the Apex Defense Consulting library).

43 C. Daryl Cameron, Cendri A. Hutcherson, Amanda M. Ferguson, Julian A. Scheffer, Eliana Hadjiandreou & Michael Inzlicht, *Empathy is Hard Work: People Choose to Avoid Empathy Because of Its Cognitive Costs*, 148 J. Exp. Psych. 962 (2019), https://psycnet.apa.org/manuscript/2019-20830-001.pdf (on file with the Apex Defense Consulting library).

44 Brené Brown, Dare to Lead: Brave Work. Tough Conversations. Whole Hearts. 142 (2018).

45 Donna M. Webster & Arie W. Kruglanski, *Individual Differences in Need for Cognitive Closure*, 67 J. Pers. & Soc. Psych. 1049, 1049 (1994), http://www.communicationcache.com/uploads/1/0/8/8/10887248/individual_differences_in_need_for_cognitive_closure.pdf (on file with the Apex Defense Consulting library).

need for closure, with some individuals having a higher need for closure, and others evincing a lower need. But what is most interesting for our purposes is that when humans are faced with a time pressure or an unpleasant experience, the innate need for closure increases and appears to result in a tendency to rely on primacy effects, to render stereotypically-driven judgments, and to anchor judgments on initial estimates (even when those estimates are irrelevant or flawed).[46]

Put more simply: people like closure, are highly motivated toward closure when faced with unpleasant activities or time-sensitive tasks and are more likely to default to early impressions or anchors when those conditions are met. Our jurors, confronted with the unpleasant experience of living another's pain, the time pressure associated with jury duty, and the natural desire for closure, are easy targets for plaintiffs' lawyers, who tap into anchoring and other bias schemas to manipulate jurors from the first minute they enter the jury box.

Add this to jurors' general lack of familiarity with the law or legal proceedings, their unfamiliarity with the case (its facts, parties, context, or backstory), the fact they are assigned a weighty responsibility in assessing liability and damages (impacting both the plaintiff and the defendant, as well as untold others), and a shocking lack of guidance from jury instructions, and jurors are primed for confusion at best and manipulation at worst.

Jurors Genuinely Want to Do What is Right, But Have Difficulty Assessing What "Right" Is

We believe most jurors genuinely want to do the right thing. They may not have willingly signed up for jury duty, but once they accept their participation as a reality, we find they pay attention, care, and desire to serve their civic duty with honor. When we speak to jurors after a verdict, we are grateful for their depth of investment in the case and the care they put into deliberations. Some attorneys believe that jurors will assume the role of a

46 *Id.*

"hero" in order to speak up for what is just and right.[47] Perhaps it is the unfailing optimist in us, but we really do have faith in jurors to do what they think is right.

The problem? Jurors do not always know how to assess what is "right," especially when it comes to noneconomic damages. Plaintiffs' attorneys skew jurors' analysis with creative arguments and capitalize on humans' preferences to avoid pain and seek closure.

Plaintiffs' lawyers have, once again, cornered the market on using psychology in trial. They have tapped into psychological principles at play in every decision humans make. The plaintiffs' bar rarely leaves pain and suffering unaddressed. The tactics they employ in their pain and suffering arguments are rooted in psychological concepts designed to capitalize on patterns of decision-making and exploit emotional vulnerability.

THE "BECAUSE" EFFECT CONVEYS LEGITIMACY ON PLAINTIFFS' COUNSEL'S ASK

The "Because" Effect was coined in a 1978 paper that explored the amount of reason behind human decision-making by assessing the impact of being given a reason for a request (even when the reason given was objectively nonsense or conveyed no new information).[48] The experiment involved posing a request to people in line to use a copier. There were three scenarios run in the experiment: in the first scenario, the experimenter approached the line of people and posed a request only ("Excuse me, I have 5 pages. May I use the Xerox machine?"). In the second scenario, the experimenter approached and offered "placebic" information that did not actually convey a reason ("Excuse me, I have 5 pages. May I use the Xerox machine, because I have to make copies?"). And, in the final scenario, the experimenter approached and offered real information that did provide a reason ("Excuse me, I have

47 Carl Bettinger, Twelve Heroes, One Voice: Guiding Jurors to Courageous Verdicts (2011).

48 Ellen Langer, Arthur Blank & Benzion Chanowitz, *The Mindlessness of Ostensibly Thoughtful Action: The Role of "Placebic" Information in Interpersonal Interaction*, 36 J. Pers. & Soc. Psych. 635 (1978), https://jamesclear.com/wp-content/uploads/2015/03/copy-machine-study-ellen-langer.pdf (on file with the Apex Defense Consulting library).

5 pages. May I use the Xerox machine, because I'm in a rush?"). The experiment then measured the compliance rates in all three scenarios and revealed significantly higher compliance rates for the second two scenarios than for the first, but virtually no difference between the second and third scenario. So, giving *any* reason (even one that reveals no new or helpful information) results in higher compliance rates.

How does this apply in a jury trial? Plaintiffs' lawyers ask for big numbers because that is the best way to get a Nuclear Verdict, as we discussed in Chapter 11. Plaintiffs' attorneys' most common arguments about pain and suffering, laid out in Appendix A, offer a "reason" to support the astronomical ask, even though the "reason" often has nothing to do with the case or plaintiff, does not convey any actual information, and was never admitted as evidence.

The Fighter Jet[49] argument is a prime example of this, as is the Minutes/Hours/Days argument, that purports to provide jurors a formula to support a massive verdict, even though the dollar figures assigned to the formula are just as arbitrary as the ask itself (and in direct contradiction with the law, which affirmatively states there is *no* formula!). Jurors are persuaded into believing a high noneconomic damages award serves what is "right" *because* there appears to be a rationale behind it. Unfortunately, what jurors do not realize is that the rationale is created to justify the ask, not the other way around.

FALSE ANALOGIES CAPITALIZE ON EMOTION TO DRIVE OUTSIZED AWARDS

Another tool deployed by plaintiffs' lawyers is the false analogy fallacy, where an argument is made that identifies similar traits or characteristics between two or more things in order to support an invalid conclusion that the items must be alike in other ways.[50] This fallacy is ripe for use in circumstances involving unknown facts, or conditions that require extrapolation or

49 *See* Appendix A (providing a more in-depth discussion on the Fighter Jet arugment).

50 NJ Lechnir, *How to Spot the False Analogy Fallacy for Better Thinking and Mental Health*, MEDIUM (Sep. 13, 2023), https://medium.com/@njlechnir/how-to-spot-the-false-analogy-fallacy-for-better-thinking-and-mental-health-333496e39e6c (on file with the Apex Defense Consulting library).

conjecture. It provides a path to understand or guess at what is not seen, by drawing comparisons between that which *is* seen.

The way this shows up in noneconomic damages arguments is often in some version of the *Mona Lisa* version of the Inanimate Objects argument. Using this argument, plaintiffs' lawyer will say something like this:

> The *Mona Lisa* is valued at something like $870 million. It is one of the most important works of art on the planet, painted by Leonardo da Vinci on poplar plank between 1503 and 1506. Her smile has inspired mankind for generations, and we treasure her. She hangs behind bulletproof glass in the Louvre, in Paris, protected by security guards and cameras at every angle. But if the Louvre was on fire, it would be a security guard's job to run toward the burning building, rather than away. It would be his job to save the *Mona Lisa*, because that is how much we value it. But if, when he got into the museum, he discovered a little girl crouched under the *Mona Lisa*, he would have a choice to make. Does he save the *Mona Lisa*, or does he save the little girl? We know the choice we would want him to make; we would want him to save the little girl. Because human life is worth more than even the most valuable piece of art on the planet. That little girl, her hopes, her dreams, her fears, her future—worth more than $870 million. And so, too, is my client.

The plaintiffs' lawyer just analogized his client to both this precious, vulnerable (fictional!) little girl *and* an $870 million painting! Not bad for a three-minute argument. Not only does it invite jurors to reach a conclusion that $870 million is reasonable or supported by the evidence, but it is emotionally compelling! How does the defense come back from *that*? Two words: The Apex.

The Apex: How the Defense Frees the Jury and Delivers Justice Through Reasonable Pain and Suffering Damages

"Receive what cheer you may. The night is long that never finds the day."
– William Shakespeare, *Macbeth*

Our study of 100 Nuclear Verdicts confirmed what we have seen in our trial practice: plaintiffs' attorneys craft and deliver compelling, creative arguments to persuade jurors to award large dollar awards for pain and suffering in almost every Nuclear Verdict. The stories they tell are almost always tragedies: heartrending loss, darkness, misery. They tell stories that follow a predictable pattern that cultivates anger and invites blame. They *have* to tell a story of pain and suffering if they want to maximize their paycheck.

Our analysis also confirms what we see time and time again: defense attorneys typically do not *Argue Pain and Suffering*. This is unfortunate for many reasons, but especially because the defense has a more compelling story than plaintiffs' counsel when it comes to pain and suffering. Jurors love our story because it genuinely acknowledges pain, validates from a place of empathy, delivers closure, and provides guidance on how to do the right thing. It works because humans love good news.

The Apex provides **two essential elements** to effectively *Argue Pain and Suffering*. Defense counsel must discuss with the jury:

1. **The impact of the accident on plaintiff's life; and**
2. **The impact of money on plaintiff's life.**

This approach to arguing pain and suffering through storytelling gives the jury exactly what it needs to come to a fair award. The Apex taps into the psychological truths outlined above. It empathetically frames the amorphous element of damages so jurors can fairly assess plaintiff's pain and find closure in their deliberations. This method guides the jury to assess what is fair and reasonable (what the law requires!) when it comes to damages by tapping into the "because" effect and providing a real, applicable analogy for the jury.

The Apex requires the defense team to truly get to know plaintiff and gather the evidence to support our defense number and pain and suffering arguments at trial. We must ask thoughtful, creative, and perhaps difficult or uncomfortable questions in discovery. As much as our brains are wired to avoid pain, we cannot look away when plaintiff claims he has suffered pain. We must be vulnerable enough and brave enough to get into the pain with plaintiff, especially in deposition, to understand what it is really like to have his experience. Then, with the right evidence, we will be prepared to *Argue Pain and Suffering* if the case must be tried.

The *Argue Pain and Suffering* element of the Core Four provides the foundation for the jury to assess what could be the most significant component of the final verdict. The jury's determination of a pain and suffering award often determines whether the case results in a Nuclear Verdict. The Apex equips the jury with the tools to do the right thing by both parties, not just plaintiff and his attorneys. Jurors leave jury duty having agreed with The Apex framework, knowing that they have helped plaintiff, and feeling good about fulfilling their civic duty.

THE IMPACT OF THE ACCIDENT ON PLAINTIFF'S LIFE

The first element of the defense's pain and suffering argument must address the impact of the accident (or incident) on plaintiff's life. The defense must acknowledge, in a genuine and empathetic way, that the incident at the core of the case has had an impact on the plaintiff. We would not be here if it did not! This, again, validates plaintiff's experience and works to defuse juror anger.

The defense must then go further to find and share the good news in the case. What is plaintiff's life really like after the accident? This is not an opportunity for a "gotcha" moment. This is not about "catching" plaintiff in a lie. This is not an argument the defense gathers through *sub rosa* (or surveillance) investigation. Rarely does an investigator lurking in the bushes capture surveillance footage that is as impactful as the defense hopes.

This is about getting to know this plaintiff, as a human, and sharing the many things he *can* do. Every person deserves joy! The plaintiff deserves fun, fulfillment, passion, independence, and hope. This is what we want for plaintiff. Plaintiff's reality after the accident is usually much closer to his reality before the accident than his attorney would have the jury believe.

Our closing argument should be centered on hope. Even in the most catastrophic cases, the defense team must develop a way to talk about the loss that highlights the good and injects hope in plaintiff's life while empathetically acknowledging the hard. Where is the day that follows the night? Importantly, draw upon the foundation of The Apex: *Be a Good Human*. This means we cannot gloss over true loss or sticker rainbows over tragedy. We cannot inject toxic positivity and walk away. *Be a Good Human* is always step one.

Examine in discovery what plaintiff loves to do and what causes him pain, stress, and anxiety. What are his passions? What does he do for fun? What brings him joy? What was it like to engage in these activities before the accident? Has he engaged in them since the accident and to what extent? If he cannot, what brings him joy after the accident? Can he do any aspect of these activities today? Do his doctors predict he will be able to return to these activities in the future, with or without limitations? Has he gotten better at all? Will he? What keeps him up at night? What worries him?

The answers to these questions should give the defense meaningful information to tell the jury a vivid, accurate story of what plaintiff's life is really like after the accident. This also allows the defense to acknowledge with the jury the impact of the accident on plaintiff's life. We must acknowledge plaintiff's pain and suffering before (and while) redirecting the jury's focus toward hope and the good news.

THE IMPACT OF MONEY ON PLAINTIFF'S LIFE

The second element of the defense's pain and suffering argument must discuss the impact of money on plaintiff's life. Specifically, defense counsel must show the jury how the defense's number for pain and suffering will have a meaningful impact on this plaintiff. This is where we show our work: we have cared enough to get to know *this specific plaintiff*, and our number is directly applicable to *his life*.

This element carries the added benefit of reminding the jury the actual value of a dollar! As detailed in Appendix A, plaintiffs' counsel often talk to the jury about hypothetical briefcases full of money, irrelevant celebrity or famous athlete salaries, and speculative values of famous works of art in closing argument. Jurors often have a hard time remembering what real things actually cost.

To bring the jury back down to earth, we must discuss the value of money to plaintiff specifically. We should support our defense number by providing the jury the context of how much money plaintiff makes in a year. We should also contextualize our defense number by examining the costs of plaintiff's passions compared to the defense's requested pain and suffering number.

To argue the impact of money on plaintiff's life, The Apex requires us to explore the value of money to plaintiff in discovery. Again, we must ask specific, potentially uncomfortable questions in discovery to develop relevant evidence to introduce at trial on this issue. We must discuss money with plaintiff in deposition, even if he is not making a wage loss claim. Is plaintiff working? How much money does plaintiff make a year? Does plaintiff own his own home? If not, how much does he owe on his mortgage? Does plaintiff have student loans? Is he saving for his kids' college education? Does anything worry plaintiff about money?

When the defense sponsors a reasonable damages number, as discussed in Chapter 11, and introduces evidence about plaintiff's financial situation at trial, this element of The Apex approach to pain and suffering highlights how the defense number is significant to plaintiff and reasonable to the jury. The Apex method for arguing pain and suffering shows jurors that it does not take an award of generational wealth to have a meaningful impact on plaintiff. Giving the jury the context of the value of money to plaintiff shows how our damages number, a number much less than plaintiffs' counsel's number, is going to have a meaningful impact on plaintiff's life. After all, plaintiff's life matters here—not the *Mona Lisa* paraded through plaintiff's counsel's closing.

This aspect of The Apex approach to pain and suffering is the most difficult for the defense to craft and feel comfortable delivering. But when executed with genuine empathy, this argument allows jurors to see, if they find liability, they are doing the right thing and helping plaintiff by awarding the defense number in the case. This element of The Apex gives power, credibility, humanity, and reasoning to the defense's sponsored number. The Apex strategy for arguing pain and suffering restores reason and relevance to the assessment of pain and suffering while freeing jurors from manipulation and empowering them to do what is right.

UNITE THE ELEMENTS IN A STORY FOR THE JURY

"Happiness is not in the mere possession of money; it lies in the joy of achievement, in the thrill of creative effort."
—Franklin D. Roosevelt

After the defense has discussed for the jury the impact of the accident on plaintiff's life, including sharing the good news about what plaintiff's life is really like after the accident and discussing the impact of money on plaintiff's life by talking about value of money to plaintiff, it is time for the defense to craft and deliver a compelling argument about how our defense number is going to make plaintiff whole. We must argue that our number is fair and reasonable and will make a meaningful difference in plaintiff's life because it will bring joy and restore hope. When possible, our argument should tell a story about how we are bringing plaintiff's passions back to his life or allowing him to live out his passions with greater ease with our sponsored damages number.

Bob provided in-depth examples of tying these concepts together in *Nuclear Verdicts*. For ease of reference, we provide only a few examples here. If plaintiff lies awake at night wondering how he will be able to pay off his $75,000 in student loans if his second surgery is unsuccessful and he is unable to go back to work, explain how an award of $250,000 for pain and suffering pays off plaintiff's student loans to ease his anxiety and still leaves money in the bank. If plaintiff has small children and enjoys getting the family together for a trip to Disneyland, explain to the jury how many trips to Disneyland our pain and suffering number can provide. An award of $250,000 for pain and suffering covers a trip to Disneyland every year until all of plaintiff's children go off to college. If plaintiff has grown children who live all over the country, $250,000 flies the family in to make memories together once a year for the next 25 years.

Any of these examples require defense counsel to ask the difficult questions in discovery, evaluate the loss plaintiff sustained, and get creative about how to bring more joy and hope into plaintiff's life. These examples achieve this. These are not false analogies like those provided by plaintiffs' counsel. All these arguments are "fair and reasonable," because they are tied to the loss *this* plaintiff sustained and what will meaningfully make this plaintiff whole.

False Barriers to Arguing Pain and Suffering

The Apex calls us to *Argue Pain and Suffering* in every single case, even when we are seeking a defense verdict. Defense teams cite many reasons why they cannot or should not *Argue Pain and Suffering*. We discuss the primary two reasons below.

"I WANT A DEFENSE VERDICT"

The primary reason we hear defense counsel decline to *Argue Pain and Suffering* mirrors the false barriers to *Accept Responsibility* and *Give a Number*: "I cannot argue pain and suffering because I am asking the jury to award a defense verdict. The jury will never get to noneconomic damages when they deliberate. To argue it is a waste of time and a sign of weakness." Some defense teams believe that arguing pain and suffering undercuts our arguments against liability.

Look up at the apex: How is *not* arguing pain and suffering going to validate plaintiff and defuse juror anger?

We are in the business of mitigating risk. If we lose on liability and the jury decides we owe damages to the plaintiff, what benefit are we serving our client if we do not argue damages? What is going to happen if the jury decides to award damages, and they have only heard one framework for awarding pain and suffering at trial? What if that one narrative is about billion-dollar fighter jets and rare paintings worth hundreds of millions of dollars? Is that jury going to come back with a reasonable verdict?

Fortunately, our analysis of 100 Nuclear Verdicts provides the answer to these questions. When the defense declines to *Argue Pain and Suffering* in closing argument, the jury awards an even higher verdict than when the defense chooses to speak to this element of damages.

We *Argue Pain and Suffering* in every trial at Tyson & Mendes, and we get defense verdicts all the time. Why? We believe it comes down to reasonableness. Our theory on this is similar to our theory on why a defendant is more likely to get a defense verdict if they *Give a Number* than if they do not, as discussed in Chapter 11. We believe presenting a reasonable argument for pain and suffering, an argument that is tied to *this plaintiff's* experience and life, is more credible than the false analogy arguments presented by plaintiffs' counsel. Presenting a reasonable argument in this area increases our credibility with the jury in others, including our liability arguments.

Thus, even when seeking a defense verdict, The Apex mandates the defense always *Argue Pain and Suffering* to the jury.

"THERE IS NO GOOD NEWS IN THIS CASE"

The second most frequent false barrier to arguing pain and suffering we hear from defense teams sounds something like, "I cannot argue pain and suffering because this case is too catastrophic. There is no good news in this case." We hear you. We have been there.

The truth is that many "large loss" cases settle. Settlement is likely the best outcome for the plaintiffs who have experienced catastrophic loss of some kind; these plaintiffs are "spared" the experience of a jury trial and defendants are "spared" the risk of a Nuclear Verdict. Some cases, unfortunately, proceed to trial. In most of these cases, we find the defense either does not *Argue Pain and Suffering* or does not present a reasonable, compelling argument.

In the most tragic of cases, it is incredibly difficult to address the pain and suffering of those who have suffered the unimaginable: a father's life taken too early, a mother who has lost all use of her arms and legs, or a child who has suffered unthinkable abuse at the hand of a trusted adult. Again, we cannot look away from plaintiff's pain and suffering, especially in the most catastrophic of cases. The jury is forced to look at it. So must we, and we must handle it as the good humans we are.

When we really look at the toughest cases, it is rare to find zero good or happiness in a plaintiff's life post-accident. For example, in a quadriplegic or paraplegic case, sometimes the family grows closer together through the tragedy. If so, highlight it for the jury. Do not overstate the joy. Do not sticker rainbows over the tragedy. Simply acknowledge the truth. Acknowledge any joy, any good news, if it exists.

If no good news exists for the plaintiff today, we must create it for them. The Apex calls us to give the plaintiff hope. As we discuss in Chapter 2, *Be a Good Human*, we must dig for hope if it is not readily found. Is there any existing or emerging medical technology that could improve plaintiff's life? Research it. Find it. Hire the experts. Include the cost in the defense life-care plan. Give plaintiff and the jury hope in your plan for his future.

In a wrongful death case, do not shy away from the family's grief. It is real, it is deep, and it must be honored. Ask the toughest questions. What do they miss most about their loved one? How did they used to spend time together? How do they honor their loved one today? Include a portion of your defense damages number for noneconomic damages to support the memory of the decedent. Hire a grief counselor for the plaintiffs and include the cost for ongoing grief counseling in your defense number at trial. Give plaintiffs hope that they can move on and be happy again.

In a sexual assault and molestation case, what therapy or counseling does plaintiff need to address the trauma and heal as they mature? Hire the experts. What activities does plaintiff do that brings him joy? Include the costs of these activities in our defense number. Go above and beyond to pour into the plaintiff. Give the plaintiff hope for a full and fulfilled future as part of our pain and suffering plan.

Acknowledge the truth of the pain and suffering. Create, find, and deliver hope to the plaintiff. That is the calling of The Apex.

CASE STUDY OVERVIEW: *ARGUE PAIN AND SUFFERING*

Our study of 100 Nuclear Verdicts confirmed three things: (1) noneconomic damages are the biggest component of outsized awards, but (2) the defense rarely argues them. And, (3) when the defense chooses to address noneconomic damages, verdicts tend to be lower. We also saw that plaintiffs' lawyers essentially "copy + paste" each other's arguments. We tracked the most common plaintiff arguments for pain and suffering and analyzed their impact on final result. Keep reading for some good news (the theme of this chapter!).

Methodology

As with all our data categories, we standardized across all 100 cases as much as possible to ensure consistency and clarity of results. Specifically, we tracked whether the defense advanced *any* argument about noneconomic damages. If the defense addressed it at all in their closing arguments (even if they did not touch on either of the two elements The Apex mandates), we counted it as an application of The Apex. This was a little painful for us, we must be honest.

Any good trial lawyer will tell you that merely reading jury instructions is not argument, and it certainly is not advocacy. However, for the sake of consistency, we counted *any* reference to noneconomic damages by the defense as an "argument." We also tracked whether the defense applied any aspect of The Apex by addressing the impact of the accident and the impact of money on plaintiff's life. We considered no mention of noneconomic damages an omission of The Apex. In addition, we tracked how plaintiffs' lawyers argued pain and suffering. We identified six frequent arguments, tracked how often each was used, and measured their impact on overall verdicts.

Hypotheses

We had four hypotheses related to pain and suffering arguments. First, we hypothesized that in most Nuclear Verdicts the defense does not argue or mention pain and suffering in closing argument in any way. Second, we hypothesized that if the defense addresses pain and suffering in these cases, the arguments are typically limited to referencing the relevant jury instruction, such as simply stating the noneconomic damages must be fair and reasonable. Third, we hypothesized the defense rarely uses The Apex by arguing both elements of pain and suffering in Nuclear Verdicts. Fourth, we hypothesized that plaintiffs routinely advance creative and compelling pain and suffering arguments.

Results

Our case study supported all four hypotheses. We found the defense rarely addressed pain and suffering in any way and some form of "fair and reasonable" is the most common argument used by the defense. In only two cases did the defense argue both Apex elements of pain and suffering. As we all know, our analysis confirmed that plaintiffs' counsel routinely deploys creative noneconomic damages arguments.

CASE STUDY DISCUSSION: THE DEFENSE USUALLY LEAVES THE BIGGEST COMPONENT OF NUCLEAR VERDICTS UNTOUCHED, BUT ADDRESSING IT CARRIES MASSIVE BENEFITS

Our study confirmed that noneconomic damages are, in fact, the biggest damages component of Nuclear Verdicts. In all Nuclear Verdicts analyzed, the economic damage awards tended to be significantly less than the noneconomic damages awards. Punitive damages were only available in 41% of the cases studied, while noneconomic damages were available in all 100 cases analyzed. This highlights, once again, the impact and importance of arguing pain and suffering damages.

Our analysis reveals that defense counsel approach pain and suffering in only four ways when the case results in a Nuclear Verdict: (1) the defense does not address pain and suffering at all; (2) the defense reiterates the law and reminds jurors that any final award must be fair and reasonable; (3)the defense argues impact of accident on plaintiff's life or that plaintiff is not as hurt as plaintiff's counsel claims;[51] and/or, (4) the defense argues the impact of money on plaintiff's life. Our study did not reveal any new methods or approaches to defending against excessive pain and suffering damages. This makes sense, because we strictly examined Nuclear Verdicts.

In Most Nuclear Verdicts, the Defense Does Not Mention Pain and Suffering in Closing Argument

Defense counsel avoids talking about pain and suffering *at all* in most Nuclear Verdicts. **In 69% of Nuclear Verdicts, the defense did not address pain and suffering damages in *any way* in their closing arguments.**

Frequency of Defense Arguing Pain and Suffering

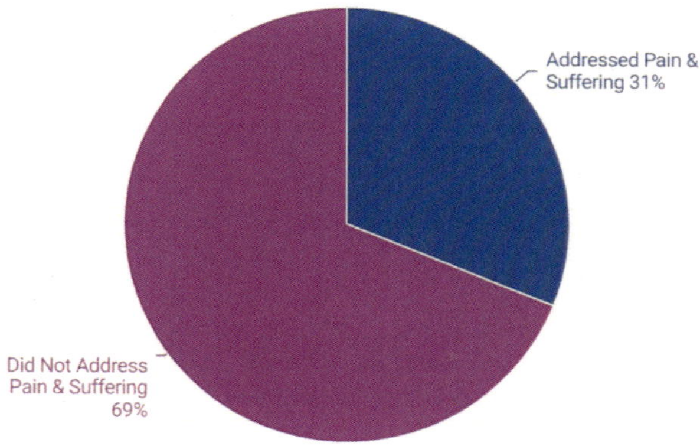

When the defense chose not to even mention pain and suffering in closing argument, the average Nuclear Verdict was 91.3% of plaintiff's counsel's

51 Arguing the plaintiff is not as hurt as they claim would be an improper application of The Apex—the impact of the accident on plaintiff's life. The Apex is not a "gotcha" moment. It is not about calling plaintiff a liar. It is about telling the good news about what plaintiff can do and giving the plaintiff hope.

request. This statistic confirms what we know to be true. If the defense does not provide a framework for the jury to use to analyze pain and suffering, the only narrative the jury will have when it is time to deliberate is the creative narrative and accompanying astronomical verdict request from plaintiffs' counsel. This scenario is ripe for an unjust award.

When Defense Counsel Provides Any Argument, It Helps!

As previously shared in other Parts of this book, where the defense did not use any component of the Core Four, the verdict averaged 148.6% of plaintiff's ask.

Failure to Use Any of the Core Four =
Verdict Almost 50% Higher than Plaintiff's Ask

Defense Approaches to Arguing Pain and Suffering

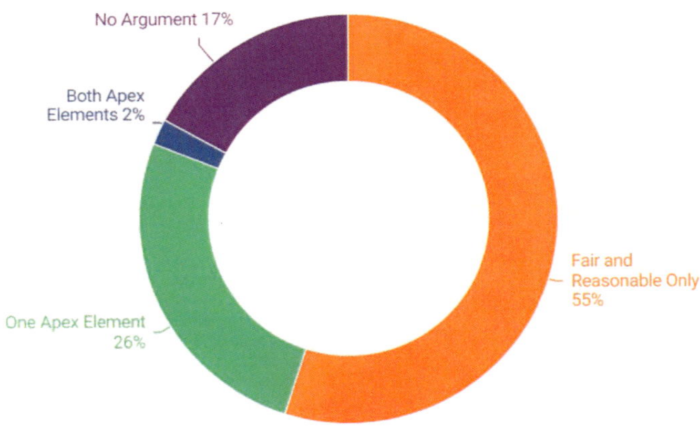

The defense chose to argue pain and suffering in any way in 31% of cases we analyzed. In these cases, the defenses' "argument" over half of the time (55%, to be exact) was merely that the noneconomic damages must be "fair and reasonable," while in 17% of the cases the defense merely said the phrase "noneconomic damages" or "pain and suffering" without any commentary (i.e., argument). **Put another way: the defense routinely disregards the biggest component of Nuclear Verdicts altogether, and when they do address it, they tend to simply read the jury instruction to the jury.**

In the 31% of cases where the defense addressed pain and suffering, the awards tended to be lower. When the defense offered any argument as to pain and suffering, the average verdict was 88% of plaintiff's ask, compared to 91.3% of plaintiff's ask in cases where the defense ignored pain and suffering altogether.

Argue Pain and Suffering in Any Way =
Verdict 12% Less than Plaintiff's Ask

We expected to see a greater difference between these two numbers, but it is worth noting that we did observe a decrease in average verdict compared to plaintiff's ask. And, as you will see below, the *way* defense argues pain and suffering is really where the magic happens.

The Apex Approach to Arguing Pain and Suffering Works, But Is Rarely Used

We also tracked whether the defense argued either or both elements of pain and suffering set out by The Apex and found the defense rarely employs both elements. We found **only two cases—2% of our study**—where the defense argued both impact of the accident and impact of money on plaintiff's life. In those cases, the verdicts averaged 78.7% of plaintiff's ask.

Argue The Apex Pain and Suffering =
Verdict 21.3% Less than Plaintiff's Ask

Impact of Arguing Pain and Suffering on Overall Verdict Size

Verdict Amount as Percentage of Plaintiff's Ask

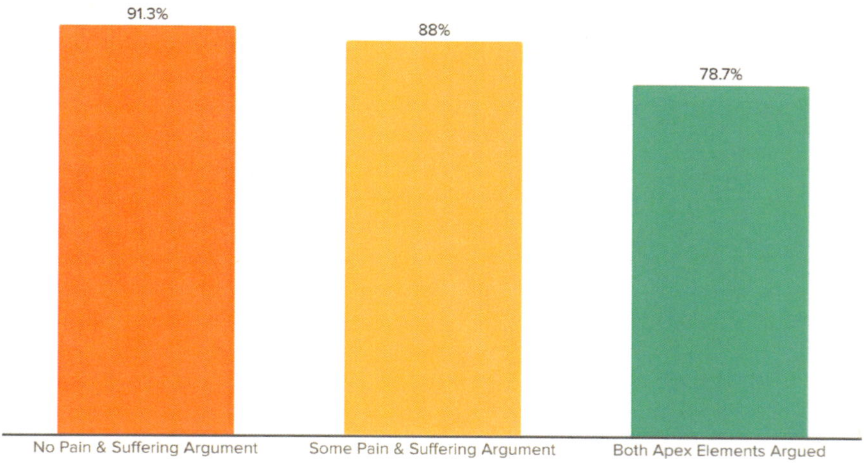

While offering any kind of argument as to pain and suffering is helpful for the defense (resulting in an average verdict 88% of plaintiff's ask), specifically arguing both elements of the Apex drops the average verdict compared to plaintiff's ask even further. While the data reflects the defense arguing both elements of pain and suffering in those two cases, neither defense counsel provided specific examples of what the defense's proffered number could actually *do* for the plaintiff, and instead offered general statements that the suggested number could help plaintiff "do whatever they choose." Again, in zero cases did the defense use all Core Four strategies.

In 26% of all Nuclear Verdicts, the defense engaged only one element of The Apex approach to pain and suffering. We anticipated the most common way to argue pain and suffering (second to simply referencing jury instructions) would be to argue the impact of the accident or incident on plaintiff's life. This tends to be the easiest element of pain and suffering for the defense to broach, because the typical defense approach involves trying to impugn plaintiff's character by arguing they are not as injured or affected as they claim. This is not a true application of this element of The Apex, however. As we noted, the heart of this element for The Apex is *hope*, not *entrapment*. The data bears out that arguing this element alone and in this "gotcha" way is damaging to the defense.

If the defense argued pain and suffering using either of the Apex elements, the defense was substantially more likely to argue impact of the accident or incident than they were to argue impact of money. This was to their detriment. The defense argued impact of the accident or incident but *not* impact of money in 21 cases. And, in those cases, the average verdict was 122% of plaintiff's ask.

This makes sense! If the jury is already angry and the defense then asserts that plaintiff is a liar without offering any humanity, hope, or empathy, the jury is further angered to deliver every penny of plaintiff's ask—and then some. We believe the jury will draw their own conclusions about the plaintiff's credibility without defense counsel attacking it during their pain and suffering arguments. The point of the first element is to share hope for the plaintiff's future well-being and life. It is a fine line that requires finesse in delivery, and we saw this element applied effectively only a handful of times.

And though it was rare, we identified five cases where the defense argued impact of money on plaintiff's life but not impact of the accident/incident on plaintiff's life. What happened there? The average verdict dropped to 72% of plaintiff's ask. As we said previously, money is why everyone is in the courtroom. Talking about its impact is uncomfortable, but it is necessary, and it carries tremendous benefit for the defense.

We noticed the average verdict was lower in these cases than in the two cases where the defense argued both elements of The Apex. The difference between these two scenarios is minimal (72% compared to 78.7%). The takeaway here is that the defense routinely leaves on the table one of its most impactful tools in preventing outsized noneconomic damages: arguing the impact of money. The Apex offers a clear framework for addressing both plaintiff's doom and gloom narrative, and the astronomical numbers they propose. The defense must address both elements.

Plaintiffs Use Manipulative Arguments to Generate Anger and Drive Outsized Pain and Suffering Awards

Our analysis confirmed another truth from our trial practice: plaintiffs' counsel know noneconomic damages are fertile ground for outsized jury awards. This is where plaintiff's counsel make their money. Plaintiff's counsel argued pain and suffering in 64% of cases.

Plaintiff vs Defense Arguing Pain and Suffering

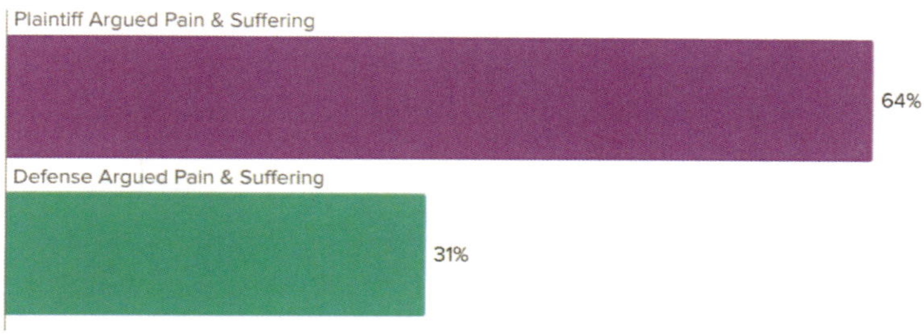

Specifically, plaintiffs' counsel argued noneconomic damages by catastrophizing or graphically describing plaintiff's injuries and advancing creative arguments about pain and suffering (those contained in Appendix A). Just as we suspected, these manipulative arguments are highly effective, particularly in cases where the defense does nothing to address pain and suffering.

In the 36% of cases where plaintiffs' counsel did not argue pain and suffering, the average verdict was 58% of plaintiff's ask. But, where they *did* advance one of these arguments, the average verdict rose to 94.9% of plaintiff's ask.

The most common plaintiff arguments were Elements of Damages (35% of cases) and graphically describing plaintiff's injuries (35% of cases). Despite being regularly used, arguing Elements of Damages was the least effective argument, resulting in an average of only 49.2% of plaintiff's ask. Conversely, the most effective argument for plaintiffs was Famous Athlete Salaries, resulting in an average verdict 132.3% of plaintiff's ask. These results make sense to us and speak to why this type of inflammatory argument has been disallowed in certain states.

The Texas Supreme Court addressed the use of manipulative and misleading noneconomic damages arguments in 2023 in *Gregory v Chohan*.[52] In that case, the court took up plaintiff's counsel's use of a commonly observed pain and suffering argument: using inanimate objects such as an F-18 fighter jet and a famous painting (in that case, a $186 million painting by Mark Rothko). The Texas Court rightfully disallowed these types of arguments, concluding:

> The self-evident purpose of these anchors, however, is to get jurors to think about the appropriate damages award on a magnitude similar to the numbers offered, despite the lack of any rational connection between reasonable compensation and the anchors suggested. *Unsubstantiated anchors like those employed here have nothing to do with the emotional injuries suffered by the plaintiff and cannot rationally connect the extent of the injuries to the amount awarded.*[53]

For all the psychological reasons we have already discussed, conflating entirely irrelevant valuations with a nebulous and emotional question (for example, what is the value of a family's loss?) is plainly manipulative and, in some states, also against the law.

The second most effective argument for plaintiffs was to graphically describe plaintiff's injuries, which resulted in an average of 124.3% of plaintiff's ask when used in conjunction with one or more of the arguments in Appendix A. However, graphically describing plaintiff's injuries as the *only* pain and suffering argument produced the greatest return for plaintiffs: in those cases, the average verdict was 154.8% of plaintiff's ask. Describing another human's suffering in graphic terms obviously produces a visceral reaction, and one that sticks around in the deliberation room.

What happens in cases where plaintiff's counsel uses one or more of these arguments *and* defense says nothing to address pain and suffering? In all cases where plaintiff's counsel argued Elements of Damages, the average verdict was 49.2% of plaintiff's ask (remember, despite being the plaintiffs' bar's

52 Gregory v. Chohan, 670 S.W.3d 546 (Tex.2023).

53 *Id.* at 558 (emphasis added).

favorite way to argue pain and suffering, it is the least effective). However, when plaintiff's counsel advanced that argument *and* defense said nothing, the average verdict rose to 79.3% of plaintiff's ask. Put another way: the most common plaintiff's argument for pain and suffering is only truly effective when the defense does not address pain and suffering at all.

THE DATA-BACKED CONCLUSION: ARGUING PAIN AND SUFFERING IS CRITICAL TO REDUCE DAMAGE AWARDS

The defense should take heart in the conclusion from the research and analysis: **when the defense chooses to address pain and suffering in any way, it has a measurable impact on reducing damages, even in Nuclear Verdicts.** "Pain and suffering" is a nebulous concept and jurors appreciate reasonable arguments that offer guidance for how to address it. Left unchecked by any of the Core Four, verdicts averaged 148.6% of plaintiff's ask. Arguing pain and suffering in any way resulted in a 73.4% decrease in the final verdict.

Our jurors arrive in the deliberation room as the same layered, complex humans they were on the first day of jury duty. They are tasked with heavy concepts and hard decisions, and they are psychologically vulnerable. We must protect them from manipulation, and we must equip them with the tools to know the unknowable. The Apex offers the framework; the defense need only enter the ring.

CHAPTER 15

TIME FOR CLOSURE

BOB'S ALTERNATIVE, APEX CLOSING ARGUMENT

ACCEPT RESPONSIBILITY, AGAIN

AS I HAVE SAID SINCE the first day we met, we are sorry. We wish this had never happened.

This was an accident, a mistake. We own it, and we accept responsibility for it. We are here for you, ladies and gentlemen, to hold us accountable. And how do you do that? You award what's fair and reasonable, nothing more, nothing less.

GIVE A NUMBER, AGAIN

Again, if you believe everything Mr. Raines is claiming in this lawsuit, the total fair and reasonable number for all damages is $3.2 million. Let me share on the screen here the exact breakdown I believe is reasonable damages:

$279,375 in past medical expenses (stipulated)

$474,956 in future medical expenses

$95,729 in past lost wages (stipulated)

$354,185 in future medical expenses

$2,000,000 in pain and suffering

$3,204,245 = TOTAL VERDICT

Let's talk now about noneconomic damages, commonly referred to as "pain and suffering." I know many of you had questions when we were first picking a jury as to how you come up with a number for pain and suffering. I told you a month ago I thought that number was $2,000,000.

But how do you get here?

Well, I believe you look at pain and suffering in two ways. First, what is the impact of the accident on plaintiff's life? And second, what is the impact of money on plaintiff's life?

IMPACT OF THE ACCIDENT ON PLAINTIFF'S LIFE

Let's talk first about the impact of this accident on plaintiff's life. How has his life changed? What things can Mr. Raines not do now that he used to do before this accident?

Mr. Raines' life has changed in many ways. He and his counsel have shared that with you. But in many ways, Mr. Raines' life has not changed very much. For instance, he still regularly uses his computer. This was something he spent a lot of time doing before the accident, and he is doing it now. He also continues to enjoy a lifelong passion of his—playing video games. He plays video games with his friends regularly.

Mr. Raines can still use a telephone, he can walk, he can drive himself, and he is as sharp and articulate as ever. And you know what else? He is just as driven and committed as ever. How do I know this? Because he has not given up on his biggest passion, painting.

No, Mr. Raines cannot paint like he used to with his right hand, not yet. But he hasn't given up either. He started drawing with his left hand, and now he is painting lefty. He has even set up an art studio, where he continues to express himself and follow his passion.

What about him personally? How has his life changed? Well, there is some good news. His relationship with his family has actually improved. Mr. Raines is closer than ever with his mother. He is still in very close contact with his friends from high school. Mr. Raines even has a girlfriend now. He is able to spend quality time with his dearest friends and family members. This is super-important for Mr. Raines, especially after all he has been through.

What does his future look like? Well, let's look to his doctors. No doctor has ever told Mr. Raines or any of us that he is unable to work again. Mr. Raines is not permanently disabled. This is great news! You want to know why? Because I think we have all seen the incredible things Mr. Raines has been able to do in his life when he has put his mind to it.

You saw how well he did in school. He told you how hard he worked, how he would pull all-nighters studying. He is a strong man, and I believe in him, much like you do. His life has gotten harder, but he has overcome challenges in the past. And now, with the support of his family, his girlfriend, and his close friends, I believe he will again overcome this challenge, too. $2,000,000 helps him do that.

IMPACT OF MONEY ON PLAINTIFF'S LIFE

We take the plaintiff as we find him. This is what plaintiff's counsel has been talking about. How do we find him? You have to look at the value of money to Mr. Raines. Attorneys who do this kind of work will often look to the plaintiff's lifestyle to get a feel for the value of money to the plaintiff. So let's look to Mr. Raines' life. What does he like to do? What does he enjoy, and let's see if we can give him some of that back.

We know Mr. Raines likes to use his computer. He is very good at computers. Well, $2,000,000 is a lot of computers.

What about painting? You have heard this is a passion of his. You know he is a fighter and will never stop painting. He wants to do this, and he will do this. You heard him testify about an etch drawing he did in the style of a Gustave Dore—a mythological representation of Heracles defeating the giant snake monster. It's Heracles overcoming adversity. This is Mr. Raines. He is this warrior.

How can we help Mr. Raines? $2,000,000 gives this fighter the tools, supplies, and space to try new mediums and to follow his passion. Obviously, $2,000,000 is more art supplies and computer equipment than any one person could ever buy in a lifetime.

What else could we do to address Mr. Raines' very real pain and suffering? We know he liked to go camping with friends and family. It is more difficult now, but a friend testified during this trial about the cost of highly technical, lightweight equipment that would make it easier for Mr. Raines. But for $2,000,000, he could obviously afford to rent cabins for him and his friends, multiple times a year, every year, for the rest of his life.

What else have we learned about Mr. Raines over the last month? We know he really enjoys video games. $2,000,000 is a lot of video games. It also pays for trips every year for Mr. Raines and his friends to go to video game conventions. At $10,000 a trip for hotels, airfare, and the conventions for him and his friends, he could make two trips a year, $20,000, for the next 100 years with $2,000,000.

Speaking of trips, Mr. Raines enjoyed watching boxing with his father. $2,000,000 pays for a lot of trips to Las Vegas to see the biggest boxing matches every year with his dad.

He also enjoyed working out. As Mr. Raines grows stronger, if he chooses, he could easily buy gym memberships and home gym equipment if he wanted.

All these things are intended to try to give back Mr. Raines some of the joy he has lost because of this accident. Yes, it takes all of us trying to get to know Mr. Raines; what were his passions, and how can we help him now?

We all know $2,000,000 can buy all the things we just discussed. So maybe a better way to look at this is, what could happen if Mr. Raines invested $2,000,000? If he invested it in the stock market, the historical returns are 7 or 8%. If you put it in a savings account, it is more like 1 or 2%. So let's say 5%. If Mr. Raines were to take the $2,000,000 and get 5% a year, he would earn **$100,000** each year. $100,000 to spend on all the things we just discussed. To follow his passions and to be near his family and friends when he needs them the most.

Let me also say that before this accident, we know Mr. Raines was making about $60,000 a year, right? $100,000 is more than he was making before this accident. $100,000 a year is more than most Americans make in a year. It is real money. It is real money to most Americans, and it is real money to Mr. Raines.

He can travel the world and study art. Or go back to school and get a Master's degree if he likes. He could start an art school for kids; you heard how he loved substitute teaching. Or he could become an art broker or open a gallery of his own.

$100,000 every year is real money. It enables Mr. Raines to do all the things he cares about. But you know what else it does? It allows him to keep $2,000,000 in his pocket the whole time. A nest egg. So if he is ever worried or stressed about financial issues, he has the security of knowing he is safe, because he has $2,000,000 in the bank.

How else do we know $2,000,000 is real money? Well, let me ask you this, how long does it take someone making $60,000 a year to make $2,000,000? Divide $2,000,000 by $60,000 and you get 33. It would take Mr. Raines 33 years to make $2,000,000. Let me ask you this: How long would it take someone making $60,000 a year to save $2,000,000? It might not happen in a lifetime. $2,000,000 is real money. It is real money in this courtroom, and it is real money to Mr. Raines.

Now maybe there is a feeling we are somehow judging Mr. Raines for some reason. These are all facts and evidence. But also, there is an old saying in the law that you take the plaintiff as you find him. This is how we found Mr. Raines. This is evidence that his attorney, who has the burden of proof, brought into this courtroom so you could get to know him. We take the plaintiff as we find him.

I am not judging anyone. My mom was a public high school teacher. She never made or saved a million dollars in her life, let alone $2,000,000. I don't judge my mom, and I don't judge Mr. Raines. You take the plaintiff as you find them. $2,000,000 is real money to Mr. Raines, just like it is to many of us. Don't let plaintiff's counsel tell you he needs tens of millions of dollars to get better. $2,000,000 is real, life-changing money. $2,000,000 is fair and reasonable, which is what the law requires.

ADDRESS PLAINTIFF'S COUNSEL'S "ELEMENTS OF DAMAGES" ARGUMENT

Now I need to address some of the arguments you heard from plaintiff's counsel. Plaintiff's counsel walked you through all the items the law allows you to consider when determining your verdict for pain and suffering. He threw out some really big numbers for individual hardships Mr. Raines has experienced between the accident and trial.

We just talked about what impact this accident has had on plaintiff's life. You have heard the good news. He is on the road to recovery. He has certainly experienced very real pain and suffering for his broken bones. But the law says there is no fixed standard, no formula for determining what that amount should be.

Plaintiff's counsel is trying to appeal to your emotions and trick you into awarding damages based on a formula. Plaintiff's laundry list of damages is just that—an illegal formula. I know when counsel stands before you again in his rebuttal argument, as an officer of the court, he is going to agree with me that it would be improper for you to use a formula as you deliberate. He's going to take back that argument.

In addition to being a formula, plaintiff's counsel's argument is not supported by the evidence. Where in evidence did any witness discuss that any dollar amount is what is fair and reasonable for past anxiety? Now, the anxiety is real. We talked about that. The defense has not prevented plaintiff from obtaining treatment of any of his injuries to date. In fact, our plan for him moving forward gets him every bit of help he is going to need on this road to recovery.

Instead, what you heard in the testimony from plaintiff's mother is that $2,000,000 is going to have a meaningful impact on Mr. Raines' life. My client has accepted responsibility. This is how you hold the company accountable. You award what is fair and reasonable—what is going to make Mr. Raines whole—no more and no less.

When it comes down to the verdict form, you are going to award $2,000,000 to Mr. Raines by writing $1,000,000 for past pain and suffering for the last year and a half, and $1,000,000 for future pain and suffering.

Don't let plaintiff's counsel trick you. Follow the evidence, not a formula.

ADDRESS PLAINTIFF'S COUNSEL'S "NICKEL AND DIMING" ARGUMENTS

Plaintiff's counsel mentioned that we are trying to somehow "get a deal" on what we owe to Mr. Raines in this case. He said we are trying to lowball him. That is simply not true.

We accept full and complete responsibility for the accident and for Mr. Raines' injuries. It is not our job to get the lowest verdict amount possible. It is our job to help you decide the most fair and equitable award for both sides. Fully compensate plaintiff in a fair and equitable way. Justice for all, not just for plaintiff and his attorneys.

TIME FOR CLOSURE

Finally, what else does $2,000,000 for pain and suffering do? It allows everyone to move on. An accident happened. My client accepts full responsibility. $2,000,000 is fair and reasonable, and maybe it's time for the healing process to truly begin.

Maybe you have had enough. How about no more lawyers? No more personal injury lawyers. No more lawyers referring clients to doctors, to the same doctors they have used over and over again.

How about no more hearing what I think? Maybe it's time for Mr. Raines to do what he loves, to spend time with his family, visit his dad, go camping, see friends. Follow his passion. Put this stressful litigation behind him, take the Cymbalta pain medication he was prescribed some time ago, and get out there and enjoy this beautiful weather he loves so much.

A time to heal. A time to move on. Get some closure. This accident has affected enough lives. You have seen it just in these short few weeks; imagine the last year and a half. It is time to heal, and $2,000,000 does that.

Maybe we are all a bit to blame for us being here. $2,000,000 is fair and reasonable and helps get closure. And I think it was said best by my client when he said he made a mistake. It was an accident. It was his fault. He is sorry.

$2,000,000 not only says you made a mistake, but it also holds my client accountable.

ARGUING PAIN AND SUFFERING IS HARD!

Arguing pain and suffering is not for the faint of heart. For most of us defense lawyers, it is pretty scary. There are no real laws or calculations or experts to guide us like there are for arguing economic damages. Yet this is the biggest component of most Nuclear Verdict awards, so we have to address it.

In the above sample closing argument we shared, you will note there are a few things the defense must do differently than what was done in the actual defense argument. First of all, we are very positive. We tell the good news. It is not all doom and gloom as claimed by plaintiff's counsel. The defense counsel did do a good job in this regard. We can all just do a little bit more, to really bring it home for the jury.

We need to find the positive in plaintiff's life, just like the plaintiff should. It is fair. The jury should hear both sides of the story. Sometimes there are a lot of good things happening in the plaintiff's life. Sometimes there is even some good that comes out of a tragedy. Tell the jury. Share both sides of this challenging situation. Tell the good news.

We also never say plaintiff's number. In the actual closing argument, the defense repeated plaintiff's damages number countless times. This is done very frequently in Nuclear Verdicts. In the 2025 Starbucks hot-water jury trial where the jury awarded $50 million, defense counsel repeated plaintiff's number many more times than his own defense number. Repeating a number is an extremely effective psychological tool. The concepts of priming, desensitization, and recency definitely work. That is why plaintiff's counsel do it all the time. But that is also why we should never repeat their number! We must say our number, not the plaintiff's number.

Finally, the biggest difference between our method of arguing pain and suffering and what was actually done in this trial is relating money to plaintiff's life. "That's gold, Jerry! Gold!"[54] And most importantly, it is reasonable.

From Bob: "Be an Artist"

I recently ate at a three-star Michelin restaurant in Paris, Le Cinq, for the second time. Now that is something I never thought I would say growing up on Staten Island! It was unbelievable, every part of the experience. From the minute we were escorted to our table, to the nonstop attention from the waitstaff who served and removed each of our nine courses of dinner in magical unison, to the food.

Oh, the food. It was opulent and complex, and yet simple at times. Every bite was literally an experience. In fact, and I did not share this with my group because I was a little embarrassed, my first bite of dessert almost caused me to tear up. Yes, I got emotional from taking a bite of a frozen, Neapolitan grapefruit dessert that pretty much overwhelmed me with flavor.

The emotion may have come from several sources: it was a special night of celebration, gratitude, and privilege with my wife and my law partner, Pat Mendes, and his wife, but it was triggered by a bite of food that was so incredible I almost cried. That moment, that enchanted creation, may never be replicated again. Nor should it. It was unique; it was special. It was food prepared by an artist, someone who strived to be better than anyone else and did not settle for preparing food the same way everyone else had since the beginning of time. This chef did not follow the herd, did not play it safe, did not worry what people would think about her creation.

Now contrast this with other cooks. I still remember when McDonald's opened a few blocks from my home on Hylan Blvd. and Midland Ave., right across the street from the best pizza shop ever, Nunzio's. I was about 10 years old. I was pretty excited. It was on the way to one of my basketball pickup games at Egbert Middle School. And if I had the money, I would stop in there.

To this day, I still love a Big Mac, and of course the French fries. And to this day, fifty years later, it is still consistently delicious. Nothing about the Big

54 SEINFELD: *The Fatigues* (NBC television broadcast, aired Oct. 31, 1996).

Mac or delicious fries have changed. It is dependable and repeatable, every day. The same, every day, every week, every year, year over year. Nothing new, nothing different. It works.

So the question is, especially when it comes to arguing pain and suffering, who do you want to be? A robotic line chef, playing it safe, just doing the same thing you have always done? Or do you want to be an artist, a creative Michelin three-star chef in Paris?

The McDefense

What the defense has been doing with pain and suffering arguments for many years, and it is borne out in the data, is very wrought. It is a "McDefense." Same ole, same ole. Safe, boring, conservative, expected, and unfortunately, completely destroyed by opportunistic plaintiffs' lawyers. Plaintiffs' lawyers are more creative than defense lawyers when it comes to the biggest and most important part of Nuclear Verdicts: arguing noneconomic damages. This must change.

Come on, be a "creative." Are plaintiffs' lawyers born more creative than defense lawyers? Is that the case? We do not think so. But something has happened along the way of life so that plaintiffs' lawyers are incredibly more creative than we are now. So let us do something about it. Let us do something worthwhile. Let us get a little uncomfortable.

We have all the necessary facts and law, all of the things we are comfortable with, at our disposal. Now use them. Use them to show our jury what impact money could have on *this particular plaintiff*. Not some sports star or the Kardashians or whatever other insulting analogy plaintiffs' lawyers use to exploit and manipulate jurors.

Let us do something special, something unique, something fair. Do not just punch holes in plaintiffs' counsel's arguments. Have our own story. Make it powerful and persuasive and connect with the jury. These emotional arguments made by plaintiffs' lawyers to condition jurors to award large dollar amounts are simply not fair. Let us bring fairness back to jury trials.[55]

CONCLUSION

We must do better when it comes to arguing pain and suffering. Noneconomic damages are the largest component of Nuclear Verdicts, and defense counsel most often chooses not to talk about them, let alone argue them, to the jury in closing argument. When the defense does "argue" pain and suffering, we most often recite the jury instructions and tell jurors their award must be "fair and reasonable." This is not an argument.

The Apex provides a compelling, reasonable, lawful, and fair way for jurors to assess plaintiff's true pain and suffering. This is not an argument based on professional athlete salaries or famous works of art. The Apex's two-element approach is based on this plaintiff's life and experience. By focusing the jury on (1) the impact of the accident on plaintiff's life and (2) the impact of money on plaintiff's life, the defense can take back justice for all and avoid a Nuclear Verdict.

55 For more behind-the-scenes insight into Bob's thought process and the development of this Apex closing, join our Apex Defense Community at www.apexdefenseconsulting.com.

CONCLUSION

THE FUTURE OF JUSTICE LIES IN THE APEX

"We cannot solve our problems with the same thinking we used when we created them."
—Albert Einstein

BREAK THE PATTERN OF NUCLEAR VERDICTS

NUCLEAR VERDICTS ARE NOT RANDOM. They follow a pattern, one the plaintiffs' bar understands all too well. For far too long, the defense has played catch-up in a game it did not know it was losing. But now, we know better. And because we know better, we must do better.

This book was born out of frustration with the verdicts we saw, the cases we studied, and the industry-wide resistance to change. But it was also born from hope. Hope that when we shine a light on the pattern of Nuclear Verdicts, we can break it. Hope that when we are good humans, lead with empathy, and ground our defense in reasonableness, we can achieve real justice. Hope that if the defense bar chooses to collaborate, rather than compete, we can stop the outsized awards that hurt not only defendants and insurers, but entire industries and communities.

THE APEX—HIGHER LEVELS

As we conclude this book, we leave you with a preview of what is next: the higher levels of The Apex. While this book has focused on the foundational strategies—*Be a Good Human* and The Core Four—the full power of the Apex comes to life when defense teams also embrace the advanced levels of case themes and persuasive delivery. At trial, the most effective defense themes—*Responsibility*, *Reasonableness*, and *Common Sense*—must guide every argument and every decision. These are not just legal strategies; they are universal values that resonate with jurors, defuse anger, and restore balance in the courtroom. *Reasonableness*, in particular, sits at the very core of The Apex, and every defense strategy must flow through reasonableness to reach the apex and defuse juror anger.

But themes alone are not enough. To prevent Nuclear Verdicts, defense teams must also master the art of persuasion: *Tell Your Story* and *Care*. Caring means more than being kind; it means offering creative, reasonable solutions that give jurors a path to help the plaintiff while simultaneously delivering a reasonable verdict. When defense teams combine strategic storytelling with a sincere, human-centered approach, we build the trust and connection needed to change verdict outcomes.

JOIN US AT APEX DEFENSE CONSULTING

The Apex is not theory. It is practice. It is built on experience and over 100 real Nuclear Verdicts analyzed across the country. It gives the defense bar a roadmap to defuse juror anger, tell our story, and deliver justice with purpose and humanity. But it only works if we engage every level. We cannot skip an element. We cannot fake sincerity. Jurors are watching.

It starts with being a good human.

Then, builds upon a strong foundation through the Core Four.

Then, leans into defense themes of Responsibility,
Reasonableness, and Common Sense.

Then, presents our case with storytelling, style, and care.

All of it, together, is The Apex.

We know the obstacles: client pressures, billing guidelines, institutional inertia, and fear. But the risk of inaction is greater. The cost of staying silent, playing it safe, and pretending the old way still works costs billions of dollars and erodes faith in our civil justice system.

Apex Defense Consulting provides training to overcome our obstacles and to put these principles into practice in real trials. Through training, collaboration, and hands-on support, Apex Defense Consulting equips defense teams to climb every level of The Apex and finally break the pattern of Nuclear Verdicts.

ARE YOU ALL IN?

We did not write this book to criticize. We wrote it to empower through real life examples. To every defense lawyer, risk manager, claims professional, and carrier executive who reads this: the next Nuclear Verdict is preventable. It is not someone else's problem. It is ours to solve. We are the solution.

So…

Are you all in?

APPENDIX A

COMMON PLAINTIFFS' COUNSEL PAIN & SUFFERING ARGUMENTS

THE FOLLOWING OUTLINES AND PROVIDES examples of common pain and suffering arguments advanced by plaintiffs' counsel in Nuclear Verdicts. Join the Apex Defense Community for insight into how to challenge, rebut, and overcome these arguments in trial.

Visit www.apexdefenseconsulting.com.

"INANIMATE OBJECTS"

Description

In the "Inanimate Objects" argument, plaintiffs' counsel discusses the purported value of irrelevant, inanimate objects to position their requested dollar amount as a reasonable value of plaintiff's pain and suffering. While neither the inanimate objects nor evidence about them ever comes into evidence for the jury, the items serve as a significant piece of plaintiff's argument in closing. This works to position human life as more valuable than irrelevant and expensive objects, which blurs the line between "reasonable" and "unreasonable" numbers. Common inanimate objects used include fighter jets, artwork (such as the *Mona Lisa*), or commercial buildings.

Sample Argument

The plaintiffs' bar typically advances this argument as follows:

> A B2 Stealth Bomber is one of the most expensive pieces of equipment our U.S. military can create and deploy. It does not matter that the plane is worth $1 billion; if the plane is going down, that pilot is told to eject. We never say, "Save the plane." We always say, "Save the pilot," because human life is worth more than even a $1 billion object.
>
> This question of human losses is not about economics or salaries. It's about that: human life. The question is how much is my client's life worth? The U.S. military says life is worth more than a billion-dollar piece of equipment. The defendants would have you disagree, and sign off on a discount.

"FAMOUS ATHLETE/CELEBRITY SALARIES"

Description

In the "Famous Athlete/Celebrity Salaries" argument, plaintiffs' counsel references a celebrity's reported worth or a famous athlete's salary to justify their astronomical ask of the jury. This argument is particularly effective at distracting jurors from the actual evidence in the case, convoluting the true value of a dollar, and urging jurors to act emotionally in awarding a large damages number to send a message that plaintiff is "worth" as much as an overpaid celebrity or sports star. Plaintiffs' lawyers often use hometown sports stars in this argument.

Sample Argument

Here is an example:

> Life itself is incredibly precious. It might be the most precious thing there is, but it's hard to put a dollar figure on what it's worth. We all tune in on Sundays to watch our

> Dallas Cowboys play their hearts out. They play to win, and Dak Prescott leads them to glory more often than not. And man, he should for the kind of money he makes. He makes $60 million a year. He got an $80 million signing bonus. That's big money, and he makes it playing football. He's a good quarterback, but he's got his health.
>
> My client lost everything, and the defense wants to tell you his pain and suffering is only worth minimum wage because that's what he was making at the moment their negligence cost him everything. Really? His family would tell you he's more valuable to them than Dak Prescott. He's worth more than $80 million. He was the quarterback of his family, and now he's sidelined for life.

"MINUTES/HOURS/DAYS"

Description

Here, plaintiffs' counsel creates an arbitrary formula in the "Minutes/Hours/Days" argument to persuade the jury to award a large pain and suffering verdict, even though the law says no such formula or fixed standard exists. This argument is effective because it allows plaintiffs' lawyers to assign a seemingly minimal dollar figure to each category of damages (this argument is frequently married to the "Elements of Damages" argument explained below), and then multiply out that low dollar figure by each minute, hour, day, or year of pain and suffering for each category. This tethers jurors to a formula that is arbitrary, irrelevant, and appears to justify an exorbitant ask.

Sample Argument

Below is an example of this argument:

> So, how should we value Josh's pain and suffering? Let's do this. Let's start from the moment he was pinned under force of the defendant's truck and work forward to today. That moment was 6 years, 3 months, and 28 days ago. What do they think his pain was worth in that moment when his

> bones were snapping and he was struggling to catch his breath, wondering if he'd ever see his baby daughter?
>
> Maybe the defendant thinks those 6 years, 3 months, and 28 days were only worth minimum wage. So, let's do a little math and see what that works out to be.
>
> There are 365 days in a year. So, that's 2,190 days in 6 years, plus 90 days in 3 months, plus 28 days. So, we've got 2,308 days of past pain and suffering to account for.
>
> How many hours is that? There are 24 hours in a day. 2,308 times 24 equals 55,392.
>
> Our state's minimum wage is $17 per hour. 55,392 times $17 per hour equals **$941,664 in past physical pain.**
>
> You heard he's got another 32 years left of this day-in, day-out suffering. Discomfort while he's sleeping. Bone-splitting pain while he's awake.
>
> So, some more math: That's 11,680 days left. 280,320 hours left of future pain and suffering. That's **$4,765,440 in future physical pain.**
>
> Now, let's look at past humiliation…

"ELEMENTS OF DAMAGES"

Description

In the "Elements of Damages" argument, plaintiffs' counsel identifies different "elements" of noneconomic damages, usually tied to specific elements or categories of noneconomic damages available in the applicable jury instructions. These elements vary by state and can include things like loss of enjoyment of life, anxiety, grief, disfigurement, humiliation, physical pain, and similar categories. Plaintiffs' counsel often deploy this argument in tandem with the "Minutes/Hours/Days" argument referenced above to maximize the jury's verdict.

Sample Argument

Plaintiffs' attorneys make this argument as follows:

> The law shows you the categories of noneconomic damages, and the law will tell you that if we've established these losses, you must award money for each of them. So, let's break it down.
>
> As you've seen, the jury instruction says my client is entitled to damages for past and future physical pain, mental suffering, loss of enjoyment of life, disfigurement, physical impairment, inconvenience, grief, anxiety, humiliation, and emotional distress.
>
> Starting with loss of enjoyment of life, what does my client have to look forward to? He is no longer able to enjoy his life; this accident fundamentally changed his entire reality, in countless ways. His entire goal now is just to stay alive. He is no longer hiking, no longer walking his dog. He is not going to pick his children up from school and hear about their day. He's not playing soccer with them. He's missing out on family vacations. He is not going to walk his daughter down the aisle. He will never hold his grandchildren. And while he's here, alive, he's a shell of the person he was. His life is pain, anxiety, fear, disappointment, and sadness for all that this experience has taken from him. So for that loss of enjoyment, it's $20 million.
>
> What about his face and his body, his disfigurement? He used to be a body builder. He loved going to the beach. Now, when his wife wheels him through the grocery store, people stare. He sees them staring; he knows what he looks like. He's disfigured. So for disfiguration, $7 million.
>
> And he must now depend on his wife for all his needs. If he needs to use the bathroom, she helps him. He cannot feed himself. He is completely dependent on her. For the humiliation this causes him, it's another $5 million.
>
> . . .

"FUTURE INFLATION PROTECTION"

Description

Using this tactic, plaintiffs' counsel leverages inflation as a concept to justify a significantly higher damages award from the jury. They argue a higher award is required to ensure plaintiff has the means to live in the future. The plaintiffs' bar often couples this argument with a "No Mulligans" type of argument (more on that below). Plaintiffs' counsel will highlight how the value of a dollar has changed over time by pointing to a specific year in the past (often the same number of years in the past as plaintiff's future life expectancy) and reminding jurors how much things used to cost in that year. The implication is that whatever jurors award today must provide for plaintiff in the years to come, even in the face of rising, untold, unspecified inflation.

Sample Argument

Here is how the argument looks in practice:

> You heard my client has 36 years of life left, a far cry from what she had before the defendant put profits over safety and caused her to lose everything. What we do today, what you sign on that verdict form, must reflect not only the seriousness of this case, but how long she must live with these human losses. What will happen over the course of 36 years? Things change. Life changes. The value of money changes.
>
> 36 years ago, it was 1989. George H. W. Bush was president. Poison reigned supreme on the radio. And a carton of milk cost $1.17. A loaf of bread was $0.67. And a dozen eggs cost a single dollar. Money went a lot further then, and money today goes further now than it will over the next 36 years of excruciating life awaiting my client.
>
> Full civil justice is what it's going to take, and that means full civil justice for the years and the many rising expenses she'll have to face in the future. What's the value of a dollar in 2061? I know that's far away. What will be the cost of someone coming to her house every single day to take care of her? She needs full-time care, around the clock. We know

> what that costs today, but we aren't just compensating her for 36 years of today. We're talking 36 years into the future.

"ANSWER AN AD/BRIEFCASE FULL OF MONEY"

Description

In the common argument in which counsel proposes an "Answer an Ad" or a "Briefcase Full of Money" scenario, plaintiffs' counsel violates the Golden Rule (which precludes lawyers from asking jurors to put themselves in the shoes of a party). Here, plaintiffs' counsel urges jurors to consider who would willingly answer a newspaper (or online) ad calling for someone to experience plaintiff's specific losses and pain in exchange for money. A modern spin on the argument occurs where plaintiffs' counsel asks jurors if they would accept a briefcase full of money in exchange for what plaintiff went through. This argument is deeply emotional; it personalizes the plaintiff's loss for the jurors themselves while also implying the defense intentionally subjected plaintiff to the pain she now experiences, though that is rarely the case.

Sample Argument

Here is how the plaintiffs' bar commonly presents this argument:

> You heard from Robin's friends, her boyfriend, and even her boss. You know what this accident did to her, at every level. And I told you at the start of this case we'd be asking for $21 million, and maybe that felt like a big number the first time I said it.
>
> But let's go back in time. Let's go back to the moment just before Robin slipped on that puddle of oil in Taco Taco. The moment before she fell and her life changed forever.
>
> Let's suppose Robin is walking to the restroom, and a tall man in a black suit walks up to her holding a big briefcase. He says, "Robin, I have a deal for you. Inside this briefcase is $21 million. And it's yours. You can have it. But in exchange for it, you are going to slip and fall on the floor ahead. You will go through three spinal surgeries. You will lose the

> memories of giving birth to your twin girls. You're going to suffer personality changes that make those girls not want to play with their mommy anymore. Your marriage is going to fall apart. You're going to be at increased risk of dementia, and you won't be able to work at the dentist's office anymore. You won't be able to be a dental hygienist anymore at all, in fact, and if you ever work again, it'll be at a computer and you'll be in horrific pain the whole time. And, you'll have daily migraines that limit your ability to go outside, so you won't be able to garden anymore, either. You'll have two more surgeries in the future, and I can't even tell you if they'll help one iota."
>
> Do you think Robin takes that deal? Would you? Would anyone?

"NO MULLIGANS"

Description

In the "No Mulligans" argument, plaintiffs' counsel empowers the jury by arguing the jury's verdict is plaintiff's only chance at justice. This conveys to jurors the seriousness (and permanence) of their decision, and works to drive up damages using speculation, even though jurors are specifically instructed they may not speculate when deliberating. By telling jurors that the plaintiff cannot come back to court in the future *if* the award is not enough, plaintiffs' counsel argues jurors should increase the dollar amount awarded to reduce the likelihood of an inadequate result. This argument often appears in conjunction with the "Future Inflation Protection" argument discussed above.

Sample Argument

This is how plaintiffs' counsel makes this argument in trial:

> Members of the jury, you have been so diligent and focused throughout trial. I've seen you taking notes and really listening to all the witnesses testify, and for that, I thank you. Jonathan thanks you, too.

That's really how this has to work, because we can't come back in ten, twenty years, after you've signed your verdict form and left the courthouse. What you decide today is Jon's life, long after you've finished your civic duty. It's an awesome power, and it's one I'm glad you have—you can decide what is right, and your words matter. They echo through these halls, and they'll have lasting impact.

That number you write on this line, it has to be intentional. This is our only shot to get it right for Jon. We can't come back down the road if it isn't enough, if he needs those three additional surgeries the defense is trying to get a discount on. We can't come back—this is it.

BOB'S ACKNOWLEDGMENTS

NO ONE ACCOMPLISHES ANYTHING SIGNIFICANT alone. You always have support. But some of us are also lucky enough to have someone pushing us. You may not always feel lucky this person is pushing you to do more, to achieve more, to challenge yourself, to pursue every opportunity, to work harder, to get stronger, to set new and bigger goals, to stretch, to grow, to not rest, to not give up, to not care what others are doing or saying, to be yourself, and to be your best self.

Sometimes, you wish that person didn't push so hard, either with his words or just knowing look—like, hmm, that's it? You can't do anymore? You really are going to give up? Sometimes, you wonder why that person pushes you so hard. In my case, the reason is love. Love is why this person has pushed me my entire life.

And for me, that person was my Dad. As I write this, he is dying. When this is published, he will most certainly be with Jesus, in Heaven. He will never read this book or this acknowledgment. Losing my Dad will be the biggest loss of my life. Where will I find the motivation?

Maybe now I am just blessed to have support. The support of my loving and amazing Mom, who has always inspired me to write and learn and be kind. Thank you, Mom. My beautiful wife, Jenny, who is just incredible. She accomplishes more in a day than I do in a week and is always there when I need her. My three awesome kids, Faith, Mary, and Bobby, who are always surprising me with their brilliance and hard work. And my sister, Denise. It can be challenging to work with family, but you have helped us immensely for many years now. I am forever grateful for your support, leadership, guidance, and love. Thank you.

This book would not have been written without Cayce Lynch. Bash on millennials if you want, but Cayce is one of the most impressive people I have ever met. She is the real deal. Thank you also, Ashley Fetyko, for your relentless effort to make this happen and your everyday creativity and enthusiasm. Can't wait for your next idea!

Pat Mendes. I could go on and on about how great Pat is. If you know, you know. I am very blessed to call you my best friend and partner. Much more to come, my friend. Thank you, buddy!

Thank you to my in-laws Mike and Linda Murphy, and my partners Susan Oliver (quite the journey, my good friend), Lynn Allen, Jim Sell, Dan Fallon, Kristi Blackwell, Jake Felderman and one of my favorites of all time, truly inspiring to me, although I love to tease her, Mina Miserlis! Thank you also to Brynne MacEachern, Sarah Hickey, Carmen Lam Freeman, and Juli Attaway. You make our firm a better place, and we appreciate all you do.

I have also had a ton of support from great friends like Jerry Meis (literally the best ever!), Karyn Meletis, Brooke Bucknum, Pat Kilkenny, Abe Badani, Chris Musgjerd, Mike Ripley, Randy Nunn, Tom Savino, Joe and Judi Zappia, and my favorite paisan, Marc Lanci. And the support and inspiration that lives on from those who have passed, Fr. John Stack and Mort Shaevitz. I miss you dearly.

Finally, God gave our family an angel 19 years ago. That angel is named Andrea Ponce. Andrea was our nanny for many years and now good friend. We could not have made it through this incredible journey of life without you. Thank you and your beautiful family, Eric, Eric, and Jacob, we love you!

So I am not being pushed anymore. It feels strange, empty, sad. It will feel worse by the time you read this. I am not sure what I will do to fill this huge gap in my life, in my being. Maybe, because of all the support and "pushing" I have received, it is time for me to support and push others. I know I can never have the impact on others that my Dad had on me, but I will try.

I love you, Dad.

CAYCE'S ACKNOWLEDGMENTS

TO EVERYONE MENTIONED BELOW, I could not have co-written this book without your meaningful contributions and impact on my life. First and foremost, I praise and thank God, who has granted me innumerable blessings and opportunities. This I know is true: the most precious things in my life are due to His divine design and intervention.

To Those Who Helped Bring this Book to the World:

Bob Tyson—Bob, it is impossible to sum up in a single paragraph the positive impact you have had on my career and life. Thank you for believing in me since the day you interviewed me to join Tyson & Mendes as a brand-new lawyer. Thank you for your mentorship and guidance. Most notably, you taught me how to take depositions, talk to clients, write an introduction, defuse juror anger, and make an audience laugh. You have taught me how to lead and given me the confidence to make difficult decisions. Now, we have written a book together! Thank you for giving me this opportunity. Above all, thank you for being a friend.

Pat Mendes—Thank you for seeing something different in me, even as a young associate. Thank you for taking a half-day to attend the swearing-in of a new TM attorney back in 2013. Thank you for your leadership, mentorship, and friendship. Thank you for your quiet encouragement when I needed it most. Thank you for having my back, challenging me, and helping me grow into the kind of person and leader I am proud to be.

Ashley Paige Fetyko—This book and "The Apex" framework would not exist without you, without question. Thank you for taking this frazzled project by the reins and guiding it every step of the way over the nish line. Thank you for agreeing to become a data mastermind, against your better judgment. Thank you for your analysis, creativity, writing, and editing. Thank you for sharing your trial expertise with me. Thank you for joining me on this journey of working motherhood, for being my "mirror," and for every permission slip. You will never fully appreciate how much I admire, respect, and love you like a sister!

Mina Miserlis—Thank you for being my mentor and friend. Thank you for teaching me the "TM Methods" that have now become "The Apex." Thank you for sharing your brilliance with us as we shaped The Apex from the foundation up. Thank you for collaborating with every attorney in our rm in your role as our Chair of Complex Trials to ensure we deliver best-in-class trial skills to defuse juror anger across the country. It is not an easy job, and you do it brilliantly. As my dear friend, thank you for supporting me through every era of my professional and personal journey. Having you in my life makes me a better human and a better lawyer—with far more laughter involved!

Grace Shuman—Thank you for over three years of painstaking analysis, editing, and citing. I understand if you never want to read a closing argument transcript ever again. "Long live all the mountains we moved" to write this book! We are incredibly grateful to you.

Kira Giannoni and Mario Yepez—Thank you for your design genius, including cover design, graphics and graphs, and formatting. You continue to amaze me with your creativity and ability to communicate through design. Tyson & Mendes is SO LUCKY to have you.

Dr. Beverly Burrow—Thank you to my long-time friend and editor of this book! We surely have come a long way from your helping me iron out a little idea for a high school project on Latin and Greek roots. Thank you for your encouragement and for embracing our philosophies in this book. Thank you also for asking questions and for your red pen! You made this book better. Period.

Denise Tyson—Thank you for all your data analytics, insights, and patience for this book. We appreciate your help very much. Separately, thank you for your guidance and leadership on all things "finance." I am incredibly grateful to continuously learn from you. You have done some amazing things for Tyson & Mendes with **Trish Ogden**, **Brian Hunt**, **Christy Ninteman**, and your whole team. We appreciate you.

Erin Pedersen—Thank you for sharing your guidance and assistance in obtaining hard-to-find trial transcripts. Thank you for your long-standing friendship and support and for (almost always) including champagne. Big hugs!

Dr. Jennifer Staples—Thank you for educating us on the power of validating to defuse juror anger. We have grown professionally just by being in your orbit!

So many others had a hand in the analysis and creation of this book: **David Ramirez, Alla Policastro, Jefferson Cheney, Mitchell Siegel, Genesis Franco, Kiran Gupta, Laura Desjean, and Thomas Meis**. Many thanks to each of you for your significant contributions!

To my other Equity Partners—**Jake Felderman, Jim Sell, Lynn Allen, Susan Oliver, Dan Fallon, and Kristi Blackwell**—thank you for believing in this project. Thank you for enthusiastically embracing The Apex. Thank you for your collaboration and support as we lead and grow this firm together. I am blessed to have you in my corner, truly.

To Those Who Invested in Me:

Professor Eric Yamamoto—Thank you for teaching me how to be an attorney. From analysis, writing, and "what's really going on," this book would not exist without you. My career would not exist without you. I carry the Aloha Spirit in my bones because of you. Thank you, my dear friend.

Dr. Mort Shaevitz—How I wish I could still talk to you, Dr. Shaevitz! Thank you for the countless hours of mentorship and guidance you shared. From the formal advice you shared with me in breakfast meetings to the informal way you always checked in on me, you shaped me and Tyson & Mendes in more ways than you ever knew. Your legacy lives on every day. We strive to make you proud!

Barbara Sutherland—To the dearest gal pal and mentor a girl could ever ask for: thank you. Learning from you over the last decade has brought so much joy and confidence to my life. Cheers, my love!

Cheryl Farrell—Thank you for all your mentorship and guidance when it comes to Organizational Storytelling. Your work and friendship have had a meaningful impact on my life, and I look forward to what the future holds!

Phil Rudolph—"Don't aim at the brick; aim through the brick." Thank you!

Frances Nuar—"You have proven yourself. Now it is time to care for yourself." Your words sit on a sticky note on my desk, and I hold tight the many lessons you have already taught me. Thank you for making me feel seen.

Corey Hoffmann—Without your encouragement, I probably would have abandoned all my plans for law school. Thank you for lending your support during such a critical time in my life. I would say it all worked out!

Chuck Ford—Thank you for being my first real mentor and creating the opportunity for me to roll up my sleeves and try. You had the faith in me to just let me learn by doing. You changed my "hope" that I could succeed into a (headstrong) "knowledge" I would succeed. Thank you, friend.

To My Village:

Carmen Lam Freeman—The equity partnership calls you the "heartbeat" of Tyson & Mendes. To this accurate description, I also add, "my angel." I cannot imagine my life without you in it and am so fortunate that Tyson & Mendes brought us together over 7 years ago. Thank you for sharing your gifts with me and helping me be the best version of myself—leader, attorney, mother, and friend.

Julianne Attaway—Thank you for partnering with me all those years ago. I am incredibly proud of what you have built here at TM. Most importantly, I am grateful for your friendship.

Brynne MacEachern—Thank you for "growing up" with me at TM. It is incredible to see where life and this firm have taken us. I am fortunate to get to work alongside someone I trust so very much—YOU. Your laughter is such a special and distinct part of the joy that you bring to all of us. Thank you for bringing heart, empathy, and understanding to what we do every day.

Jordann Rawls Reis—How blessed are we? It is not often we meet a kindred spirit, but to also get to work together?! There is no better ambassador and evangelist of Tyson & Mendes on the planet than you. Thank you, sweet friend.

I could not succeed in my professional career without the village of support I receive in my family life from so many incredible women since becoming a mother. Thank you to **Sonia Lopez, Sarah Nightingale, Dr. Isabel Smith, Pamela Bundy, Maggie Miller, Jansen Gutierrez, Kaley Garrett, and Fiona Sales.**

To My Family:

Thank you to my whole family. You are woven into the very core of who I am today. I carry my grandparents with me always, especially my great-grandfather and namesake, **Morris Cayce Nance**. Thank you especially to **Pam Hall** and **Nash Peterson**, from whom I have learned so much.

Lynch Family—Brian, Nancy, Sandra, Suzanne, and Kevin: I am so blessed and grateful that you welcomed me into your family. To my beautiful and brilliant nieces, **Sophronia** and **Madison**, I adore you. Thank you for being the best big cousins to Laurel and Cora. I always have your back and cannot wait to see what incredible things God has in store for you!

Robins Madril Family—Niki, Joe, Emma, Maddie, Michael, and Bumpa: Thank you for being my bonus family and supporting us every step of the way. I cherish our annual visits more than you will ever know!

Spencer, Rose, and Jackie—I always look forward to the next time we get to be together. Spencer, I won the lottery when God gave me you as a "little" brother. You were my first friend and now my longest-running friendship. I am grateful we are on this parenthood journey alongside each other; just two kids figuring it out as we go! **Rosie**, you are such an inspiration to me. I won the lottery a second time when you said, "I do." I love you, sister! **Jackie**, look for your Aunt Cayce in the front row of your first headlining tour. Thank you for sharing your many gifts with us, little dude. We love you!

Mama and Daddy—I owe it all to you! Your love and sacrifices served as the foundation of everything I have built, including this book. Thank you for instilling in me both the discipline to work hard and the grace to know my best is good enough. Your unwavering belief in me brought me through my hardest days and made my proudest days possible. I have loved watching you become "Missy Bee and Papa" to Laurel, Jackie, and Cora. I pray and work to replicate your values and lessons in my own daughters. Thank you for continuing to pour into our family in such special and meaningful ways.

Laurel and Cora—You are the joy of my life! You may be too little to read these words now, but one day I hope you will see them and know you inspired every page of this book. Thank you for your grace as I spent Saturdays in my office working on this project instead of on the swing set with you. Thank you for teaching me more about love and resilience than I ever thought possible. I get deep fulfillment from witnessing you explore and share your gifts with the world. Always remember:

> *I love you forever, no matter what. I love you just the way you are.*
>
> *There is nothing you will ever do that will make me love you less.*
>
> *Daddy loves you like that; your sister loves you like that; and Jesus loves you like that, too.*

Mike—Thank you, M. Thank you for being an equal partner alongside me on this beautiful, crazy story we are writing and living together. Thank you for supporting my dreams and ambitions while keeping my feet firmly planted on the ground. You are an incredible father. I love the life we continue to build. While I wish time would slow down, I am so excited to see what our forever holds. I love you. —C

www.ingramcontent.com/pod-product-compliance
Lightning Source LLC
LaVergne TN
LVRC081519210926
848486LV00022B/414/J